DEVIANCE

DEVIANCE

The Essentials

HENRY VANDENBURGH

Bridgewater State College

Upper Saddle River, New Jersey 07458

Library of Congress Cataloging-in-Publication Data

Vandenburgh, Henry.
   Deviance: the essentials / Henry W. Vandenburgh.
      p. cm.
   Includes bibliographical references and index
   ISBN 0-13-094113-1 (alk. paper)
   1. Deviant behavior. I. Title.

HM811.v36 2004
302.5'42–dc21   2003052832

Publisher: Nancy Roberts
Executive Editor: Christopher DeJohn
Editorial Assistant: Veronica D'Amico
Senior Marketing Manager: Marissa Feliberty
Marketing Assistant: Adam Laitman
Production Editor: Cheryl A. Keenan
Asst. Manufacturing Manager: Mary Ann Gloriande
Copyeditor: Virginia Rubens
Proofreader: Beatrice Marcks
Formatting and Art Manager: Guy Ruggiero
Illustrator (interior): Mirella Signoretto
Cover Art Director: Jayne Conte
Cover Designer: Bruce Kenselaar
Composition: Laserwords Ltd.
Printer/Binder: RR Donnelley & Sons Company
Cover: The Lehigh Press, Inc.
Typeface: 10/12 New Century Schoolbook

Pearson Education LTD.
Pearson Education Singapore, Pte. Ltd
Pearson Education, Canada, Ltd
Pearson Education–Japan
Pearson Education Australia PTY, Limited

Pearson Education North Asia Ltd
Pearson Educación de Mexico, S.A. de C.V.
Pearson Education Malaysia, Pte. Ltd
Pearson Education, Upper Saddle River, NJ

10 9 8 7 6 5 4 3 2 1
ISBN 0-13-094113-1

For Nancy

Brief Contents

Contents

PART II   PERSONAL DEVIANCE

7   Drug and Alcohol Abuse   77

8   Mental Illness   97

9   Sexual Deviance   111

PART III   SOCIAL DEVIANCE

Preface

As an undergraduate, I was partly drawn to sociology by studies of deviant behavior. Some of the best and most interesting academic writing I saw was in the qualitative studies of deviance I read during those years. This writing had an immediacy and truth to it that not even history, known for its interesting studies, seemed to offer. In spite of the occasional bizarre nature of the material, deviance studies were oddly reassuring. They seemed to tell the truth about the construction of unusual nooks and crannies in the social order—and they went into detail. Not even history with its grand sweep could offer this.

In addition, deviance studies, and deviance *theories* for that matter, seemed to bring life and humanity to the issues that psychiatry and psychology also dealt with. From a deviance perspective, you could get a sense of what was in it for people to be deviant, how they put their worlds together to defend their status and self-esteem in their own minds, and how they protected themselves from the public. I was hooked on studying deviance, in short. Small wonder, then, that years later I wrote my dissertation on business deviance by psychiatric hospitals.

Later, however, as a teacher of deviance, I noted that the students had changed since my undergraduate days in the late 1970s. Unlike the social critics and countercultural travelers we oftentimes were, today's students are usually more job-oriented. They're frequently destined for careers as police and probation officers, social workers, nurses, human resources officers, and any of a number of other middle-level professions. Many if not most are already working in their chosen fields, or in a preparatory position for entry into those fields. Also, chances are that some of these students would not have attended college 30 or 40 years ago, instead going immediately into technical or on-the-job training after high school.

This development explains the reason for *Deviance: The Essentials*. It's intended as a reduced-form text, very accessible to today's students, which, at the same time, conveys some of the interesting and unusual things to be found in deviance studies. As such, it attempts to convey much of the key information that might also be found in a large-form deviance text, but in a way that economizes on reading. Since this is in no way a reader, I hope that instructors adopting this text will also adopt a book of readings as its companion.

In orientation, this book tries to achieve a compromise between a pure sociology approach (in which official definitions of deviance are generally problematized) and one that is likely to be more useful for today's students, many of whom are destined for human services careers. Accordingly, "official" definitions of mental disorders are taken more seriously than they might be in more critical texts, as are those for crime. Psychiatric medications and illegal drugs are explored in greater detail, because, based on my own predoctoral experience as a human services worker, this information is eminently useful across the spectrum of social and public services, and is rarely taught.

Each chapter consists of text, one vignette illustrating a form of deviance, and one or more tables or figures. A reasonable plan might be to cover one chapter a week, with one or two readings from a companion reader for illustration. This book is chiefly intended for undergraduate students of deviance in sociology and criminal justice, although it can easily be incorporated into other curricula. Interdisciplinary in nature, it can also be utilized in psychology and anthropology courses, since it illustrates psychological and biological theories as well as the sociological theories more traditional in deviance courses. It's easy to read, and can be used by all levels of college students.

PLAN OF THE BOOK

This book is organized in three sections. **Part I, Foundations of Deviance**, contains six chapters discussing the various theories and methods for explaining and studying deviance. Chapter 1, *The Nature of Deviance*, discusses the definitions of deviance and presents methods for studying it, including participant-observation, survey research, secondary data analysis, and content analysis. Chapter 2, *Deviance in Premodern Society*, delineates the nature of deviance and deviants in primitive societies, ancient societies, the Middle Ages, and the Renaissance. Chapter 3, *Classical or Deterrence Theory*, discusses the role of rationality in encouraging and discouraging deviance and crime. Chapter 4, *The Age of Positivism*, covers the use of objective science in studying deviance (including some important mistakes made by early science). Chapter 5, *Modern Sociological Theories of Deviance, Part 1*, explores macrosocial theories and their role in explaining deviance. Chapter 6, *Modern Sociological Theories of Deviance, Part 2*, discusses more critical and microlevel theories.

Part II, Personal Deviance, explores specific types of deviance at the microlevel. Chapter 7, *Drug and Alcohol Abuse*, discusses addiction and presents a model that can be used to analyze all forms of addictive behavior, including those not involving addictive substances. Chapter 8, *Mental Illness*, examines mental problems and the individuals and institutions that attempt to deal with them. Chapter 9, *Sexual Deviance*, notes the different types of sexual behavior in which humans engage.

Part III, Social Deviance, explores deviance on a broader level than the merely personal. For this reason, it includes material on crime, as well as simple deviance. Chapter 10, *Organizational and Vocational Deviance and Crime*, discusses the ways in which organizations and individuals commit crimes and practice deviant behavior in the context of work life. Chapter 11, *Cults, Charisma, and Terrorism*, details the ways in which cults provide deviant and sometimes dangerous lifestyles for their members. Chapter 12, *Domestic, School, and Workplace Violence and Abuse*, examines ways in which bullying and violence occur in these important but often overlooked contexts. Chapter 13, *Cyberdeviance*, discusses ways that deviant or criminal activities take place through computers or the Internet. Chapter 14, *Crimes Against Persons and Property*, examines crimes as offenses against both fellow humans and their possessions. Finally, Chapter 15, *The Future of Deviance Studies*, discusses where we go from here in the context of social science's attention to deviance and in the context of public policy.

ACKNOWLEDGMENTS

As ever in academia, this book depended on more than my efforts alone. Ed Thibault gave his usual valuable advice, and discussions with Bruce Luske, Deborah Cohan, Rob Orrange, and Ernest Kilker were essential in bringing the book to fruition. David Friedrichs was very helpful in taking time out to meet with me to discuss white-collar crime on several occasions. Don Rebovich and the research staff of the National White-Collar Crime Center were very hospitable, and were wonderful resources. Chris DeJohn, Dick Hamlin, Cheryl Keenan and Veronica D'Amico of the editorial and production staff at Prentice Hall were helpful at every step. I want to thank four reviewers for improving this text in key ways I could not foresee: Jeffery Ian Ross, University of Baltimore; Bruce Luske, Marist College; Cheryl Banachowski-Fuller, University of Wisconsin-Platteville; and Frank G. Steyn, Kettering College. Sensei Frank Bowers helped nurture body and mind with martial arts instruction accessible to slow-learning 57-year-olds. Last, but not at all least, my wife, Nancy Claiborne, and my daughter, Lilah Vandenburgh, provided invaluable emotional support.

ABOUT THE AUTHOR

Henry Vandenburgh received his Ph.D. in Sociology from the University of Texas, Austin, in 1996. Previously, he was a licensed psychiatric technician, chemical dependency counselor, and psychiatric hospital middle manager specializing in admissions and marketing. A medical sociologist, as well as a student of deviance, he is Assistant Professor at the Department of Sociology and Criminal Justice, Bridgewater State College, Bridgewater, Massachusetts. He is also the author of *Feeding Frenzy: Organizational Deviance in the Texas Psychiatric Hospital Industry.*

PART I

FOUNDATIONS OF DEVIANCE

1

The Nature of Deviance

An Affair?

Sarah is a happily married housewife living in an affluent suburb of a big city. Her successful husband, Tom, puts in long hours at his executive job at a logistics company. She's often left at home for 12 or 14 hours at a stretch. Bored after taking care of her household duties, Sarah often logs on to the computer for hours at a time, surfing the Web or dropping in on various chat rooms. Lately, she's been enjoying a young-professionals chat. Unlike some of the more unruly rooms, this one seems to have nice, caring participants like her. One day, after a long discussion, she gets a message from Bill, one of the nice participants, to meet her in a private chat area. Bill tells her that he really enjoys her responses, and that she is one of the reasons he logs on. Flattered, Sarah discusses her personal history with Bill in a general way. Bill shares that he is recently divorced. Sarah admits candidly that she doesn't like staying at home all the time, even though she and Tom can afford for her to do so. They talk for hours—always, of course, staying within the bounds of polite discourse. As the week progresses, Sarah finds that she can't wait to get on the Web and chat with Bill. When he's not there, she frets that he may not log on that day. He always does, though, and they chat for hours. In one discussion, Bill tells her, "I almost wish you were not married." Before she knows what she's typing, Sarah replies, "I almost wish I weren't too." Both shy, Sarah and Bill have never had anything like "computer sex" (the exchange of erotic fantasies online). Still, they both live to be online with each other. When Tom is home, Sarah can think only of Bill. Tom, preoccupied with work, doesn't seem to notice any change. Is this an affair? Is this deviance?

What is deviance, anyway? Although **deviance** can be given extremely complex definitions, it will be delineated in two relatively simple ways here. In one sense, *deviance* is behavior that goes against norms, that is, behavior patterns that we expect others (and ourselves) to engage in. In another sense, deviance has a statistical definition. It's unusual behavior— behavior we seldom see others engage in. As we'll see, it's possible for these definitions to contradict each other in interesting ways.

It may seem that the information in this book is excessively relative. For many types of deviant behavior, this book refuses to make a judgment regarding the rightness or wrongness of the actions in question. This is deliberate. The function of college-level work is to pose questions that cannot be easily answered. The student needs to reach within himself or herself to find answers to these issues that he or she can live with. In some instances of deviance—such as murder—the student will probably agree that such behavior is always reprehensible and should always be prevented or punished. But there are gray areas here, too. What about murder done in the service of national defense? What if you kill someone in your own defense, or in the defense of another? Some might argue that we should still not kill in these circumstances. Others would say that this behavior is normal, human, and necessary—not "deviant" in any way.

It's unfortunate that we need to label this book, and the courses for which it has been written, "deviance." The scope of this material can range from alternate lifestyles, to individual idiosyncrasies, to hard-core criminal behavior. What makes it unique is that it encompasses behavior that departs from norms, or, alternatively, that's unusual. Such behavior has been called "deviance" in the fields of sociology and criminal justice and in some areas of psychology. For simplicity, that's what we'll call it here, too.

Deviance is thus not a simple thing at all. It's not always a matter of good and bad, or even strange versus not-strange. Everyone has deviant moments. Think of how it would feel to have a camera follow you around 24 hours a day, seven days a week. This would probably not be a comfortable experience because we expect privacy—not to have all of our behavior observed by others. Not that most of us practice very deviant behavior. We just do not want all of it to be public, on-stage, and observable.

Some very respectable people lead extremely deviant lives behind closed doors, as fiction and nonfiction accounts have reminded us countless times. Well-regarded businesspeople can be as predatory in their dealings as any serial killer; while they do not attack their victims physically, they may not care if they ruin people financially. In government as well as business, supervisors sometimes glory in abusing underlings. The payoff may be the petty sense of power they get from having great control over subordinates. And quite respectable families from all social classes may include one or more abusive parents who use their positions of authority to act the role of petty tyrants (or worse) around the house.

On the other hand, some people may live most of their lives in "deviant" subcultures. But in these settings, many are decent and predictable in their behavior. Others, of course, are exploitative, even predatory, just as they might be in "respectable" parts of society.

Deviance is thus probably part of everyone's life, worthy of study because it deals with the immoral and/or unusual aspects of human behavior. Many students of sociology and other behavioral sciences develop their lifelong interests in these fields because of encounters with the material in deviance courses. Deviance, especially when written up in good qualitative studies, makes for fascinating reading. As such, it's interesting, even pleasurable, to study.

Studying deviance can also make us more compassionate. When we study diverse lifestyles of others, including at times extremely negative behavior, we broaden our horizons and become less complacent about our own "good" behavior. At best, we see how deviant behavior sometimes works for others. Observing extremely negative behavior, we may say, "There but for the grace of God go I." Studying deviance also forces us to clarify our own values. For example, is it an affair if a married person has online computer sex with (but never meets in person) someone to whom he or she is not married? This book will not answer the question for you, but it may prepare you to think it through in terms of your own values.

DEVIANCE AS RUPTURES IN MORAL BEHAVIOR

Key to understanding breaches in moral behavior is an analysis of what this behavior actually is. For the philosopher John Locke (1988), it's essential for humans to cooperate because, if they don't, they lose their rights vis-à-vis one another. He tended, as did many social thinkers in the late 1700s, to equate human freedom with the ability to own and control property. Locke's predecessor, Thomas Hobbes (1977), had argued that, absent government, life would become "poor, nasty, brutish, and short." For Locke, government only helped set the stage for human cooperation. Unlike Hobbes, he thought that people were naturally inclined to be cooperative, but that government was needed to smooth the rough edges on this natural tendency.

Hobbes may have been closer to the truth however. He believed that humans were selfish and were not really inclined to cooperate all that

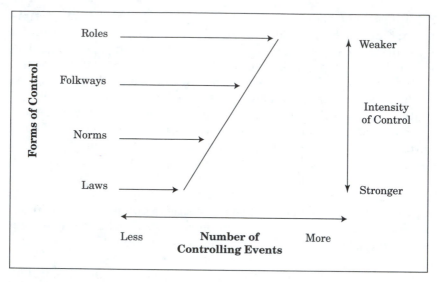

FIGURE 1.1   Forms of Social Control

much. Therefore, he felt, moral behavior had to be imposed on society, often through the offices of government.

Emile Durkheim (1976), one of the founders of sociology, agreed with Hobbes in many ways. To him, humans did better if they had limits constraining their behavior. He believed that group life gave significant comfort to individuals, even if it constrained their freedom. Modern sociologists see this control as emerging through a number of categories (Brinkerhoff, White, and Ortega 1995), as described below (see also Figure 1.1).

Roles

Roles are among the more innocuous controls, although they do exert considerable force. They are instructions we absorb about the ways to fit into a given group or setting. Often, the roles different people enact in a given group are similar, but they can also be complementary. The group's expectations of the ways individuals are to act, feel, or think places considerable limits on behavior, although roles may also provide avenues for self-expression within these definitions. We play many, many roles in the course of a day. An individual who is a powerful, authoritative parent at home may become meek as a lamb at work because he or she takes a subordinate, supportive position in the organization. Rupturing role expectations others have for us may constitute deviance, although it's also possible, given time, that the new behavior will be considered a new "deviant" role. An executive who begins constantly interrupting the boss during business meetings may (if he or she isn't fired) get a reputation for being a maverick, or "strange." He or she has found a new role based on the new behavior, one that many would agree is a deviant one.

Folkways

Folkways are somewhat more global than roles. These are general instructions for how to behave in a given society or social group in terms of style. Folkways dictate how one is to dress or speak to adapt to a given culture. In rural Bavaria, it's customary for men to wear *lederhosen* (short leather pants) during festival times, for example. Folkways are generally not emotionally charged forms of moral authority, but they do contain instructions for how to fit in. Like roles, they raise possibilities for deviance because, if some people are acting in accord with the culture and some are not, it's possible to see those who are not as deviant. Like roles, folkways do not carry a "high emotional charge" as moral behavior. They are simply issues of cultural style. It's likely, however, that in more primitive societies, folkways carried substantial moral force, and that, if we were to roll back the clock 8,000 years or so, there would be no difference between these customs and moral expectations (Durkheim 2001).

Norms

Norms are moral customs that have force behind them. They describe what's permissible and impermissible to do. An example is the norm that it's impermissible to kill someone unless one is ordered to do so in the military or is acting in self-defense or in the defense of another. Breaching norms generally brings with it a sense of guilt or shame because of our socialization (training by others) to experience these feelings. There are rare individuals who may not experience guilt, but generally the bad feeling when one breaks norms is universal. Each person expects that others will observe limitations and expectations set by norms. We are much more likely to confront others, or at least talk behind their backs, when it comes to norm violations. These violations imply that some active punishment should take place, or that the violator should at least be shunned or degraded in status. Norms include issues that speak to harming oneself or others, but, significantly for deviance, they also include behavior in which no one is harmed. Durkheim (2001) identified a close connection between religion and norms, where normative ideas were fixed in the social mind by religious beliefs, rituals, and practices.

Laws

Comparatively few norms are actually written down as **laws**—formal written requirements requiring us not to do certain things, or, sometimes, to do them. Laws usually spring from norms, although there are technical business situations or interactions with government in which social norms have not previously existed before a law is enacted. Although norms have existed as long as human groups have, laws are a relatively recent addition. They date only from the period after writing became available. The earliest form of law was the Code of Hammurabi, named for the Sumerian king who devised this body of law nearly 3,000 years BCE. Laws allow the state (here, government in all its forms) to participate in social control (making people adhere to norms). If this sounds harsh, remember that in primitive societies, social control may be enforced more savagely than in developed ones. Durkheim (1976) identified a tendency toward secularization (moving away from religion) toward more rational (and tempered) punishment as societies matured and more norms became laws. Picking someone's pocket, which was once punished by torture and lynching, is now more appropriately punished by a short stay in jail or a fine.

DEVIANCE AS DEVIATION FROM USUAL BEHAVIOR

Another useful way to define deviance is by comparing it to usual behavior. Here, the emphasis is on deviance as mundane (ordinary—not highly threatening to social norms) behavior, even if it's unusual. Some of the most fascinating deviance studies are derived from this category. Articles have been written about strippers, poachers, and women who collect beads at Mardi Gras by baring their breasts. These are things few people would ordinarily do, but, at the same time, they do not deeply offend our contemporary sense of morality. In looking at this category, it's instructive to examine how behavior comes to be defined as deviant in the first place.

Power and Deviance

Social critics from Charles Dickens to Karl Marx to Groucho Marx have noted that members of the dominant classes in society (the rich) have the ability to impose their culture on the remainder of the population. Persons who don't "behave" or show "good manners" are thought to deserve social opprobrium. Often these standards come from upper-class expectations calling for members of all classes to restrain themselves. The wealthy and middle classes have much to lose in terms of position and property if such restraint does not occur. General behavioral license might set the stage for threats to the persons and property of the well-off. The less well-off have little in common with the wealthy. So promotion of good manners in society helps socialize the lower classes not to threaten the rich and, coincidentally, helps to spark the belief that they might be able to become more like the rich (in terms of possessions and power) should their behavior warrant it.

Attempts to regulate lower-class behavior are often well-meaning. In the United States during the nineteenth century, the wives of industrialists, along with social reformers, attempted to impose the "respectability" of their own classes on working-class immigrants from Europe, who, they felt, drank too much (Gusfield 1990). They formed reform groups that worked for 60 years to abolish drinking, finally implementing the disastrous Prohibition experiment in the early 1920s. Today, the wealthy project their culture through the media, with consumption, travel, and lifestyles of the wealthy featured prominently on television and in magazines. A component of these lifestyles is sometimes respectability—the apparent avoidance of deviance. The imposition of respectability is not one-sided. Very poor people often try to imitate these lifestyles, sometimes with bizarre results as they furnish their houses with imitations of the rich goods they see in the media. The upshot of "those who have the gold making the rules" is that the mores (broad social norms) of the wealthy usually become the mores of society.

Culture and Deviance

Just as power sets the stage for definitions of deviance that favor one group over another, culture operates the same way. The United States, for example, is becoming more and more diverse. However, it's likely that most of our cultural values, hence most of our definitions of deviance, are set by the dominant culture, which is white and Protestant. When we hear statements like "Those families have too many children" or "I don't know why 'those people' have to sit on their porches and talk loudly all the time," we are hearing conflict between dominant ideas about correct conduct and the perfectly respectable (in their own eyes) notions of social conduct held by minority groups. The notion of culture and deviance should alert us to the fact that definitions of deviance can become absurd if we look at human groups closely enough. One person's deviance often is another's perfectly respectable behavior. That there are many subcultures in the United States means that there may no longer be a definition of normal behavior and one of deviance for many activities, although it's safe to say that for extreme behavior, uniform standards still apply.

Markets and Deviance

Another way to see deviance is as "exchange" (Homans 1992). Many goods and services furnished by deviant activities are in demand, and not just by poorer classes. When drug dealers sell cocaine on a city street, some of their customers come from respectable suburbs. Businessmen come to gentlemen's clubs to see strippers and get lap dances (in which a nude woman gyrates on the customer's lap), considering themselves perfectly respectable when they leave, although they may see the sex workers involved as deviant. So deviant activities can represent market locations where goods and services having to do with drugs, sex, stolen goods, and other items that are in demand but considered morally wrong or illegal are obtained.

An aspect of deviance markets is the role of **moral entrepreneurs** (Becker 1996). These individuals make careers out of alerting society to social problems, including ones involving deviance. The moral entrepreneur believes deeply in his or her cause. An example is John Walsh, who originated *America's Most Wanted*, a television show that highlights missing criminals, many of whom are arrested following publicity on the show. Walsh's son had been abducted and murdered, and he appropriately turned his outrage into a career of catching criminals. In this and many other instances, moral entrepreneurs have been a positive influence because they point out important social problems and make sure society focuses on them. Sometimes, however, moral entrepreneurs overstate a problem in order to make their own roles more important and their organizations and incomes larger. The war on drugs has sometimes been criticized as a massive example of moral entrepreneurism gone awry. Huge amounts of social resources have been dedicated to building up police and military forces to interdict drugs. Many poor people, often minority group members, have been incarcerated for long periods of time at tremendous social expense, often on minor dealing or possession charges. At the same time, treatment, the most effective way to curtail drug abuse, has been de-emphasized. The result has been a costly effort that is out of proportion to the social benefit received. It's clear, however, that individuals running the war on drugs have benefited. Massive bureaucracies have been created, employing tens of thousands of people, with large salaries and vast power for the higher-ups.

Becker has discussed the need for moral entrepreneurs to be supported by enforcers, who typically lack the moral entrepreneurs' idealism. Enforcers (for example, local police officers) have a practical orientation toward moral entrepreneurs' agendas. They want to do a reasonable amount of work on these projects, but, at the same time, they may give, say, a low-level user-dealer heroin from the police property room in exchange for information about upper-level dealers. What enforcers look for is respect from the street people they deal with, not fulfilling lofty goals.

At times, moral entrepreneurs can be destructive. One example is the series of "moral panics" created around purported incidents of nursery school sexual abuse in the 1980s. It's now clear that few, if any, of these incidents actually happened. As these panics started, however, ambitious police and prosecutors, therapists, the press, and a host of other interested parties came forward to demand that nursery school abusers be rooted out. There were a number of prosecutions based on prosecutors' and therapists' eliciting false testimony from children. Many of the alleged "perpetrators" spent time in jail; a few still languish there. We may thus suspect that moral entrepreneurism has mixed results. When these individuals identify and publicize real problems, they do society a service. When they focus energies on false issues, they hurt society, even if they benefit themselves in terms of money and prestige.

Masturbation—When "Deviance" Is Nearly Universal

As we've seen, deviance can be seen as norm violations (breaking social rules) but it can also be seen as unusual behavior (doing something few others do). That there are two ways to see deviance brings up the interesting possibility that the two definitions may contradict each other under some circumstances. One such instance is masturbation. If authorities can be believed, it's nearly universal. Nearly everyone does it or at least has done it. Researchers believe that it's part of normal sexual development, and that someone who does not masturbate has more difficulty learning appropriate physical responses during sex. Many would agree, however, that it also seems deviant. It's not something most of us would want others to know that we do. Many people probably cannot bring themselves to masturbate in front of a spouse or lover. For this reason, it's likely that it constitutes something of a norm violation, even if it's fairly universal. So here we have the interesting conundrum that one definition of deviance contradicts the other.

If you think this discussion is just a quirky theoretical one, consider the case of Joycelyn Elders. A physician and the first African American woman to become surgeon general of the United States, she was appointed by President Clinton. She quickly began speaking her mind on important health issues. The administration had no problem with this, but when she called for teaching children methods of masturbation as part of sex education, Clinton fired her. In light of the president's own peccadilloes, which came to light shortly thereafter, her firing seems particularly ironic. Here we see that sometimes the idea that certain types of behavior are proscribed will carry the day, in spite of their being almost universal.

Contrasting Deviance and Crime

In this book, "deviance" refers to relatively mild norm violations or unusual behavior. Although it, too, is a form of deviance, **crime** refers to behavior that is highly illegal. Occasionally, petty forms of crime are referred to as deviance, highlighting the fact that these are innocuous behaviors, more deviant than criminal.

STUDYING DEVIANCE

The study of deviance would not be a social science if it did not incorporate empirical study. It's worthwhile to theorize about deviance, but we also need to study people engaging in deviant behavior to see how they actually live their lives. Here we use interviews, observation, or participant-observation. In addition, we need to study deviance on a more macro or societal level. Here we use statistical or historical methods. We use either crime statistics reported by government agencies or statistics drawn from large-scale surveys. We also use large datasets from other sources and historical accounts drawn from community studies. To fail to do empirical studies would mean that the real content of deviance would constantly elude us, since it changes all the time. When deviant behavior is a social problem, we should be able to define it precisely enough to intervene accurately and effectively. When we're merely interested in studying deviance academically, then we need to accurately perceive what's occurring in order to understand it correctly. For a summary of these methods, see Table 1.1. In general, qualitative studies are more expensive, more time-consuming and pose a higher ethical risk because of closeness to subjects. Quantitative studies, although less rich in detail, are less expensive, faster and pose a lower ethical risk.

The Scientific Method

The **scientific method** is one way social science aspires to a rigorous and systematic approach. It's not the only method used, particularly for social scientists inclined toward qualitative (based on observation/interviews) or interpretive methods, but it's useful for expanding empirical

TABLE 1.1   General Types of Deviance Research

	Qualitative	Quantitative
Expensive?	Yes	No
Speed accomplished	Slow	Quick
Ethical risk	High	Low
Description	Rich	Less rich
Scope	Micro	Typically macro
Examples	Participant observation; content analysis	Data analysis using Uniform Crime Reports, National Crime Victims' Survey, other surveys; analysis of crime rates and economic indicators

Note: This table compares the advantages and disadvantages of qualitative and quantitative methods in deviance research.

(close to the observable facts) theories, and for answering specific questions. Its essence is to:

1. Formulate hypotheses (educated guesses about reality based on theory. These guesses can then be convincingly proved or disproved.)
2. Perform studies convincingly proving or disproving the issue in question.
3. Modify empirical theory to accommodate the new information.

The essence of this method is repeatability. If proposed modifications to theory are true, other social scientists should be able to use the same or similar data to come to the same conclusions. If they can't, there's a problem, and the findings aren't likely to be scientific. Although extremely useful, this method has certain drawbacks. By its nature, it's mainly suitable for measuring narrow propositions, so eternal conclusions about human nature are difficult to prove. Frequently, rigorous studies of social phenomena turn out not to be easily repeatable, so it's not clear if findings can always be generalized. It's commonly also the case that data (information—here usually statistics) are not really uniform (describing the same things or measured the same way from study to study); hence, again, findings may be difficult to generalize from. Significantly, relevant variables (inputs from specific factors) may not always be taken into account, so two studies that appear similar may in fact not be because their social environments may be different in key but unmeasured ways. Finally, a hidden implication in scientific study is the expectation of looking at unchanging subjects objectively. But human beings are actors who have the ability to evaluate and change their behavior, even to act unpredictably and irrationally. This means that objective, scientific methods often have the ground pulled out from under them by shifts in human intentionality and action. In 1964 or 1965, for example, no one could have predicted that a counterculture of hippies, protesters, and war resisters would emerge in response to racial discrimination and the Vietnam War. Emerge it did, however, and in four or five years, a sizable percentage of America's young people were dressing in outlandish clothes, smoking marijuana, and rejecting respectable college and career goals they had embraced during the first part of the decade. For these reasons, the scientific method is eminently useful, but should be used in a tightly focused way. Lieberson (1985) recommends tight statistical studies to formally describe human behavior (with a sense that this behavior is temporary) as opposed to constructing empirical theory, citing some of the difficulties I mention here.

Participant-Observation Studies

A key method frequently used in deviance research is **participant observation**. Here, observers spend time with the groups they are studying, making detailed observations and conducting interviews. Usually the observers try to be unobtrusive, so that after a while the subjects don't notice them or think of them as researchers. A common method used by observers is to wait until they return to their cars or offices before writing out or recording their field notes (written or spoken records of observations). Observers try to observe and record as much as possible—actions of subjects, conversations, and so on. That they participate along with the subjects gives them a *verstehende* (empathetic) understanding of what's going on. As observers make detailed field notes, they may also make occasional analytical notes—recordings of theoretical ideas, connections, possible patterns of causation, and the like. When it comes time to write up their studies, researchers may use these analytical notes to organize the material in the observational notes, which illustrate the theoretical sections with examples. These qualitative studies provide vivid, interesting explorations of a variety of human activities, including deviant behaviors.

Because qualitative researchers work closely with their subjects and learn so much about them, ethical considerations are important. First, researchers must not harm participants in any way. That may seem unlikely, but during the 1960s and 1970s, a number of social-psychological experiments were conducted that put subjects at psychological and sometimes physical risk, often without informing them of the danger. In the Stanford Prison Experiment (Haney, Banks, and Zimbardo 1973), a group of male student volunteers was randomly divided into two subgroups. One group became "prison guards"; the other became "prison inmates," who were "arrested" at their residences and transported to a mock prison. Over the next few days, the guards, without prompting, became extremely controlling and began harassing the prisoners, sometimes sadistically. The prisoners became passive and depressed. The experimenters called off the experiment after a few days because the experience was excessively traumatic for the participants. Some prisoners suffered psychological effects for some time. For this reason, it would be ethically difficult to conduct such an experiment today. Ordinarily, research that is harmful should not be done. In fact, sociologists and criminologists rarely use the experimental method at all, usually for reasons of this sort.

It's essential that subjects read and sign informed consent forms. These detail what the research is about, what the subject is likely to experience during it, the subject's possible reactions, and whom the subject can contact if he or she believes there has been mistreatment by the researcher. The researcher must implement what he or she promises on the form, and the subject can withdraw his or her consent at any time. University researchers go through a review process before they begin their research, approaching a human subjects' rights committee, or institutional review board (IRB). Some organizations other than universities also have IRBs. Unaffiliated researchers may request that a local university IRB review their proposed research.

Another ethical consideration is anonymity. In deviance research, especially, researchers observe subjects saying or doing embarrassing or even illegal things. For this reason, researchers typically promise subjects anonymity (no one can find out the subject's name from the research, even by indirect methods). In order to safeguard anonymity, researchers maintain the names of the subjects separately in locked codebooks, use pseudonyms, or use a code number for each subject. Related to this is confidentiality. Researchers agree not to disclose the details of subjects' behavior in such a way that the subject can be identified from it. These two issues may actually pose problems for deviance researchers, however. It's not commonly known, but researchers lack the protections from subpoena that clergy and therapists enjoy. Legally, researchers are similar to journalists. This means that police or the courts may have the right to see social science researchers' notes, provided proper legal steps are followed. In addition, researchers can be forced to testify against their subjects, particularly if legal immunity is granted the researcher. For this reason, it's possible for researchers to find themselves on the horns of a legal-ethical dilemma. To comply with the law, they may need to testify if subpoenaed. But to comply with professional ethics, they may need to refuse to testify. In similar circumstances, journalists have sometimes gone to jail for contempt rather than break trust with interviewees.

Dataset Research

While the emphasis in participant-observation is usually "micro," that is, based on the unique behavior found in various small groups, research using datasets—large compilations of uniform statistical data—is usually "macro," that is, pertaining to much larger social groups. The best-known dataset in deviance and crime research is the Uniform Crime Report (UCR) issued yearly by the FBI. The government requires legal jurisdictions all over the country to submit data on a yearly basis covering the occurrence of key (serious) "index crimes," such as murder, robbery and arson, and their disposition. The UCR provides a wealth of data, but, at the same time, there are many potential problems in seeing it as providing a good model of criminality in the United States. Reporting is anything but uniform. The best police jurisdictions in the country may reflect higher-than-normal criminality, for example, because citizens are pleased with the performance of the police and feel empowered to notify them when they identify problems. In jurisdictions where citizens feel that the police are unresponsive, they may minimize contact. When this occurs, the crime rate in those communities may appear to drop (Bell 2000). Another issue is defining index crimes. Communities anxious to make the list of the "ten best places to live in the United States" may encourage the police to charge suspects with lesser offenses so the statistics will not reflect badly on the community's rating.

Therefore, a major problem with the UCR is what's been called the "dark figure" in criminology, referring to the fact that much crime is never reported. We thus usually get a distorted picture when we explore crime from the macro perspective if we only use official datasets.

Survey Research

In order to deal with the UCR's problems, researchers also use the **National Crime Victims' Survey (NCVS)**. Here, a stratified sample (carefully selected to accurately model the United States population) is utilized. Participants are asked detailed questions about their experience as victims of crime during the past year. The NCVS has proven to be more accurate than the UCR because it's modeled on a real population, rather than based on reports. Researchers can also conduct independent surveys in deviance and crime, although these are expensive. Typically such surveys consist of demographic (personal) information and forced-choice questions in which respondents can only select certain responses. Statistical methods are used to assess relationships between the variables (issues denoted by demographic information or questions). Surveys can often be extremely valuable because they are easier and faster to do than protracted participant-observation. If we want to find out about drinking on a college campus, for example, it probably makes more sense to conduct a survey than it does to do participant-observation. The survey, although only a loose model of reality, provides us with useful summary statistics, like the average number of drinks students consume per week. It can also be used to assess whether certain demographic variables are associated with drinking—being a freshman, for example.

Content Analysis

Another way to do deviance research is by noting the content of media. Much deviant behavior is institutionalized, and **content analysis** represents a means by which to note how deviance is popularly constructed (or misunderstood). If we scan the ads in music magazines, for example, we note these media portraying adolescent gangs in an implicitly positive light. It's not unreasonable to expect that adolescents reading the magazine will be tempted to dress the dress and walk the walk of the persons portrayed in the advertising. This does not mean that they necessarily become gang members, but some of their behavior may become more and more "gang-like" because of media images. Assessing the media's effect on deviance and crime is of great interest, and many such studies have been done in recent years. Pornography and personal ads in sexually oriented magazines can be analyzed for common issues as well.

Content analysis may be accomplished by statistical means, but it's usually done qualitatively by studying a variety of items in order to see what themes they have in common. As with much other qualitative research, themes usually emerge once the researcher has made extensive notes on the pieces of media he or she has been examining. As with other qualitative field research, the researcher may keep analytical notes exploring deeper insights than are suggested by the initial descriptive notes.

SUMMARY: THE NATURE OF DEVIANCE

We explored two basic ways to define deviance, first as norm violations, then as departures from usual behavior. We examined ways in which these two definitions sometimes contradict one another. We also saw that deviance is common, and that everyone's life would probably be seen as deviant if examined closely enough. We also saw how "crime" is a subset of the broader category "deviance"—not all deviant behavior is criminal. We explored the use of research methods in deviance studies, and we saw how the scientific method is useful when these studies concern themselves with narrow questions that develop empirical theories. For broader explorations, however, we saw that the scientific method is not as useful. We examined such qualitative research methods as participant-observation studies, noting that these require a high amount of attention to ethics because of the intimacy involved between researcher and subject. We also explored secondary dataset analysis and survey research, noting that these are areas where statistical methods are frequently employed. We also examined content analysis as a method of monitoring the media's effects on deviant behavior.

2

Deviance in Premodern Society

The Persecution of a Healer

Jane is a healer in a New England town in colonial times. An unmarried older woman, she typically delivers babies and tends to the medical needs of people for miles around. A local Native American woman has shown her a variety of local plants and herbs that can be used for cures. For example, if a woman is having trouble delivering a baby, Jane has learned to give black Cohosh, an herb designed to force the uterus to contract. Lately a new minister has come to the community's church, which Jane attends. He has attended newly founded Harvard College and proclaims that he is there to do God's will. Part of his mission, he explains, is ridding the community of heathen influences, for, as he says, "The Devil is very strong in the New World, as close to nature as it is."

 The new minister loses little time in convening a special board to investigate local pagan influences. The board quickly focuses its attention on Jane. The community has a new physician, college-trained like the minister, and Jane is an embarrassment. They call her in to explain where she obtained her knowledge. She is loath to say, knowing that to do so may open her up to charges. The committee, in view of her silence, forbids her to practice. Jane now believes that it will only be a matter of days before the committee levies a sanction against her—perhaps banishment or imprisonment, perhaps worse. That week, she abandons her small cottage and joins the Native American tribe to which her original mentor belonged.

Deviance has been an issue with humans since we formed our first primitive societies. In fact, it's doubtful that society could exist at all if it were not for deviance. We seem to require an image of not following the rules in order to follow them. As Emile Durkheim (2001) pointed out long ago, in social groups where everyone behaves correctly, rules for correct behavior become more stringent. Some behavior must seem deviant; otherwise normal behavior does not seem normal. This may appear unfair, but Durkheim thought it inevitable. Behavior seen as deviant marks the boundaries of what is and is not acceptable. Because of deviance's tendency to loom large in religion, social structure itself (which partly comes from religion) depends on definitions of deviance. So, rather than a quirky sideline in social science, deviance should probably be seen as a main event. However, its forms have changed over time and from society to society. If deviance has been with us since the dawn of human history, what forms has it taken in the past?

TABOOS AND TOTEMS: DEVIANCE IN TRIBAL SOCIETIES

Durkheim (2001) said that social structure was essentially arbitrary (not derived from nature). Primitive peoples created tribes around systems of **totems**—symbols, often evoking a particular animal. This animal was **taboo**; that is, people could not kill or eat it. In fact, they usually worshiped the totem. When a tribe became more complex, two or more clans with different totems could exist in the same tribe. Once these multiclan systems were established, Durkheim believed, they facilitated the emergence of language and abstract thought because the original choice of totem was arbitrary, just as words in general were arbitrary.

Freud (1989b) thought totems and taboos served particular purposes as well—for example, to make incest less likely: Members of the same clan, even if unrelated by blood, could not mate. Totems also often symbolized the original leaders (fathers) of clans as tribes grew. When deviance occurred, it sometimes took the form of clan members sacrificing their totem animal. All clan members would be forced to partake of the animal, so that the guilt of wishing the original father-leader dead (if this had actually happened in generations past) could be shared among all clan members.

Virtually all primitive tribes are served by **shamans** (witch doctors), who see that religious customs are observed. Shamans themselves are frequently deviant sorts of individuals. They are selected because they see and hear unusual things, have unusual intuitions, or practice unusual sexual behavior. Shamans often use herbs and primitive drugs to help change their consciousness in order to play their religious roles. For this reason, the shaman is in charge of tending the region between the sacred and the profane—a clear distinction that all groups make between things religious and things worldly. At various times, as when clan members are feasting on their totem animal, it's possible to reverse the usual rules and enter a more spiritually charged world where ordinary rules are suspended. The fact that shamans tend the boundary between these two worlds also plays a key role in tribal survival. These practitioners serve the tribe's ability to change its behavior if it needs to.

The reason they can do this is simple. Tribal peoples are locked into a limited repertory of actions. Everything, in essence, is determined by custom. Durkheim (1976) described this as "mechanical solidarity," human thinking and action that is basically imitative. That is, people just do what the next person is doing, more or less. These societies are very comfortable for their members for this reason (because they do not typically face hard choices or experience much guilt), but they do not permit much innovation, even when it's necessary for the tribe's survival. If a person acts in ways deviant to tribal customs, he or she is publicly shamed—confronted and attacked verbally, perhaps even physically. But the shaman, because he (sometimes she) is capable of unusual perceptions (and may be exempt from shaming), can lead the tribe in new directions that tribal custom might not allow (Jaynes 2000). One example is the Ghost Dance movement of the American West. Native Americans, who previously had seen themselves as belonging to separate sovereign tribes, were temporarily united by shamans who taught that white people would be decimated and historic Indian lands restored if Native Americans practiced Ghost Dance rituals correctly. Ordinary tribal customs would not have permitted this type of solidarity, but the actions of shamans were capable of forging uncharacteristic unity (Thornton 1986). The implication is that deviance can occasionally promote positive actions that are incorporated into social structure.

MARGARET MEAD: SEXUAL DEVIANCE IN THE SOUTH SEAS

As a young anthropologist, Margaret Mead (2001) studied Samoa, an idyllic South Seas island. She was able to identify quite a few customs that we would consider highly deviant if they were to occur in the contemporary United States. One was the idea that children should be allowed to begin sexual exploration at a very early age. In many cases, adults (but not close relatives) actually initiated the child sexually. Mead's intellectual mentor was Freud (to be examined more closely later), whose theory of child sexuality can be read in more than one way. For conventional theorists, childhood is a time when sexual instincts are appropriately repressed. In order to fit into complex society, children must be taught to keep their sexuality under control. For more radical Freudians, however, this sexuality needs to be expressed when it begins to emerge, or else the individual grows up to be neurotic—"hung up"—and anxious. Mead's research seemed to support the second way Freud is read. The South Sea Islanders appeared to grow up more well-adjusted than we do, partly due to a lower level of sexual repression and to a sex-affirmative culture.

In the years since its publication, Mead's work has come in for criticism (see, for example, Freeman 1999). One tack has been to suggest that her findings are "procrustean"—that is, her research, however unconsciously, has been shaped to fit Freudian theory. Another, linked to this, has been to suggest that she was gullible. Critics have charged that natives, wanting to please her and sensing the results she desired, changed their stories to fit what Mead wanted to hear. But even if these charges are partly true, it's likely that forms of repression (in terms of internalized guilt) are weaker in Samoa than they are here. For this reason, it's useful to read Mead with an open mind. It's not clear that criticisms leveled against her work are all that telling in the last analysis. Many South Sea island societies have or had relaxed sexual norms. Many of these societies possessed no such thing as adolescence. So children passed directly into adulthood when they arrived at puberty. Hence, it's likely that the age of sexual socialization (training) was pushed downward in many of these groups.

MODERN PLURALISM IN STUDYING DEVIANCE

These examples of deviance in primitive societies indicate again that one person's deviance may be another's normal behavior. Just as a critique of **ethnocentrism** emerged in the 1960s and 1970s, critiques of blanket definitions of deviance have emerged apace. (Ethnocentrism is the use of local standards to judge other cultures according to the values of one's own. The Puritans deciding that Native Americans were ignorant savages is an example.) Modern social scientists are much more likely to be tolerant of the deviance of other groups or cultures because they understand that the definition of deviance, itself, is relative. Slowly a picture is emerging of social systems in which many groups use a variety of perspectives and norms. Some norms, as we've seen, tend to be universal; others are subject to local customs and tastes, especially in modern societies.

In order to understand the evolution of deviance, we need to look at the probable evolution of social control. Table 2.1 on page 22 illustrates this in broad terms. Social control in the earliest tribes was based upon imitation of others (mechanical solidarity); thinking and religion—key to justifying control—were based upon seeing nature completely imbued with spiritual

TABLE 2.1 **Evolution of Social Control**

Period	Solidarity	Thinking/Religion	Source of Control
Tribal	Mechanical	Animism	Tribe/Shaman
Ancient	Organic	Metaphysical	Lord
Medieval	Organic	Metaphysical	Lord
Modern	Organic	"Rational"	Law

meaning (animism); and authority emanated from the shaman or the tribe as a whole. Later, in ancient and medieval societies, the populace was organized in complimentary, not imitative, roles (organic solidarity—to be examined later); thinking and religion were metaphysical—in our terms, still superstitious, but with a more organized structure than animism. Authority was generally embodied in male leaders. Modern society also posseses organic solidarity, but thinking and religion are more rational, and authority derives more from law.

PATRIARCHAL PREMODERN SOCIETIES: RELIGION AND DEVIANCE

Before the advent of modernity, the most common way to define and discuss deviance was through religion. If one followed religious teachings, one likely followed the rules for social behavior as well. Durkheim (2001) said that religion was, in essence, the worship of society. With most people adhering to religious precepts, society was more or less reproduced uniformly from day to day. Perhaps, as today, members of the upper classes were often free to go their own way, although they were often required to present at least a front of respectability.

Historical Religions and Deviance: A Foundation

In order to understand the evolution of perspectives on deviance, we must understand the role of religion in historic premodern societies. As we've seen, religion was key to defining all aspects of the social order in primitive society. Western societies, and many other societies as well, evolved into **patriarchies** in historical (recorded) times. Religion was intensely important to patriarchy (Gimbutas 1991). For the first time, patriarchy introduced societies where there was great inequity. Religion was marshaled to support the power structure in these early states (Stone 1990). In many of them, the ruler was set up as a god, along with members of his family, who became demigods. There was a steep hierarchy, with high priests occupying the top rung of the ladder, followed by ordinary priests and on down until finally one reached the lowest peasant or laborer. The religious hierarchy was absolute, with secret rituals characterizing practices at the highest levels. Because the system was hierarchical, norms required of the lowest levels (which were enforced by religion) were not the same as those required of the highest levels. In most of these historical patriarchal states, religion, the state, and the economy fused in such as way as to become all of a piece. Religion seamlessly reinforced government, which, in turn, reinforced the economy. These patriarchies were very stable, forming what were later called "tributary modes of production" by some, or, somewhat more ethnocentrically, "Asiatic" modes of production by others. This last formulation is inaccurate because the first "Asiatic" economy was that of ancient Egypt, an African nation. Generally speaking, ancient patriarchies originated around the need to manage irrigation systems, such as that needed to bring the Nile River (in Egypt) to distant fields at the boundaries of the river's valley (Diop 1991).

The earliest patriarchal states, as we've seen, glorified domination by rulers who, because they had godlike attributes, were not bound by the conventional moral codes that lower-class people and slaves were expected to obey. The advent of Judaism, however, signaled a turn toward a universal law that all were to follow, including, significantly, rulers. In the Bible, Israel gets into trouble whenever its rulers and people go astray morally. This indicates that norms were beginning to be seen as universal. The other contribution of Judaism was an implicit emphasis on rationality. The rule-bound nature of the Ten Commandments indicates that a lawful structure has begun to determine morality, and, by implication, the nature of thought itself. Before the Ten Commandments, most thinking was metaphysical (imbued with superstition) or even animistic (strictly superstitious). This early moral code helped set the stage for the ultimate emergence of rational society.

Max Weber thought that the influence of the Jews, and later of the Greeks, was crucial (Bendix 1990). Much of the world practiced ecstatic religions, in which the role of rational morality was suppressed, and religions based on arbitrary superstitions. Just as today's Tibetan monks may twirl a "prayer wheel" for hours, working themselves into an ecstatic state based on this repetitive act, people in the ancient world spent much of their time in obsessive religious ritual having little to do with right conduct toward others or with realistic adaptation to the world. The adoption of formal moral codes may have helped create not only a better-behaved society (in the long run) but also a more realistic and scientific one because it began to remove superstition from everyday thinking.

This tendency toward rationality and realism in the West was probably helped along by Christianity. The original God of the Jews had been a punishing one, consonant with patriarchal practices. He often demanded sacrifices, including on some occasions human ones. The introduction of Christ meant the introduction of a new capacity for redemption and for-giveness. This helped to further rationalize morality (make it regular and functional) because it allowed for feedback. People could correct their be-havior, rather than just be seen as totally evil, beyond the pale of civilized society. Christ's rescue of prostitutes and thieves from social opprobrium symbolizes a new ideal of redemption, making morality more rational, since it allows for adjustment of behavior that's not working out.

Christianity also allowed the creation of more cosmopolitan societies because it preached a new message of tolerance for peoples in the ancient world. The Greeks and Romans, who managed to conquer much of that world, became cosmopolitan because they learned to tolerate the local re-ligions of the people they conquered. But this fact did not promote com-plete tolerance of foreigners—whom the Romans continued to call *barbari* (barbarians). Christianity began to usher in the idea that all hu-mans are essentially the same, having the same rights and duties under God. In 303 CE, Rome actually adopted Christianity as its state religion, even though it had earlier persecuted the Christians as promulgating a subversive religion.

The Middle Ages

The Middle Ages are one of the most interesting periods in the history of deviance. Christianity, when it became established in the West, set up the prospect of a moral drama to be enacted in life (LeGoff 2000). People needed to justify their right to go to heaven and sit at the right hand of God. The world was regarded as a "vale of tears," irrelevant to the true Christian soul—simply a place where the soul would be tested on its way to heaven. Even though Christianity had had a democratic emphasis at first, the idea that the world was a temporary test also justified great inequality.

The medieval world was composed of two equally important pillars. One was that of secular power. At the top was (in theory) the Holy Roman Emperor. Below him were various kings. Below them were various nobles of different ranks, extending all the way down to the knights. At the bot-tom were agrarian serfs, or common people, who farmed the land. Hold-ing this pyramid together was the theory of vassalage. This held that those on each rung of the ladder owed fealty (loyalty) to those above them. Each person had a "master." Serfs provided crops, and service in time of war, to their masters, and were bound to the land they grew up on, although as Christian souls they were technically "free." Knights and barons provided service to those above them. Society was organized as a rigid hierarchy, which was considered acceptable because all were here merely to justify their entrance into heaven by adequately performing the moral tasks required of them by their various stations. If injustice occurred, it was of little account because each soul was on earth for but a little time before joining Jesus in heaven, or the Devil below.

The religious pillar in feudal society was similar in structure to the secular one. At the top stood the pope; below him stood cardinals, bishops, and priests. At the base stood serfs as creatures of God in this instance, rather than of the emperor. The place of the serfs was reinforced by the fact that they were illiterate, and so could not read the Bible. Christ's teachings had to be interpreted for them through the words of the local priest, who spoke both the local language and Latin, the liturgical language. For miscreants (lawbreakers), there were ecclesiastical courts as well as those belonging to the secular authorities. In order to be tried in an ecclesiastical court, one would have to commit an offense against the church, or himself or herself be a clergyman or nun. In the novel *Ivanhoe* by Sir Walter Scott, a woman is tried by a liturgical court belonging to the Knights Templar, an order of military monks, for appearing to bewitch one of the knights, who has fallen in love with her. That she is a "Jewess" gives the Knights even more reason to pursue her.

As a moral tableau, medieval society was quite striking. The drama of good and evil enacted itself everywhere. If there was a famine, then it was the Devil's work and needed to be rooted out. Sometimes innocents were persecuted as followers of the Devil and made to confess under torture before either being executed or allowed to live. On their way to the Holy Land to defeat the Saracens, members of the First Crusade sacked German cities and murdered their Jewish inhabitants, largely on whim. Bloody-minded and emotional, feudal lords pursued and killed their noble enemies, usually citing flimsy moral causes as justifications. These societies were highly unstable because, although kings owed their allegiance to the emperor, and nobles owed their allegiance to kings, there was no central government strong enough to compel these entities to exist as true civil societies. Reflecting on the last days of feudalism in England during the Wars of the Roses, Thomas Hobbes (1977) commented that, absent government, life tends to be "poor, nasty, brutish, and short."

The late Middle Ages were characterized by a starkly punitive attitude toward sin and crime. Punishments were all out of proportion to crimes committed. Minor theft could be punished by flogging, mutilation, or death. Because of the notion that life was a transitory drama, it did not much matter whether the true culprit was caught and punished. A substitute might do as well. It would take several more centuries for true systems of justice to emerge. Justice during the Middle Ages was frequently nonexistent.

During this era a key issue lurking in the background was the suppression of women (Ehrenreich and English 1983). Much of the persecution of women as witches was prompted by a desire to subjugate women by branding autonomous activities they performed as witchcraft. Women (and a few men) historically practiced midwifery, the practice of delivering babies and curing mundane diseases, often using local herbs and plants. Much of the witch persecution in medieval times was designed to limit women's power by curbing these practices or forcing them underground. Because society became steeply patriarchal and religiously preoccupied, authorities intuited that the nature-religion–oriented practices were threatening to church and state alike.

The Breakup of the Feudal Moral System

Even at the height of feudalism, society was beginning to change. Feudalism in the pure sense had been an agrarian barter system with little money exchanged and only small local markets. As wealth and knowledge began to seep into Europe from the Middle East and the newly discovered Americas, trade, investment, and industry began to appear. The new society, based more on towns and less on feudal estates, allowed the emerging business class to do things that would have been considered sinful under feudalism. Lending money at interest was sinful, so much so that only Jews were allowed to do so during the Middle Ages. Within a few centuries, however, Christians lent money as well—at least some of them did. The same went for riches. Supposedly, Christians were required to eschew wealth and follow Christ in the path of poverty. Wealthy people in the Middle Ages did not actually do this, of course, but it was an ideal. With the rise of Protestantism, however, wealth became legitimate if the person acquiring it had a sober and responsible attitude toward his or her resources. In fact, in a deft twist, Protestant groups began to assert that the possession of wealth was a sign of God's grace—in other words, that wealthy people must be part of God's elect, persons destined all along to go to heaven (Bendix 1990).

The Middle Ages did not disappear easily, however. The Roman Catholic Church fought what it considered the sinful emergence of Protestantism everywhere it could. An early tactic used was the **Inquisition**, in which the Church sent inquisitors to locate heresy and deal with it. Wherever they did so, torture and murder were likely to follow. Thousands of people were burned as heretics. Most had never practiced Satanism or heathen rites, but they fell victim nonetheless. It would take another few centuries for this sort of primitivism to disappear in the West, and versions of it would persist into the twentieth century.

Protestantism and Sin

Just as the Inquisition had persecuted heretics, Protestantism rooted them out as well. For those few who believed that the demise of universal

Catholicism meant increased religious freedom, this promise was not to be fully realized for several centuries. Puritan communities punished and humiliated heretics and deviants with great zeal, sometimes burning them as witches, just as the Inquisition had. In coming to America, early immigrants founded communities that were as religiously and morally controlling as anything the Middle Ages had to offer, probably more so since the object of these "pure" societies was to construct the city of God here on earth. The main difference between Protestantism and Catholicism was the expectation that self-control would become more internal. Each church member was now expected to read the Bible himself or herself, since it was now printed in local languages as well as Latin. In theory, each person was directly under God, although in practice the local pastor and community had considerable real authority over the individual. As stated, amassing wealth and property became indications of virtue as opposed to sin, as long as the individual stewarded these resources instead of squandering them. Most American Protestant colonies became theocracies in which religious and secular authority were synonymous. The smallest infractions, such as missing church on Sunday, could be punished by whipping or being placed in stocks—public frames in which an individual could be locked, there to absorb the insults and sometimes the physical abuse of townspeople.

Most American colonies evolved a state religion of their own, even though they had fled the authority of the established Church of England. In fact, the disestablishment (changing to a system of free individual choice) of the churches of many American states did not occur until the 1820s or 1830s. This disestablishment caused much religious turmoil, leading to the emergence of a number of religious cults deviant in the societies of their day. In New York State, **Mormonism** emerged in the crucible of competitive preaching that occurred because of the new freedom to choose (Abanes 2002). The Mormons were kindly, industrious people, very typical of the early nineteenth century except for one thing. They practiced plural marriage, a system in which a husband could have as many wives as he could support. This characteristic meant that they faced social opprobrium wherever they went. Their leader, Joseph Smith, was killed by a mob when the group migrated to Illinois. Eventually, the Mormons arrived in what was to be Salt Lake City, Utah, where they founded a colony that was, in their minds, remote enough from the United States (at the time) to be safe.

Another group that became established in the same period was the highly successful **Oneida Colony** (Kephart 1982). Its founder, John Noyes, reported having a religious revelation telling him to practice "Bible Communism," a doctrine requiring group marriage. In the Oneida Colony, everyone in theory was married to everyone else. Like the Mormons, the members of Oneida were sober and industrious. In fact, some of the industries the colony created survive to this day. Sex was key to much of what went on in the colony after hours, however. Many of the young girls were initiated by the founder in special sessions he called "interviews." Men practiced birth control by holding back ejaculation during intercourse. Procreation (the actual production of children) could take place only if approved by a eugenics board, which designated which individuals (in combination) would be allowed to breed a child. In spite of Noyes's controlling personality, the settlement was a stable place to live, flourishing because of its profitable businesses. As Noyes reached old age, however, the Oneida Colony fell on hard times. He wanted his son to replace him as charismatic leader, but, as is typical with charismatic succession, the son was not up to the task. Another man, Towner, might have been suitable to replace Noyes, but the aging leader did not want him. The settlement broke up. The inhabitants reverted to monogamous marriages, and many community assets were sold to provide a foundation for their future lives.

ASSESSING THE EFFECTS OF RELIGION

For deviance, most religions provide a clear dichotomy between right and wrong, even though the terms of that dichotomy sometimes change. Many Christian religions have a concept of "sin," a condition of moral deficit one is born into or has the prospect of acquiring through his/her life if he/she does not behave. Much of what we might think of as deviant has been called sinful at one time and place or another. So the role of religion as a moderator of deviance is clear. One may act morally in order to follow the instructions given by religion. This automatically integrates one with society. But as Karl Marx pointed out, religion is often a comfort as well as a set of instructions for staying out of trouble. For poor people the world over, religion soothes the pain of living at the lower end of the economic order. Stringent religious practices often protect members from getting into trouble socially. There is no doubt that Christianity protected blacks during and after the slave era in the American South. The story of Israel described the story of African Americans, as well as ancient Jews. Religious teachings simultaneously advised caution while under the domination of Pharaoh and held out hope of a better life in the hereafter.

SUMMARY: DEVIANCE IN PREMODERN SOCIETIES

In this chapter, we've seen how primitive societies were homogeneous and required strict adherence to moral codes. The role of the shaman, however, allowed these groups to deviate from the code on occasion, and this was helpful for tribes needing to adopt new behavior based on changed circumstances. More complex societies formed where religion was used to construct and reinforce patriarchy. Most stringent may have been Europe during the Middle Ages, when deviants were punished out of all proportion to any offense they might have committed. With the advent of Protestantism, the terms of deviance changed somewhat, often still involving large punishments for minor offenses. It's notable that, in its premodern phase, America had deviant religious groups such as the Oneida Colony that used religion to justify unusual practices.

3

Classical or Deterrence Theory

Restorative Justice in Operation

Jim, a 16-year-old member of a small Pacific Coast community, has been caught by the local police vandalizing cars. Jim comes from a broken home and has been angry ever since his father left to live on the East Coast. Last year, Jim's community adopted a restorative justice model for minor crimes. In return for pleading guilty to all charges, Jim has his sentence delayed and agrees to complete all parts of the restorative justice program. If he completes them, his sentence will be vacated and his records sealed.

Jim's supervision is taken over by a board of community leaders, who outline a program for him to follow for the next six months. First he must meet with and make restitution to each person whose car he vandalized. Since Jim has no money, restitution involves cleaning up the cars personally and taking a part-time job to pay for the repairs he can't do himself. A couple of the male car owners take an interest in him during the process and agree to provide him with advice and mentorship. Jim and his mother also meet with the board, which assesses their need for supportive visits and community aid.

At the end of the six-month period, Jim and his mother are doing well. They feel included in the community for the first time. Jim, his debts paid, is taking job training after school. He continues to meet periodically with his two mentors on a voluntary basis. Jim has recently volunteered to be a peer-mentor for other young people who enter the program.

One major school of thought says that much deviant or criminal behavior occurs for "**rational**" reasons. That is, the person who breaks social norms is presumed to think rationally, calculate his or her costs and benefits in deciding to commit deviant behavior, and consciously modify his or her behavior based on consequences. Although we are used to this type of theorizing today, it's relatively new as a way to see behavior, originating in Europe only about three centuries ago. We call this way of looking at deviance—particularly crime—**classical theory** or **deterrence theory**. It partakes of one of the main modern social theories: Individuals are rational and can calculate their future behavior rationally. Classical theory is not the only modern theory of deviance, but it's one of the main schools of thought. Much of modern academic criminology is based on classical theory, since it's easy (if not always accurate) to discuss what rational persons would do, given a set of likely rewards and punishments.

THE ENLIGHTENMENT: ORIGINS OF CLASSICAL THEORY

Along with the rise of Protestantism, as described in the last chapter, came the rise of a successful business class in Europe. In order to set up successful enterprises, businesspeople needed to be able to calculate likely costs and returns on their ventures, such as trading expeditions to the New World or mills to grind grain. It wasn't long before these emerging ideas became popular in social philosophy as well. In 1775, Adam Smith wrote *The Wealth of Nations*, a work discussing the way in which markets (each participant rationally calculating which actions in production or consumption would be likely to benefit him or her) would in turn produce benefit for society. John Locke, eschewing Hobbes's vision that humans needed powerful repression by the state in order to behave civilly, wrote that humans desired cooperation with each other. Key to Locke's theory was the idea that possession of property (the administration of which required rational calculation) was essential to individual freedom. The utilitarians, Jeremy Bentham and John Stuart Mill, following in Smith's and Locke's footsteps, said that all human behavior could, in principle, be attributed to a calculation of costs and benefits. However, they took the position, contrary to Smith and Locke—who wanted to have the market coordinate most social interaction—that the state should play a major role in coordinating social life. Bentham designed a new-model prison where inmates in their cells would be on view from a central guard tower. The purpose was reform of prisoners, not their punishment. Therefore, each prisoner would be provided an individual cell in which to think over and repent his crimes, asking for forgiveness. If Bentham's prison seems a little outlandish, consider that we call prisons penitentiaries today, and that maximum security prisons often have features similar to those Bentham called for.

CESARE BECCARIA AND THE REFORM OF JUSTICE

At the dawn of the eighteenth century (the 1700s), criminal justice, such as it was, was still in a state of savagery. Punishments were all out of proportion to crimes. An individual could be hanged or beheaded for petty thievery. Felons, or those thought to be felons, were "enemies of the king" or "enemies of the state" (Foucault 1995). For this reason, the state was considered to be "legitimate" in making war on them, and outrageous punishments were commonplace. There was no need for consistency of law enforcement or punishment because it naturally fell to powerful men to administer justice. At the beginning of the eighteenth century, Europe was still in the age of the "divine right of kings." This meant that the king and his nobles were thought to be fonts of power who dispensed justice (and injustice) according to their personal judgment. Bribery and corruption were the order of the day, as people seeking justice or advantage sought to influence the decisions of the powerful. As portrayed in such films as *The Man in the Iron Mask* and *The Count of Monte Cristo* (set in the seventeenth and eighteenth centuries), people could be jailed on the basis of *lettres de cachet* (secret documents consigning an individual to prison indefinitely, often for no reason). People so confined could be tortured or kept in shackles at the whim of their jailers. The system made no attempt to differentiate between criminals, the insane, and social nuisances, confining all of them to get them off the streets.

Lawyer Cesare Beccaria (1963), however, had been influenced by the ideas of the Enlightenment, then making themselves felt all over Europe. He was appalled by the savagery and arbitrary nature of the justice system in his native Italy, and he began to advocate for legal codes precisely defining various offenses and making punishments uniform. Murder in one village would no longer be punished by a public flogging while in another village it would result in branding followed by hanging. Most significantly, Beccaria defined the germ of modern deterrence theory. A humanist, he felt that punishment for a given offense should be just what was required to stop, or deter, the criminal from committing the offense again. To do more was to practice cruelty; to do less was to be ineffective. In addition, he wrote that the usual punishment for offenses should be confinement, not the gratuitous cruelty he had witnessed in the Italian legal system.

It took many years, but Beccaria's ideas have influenced the ways we look at justice and punishment today. Implicit in them is respect for persons who commit offenses against society as people, and, significantly, respect for them as thinking beings. The deterrence concept fits well with the idea of rational choice, which is a theme in a number of social science disciplines, including economics.

THE IDEA OF PUNISHMENT: CERTAINTY, CELERITY, SEVERITY

In the early eighteenth century, punishment meant (in accordance with Foucault's "war" metaphor, above) that the state could make war on the malefactor's body. During the nineteenth century, these ideas lost currency due to the Enlightenment and the ideas of Beccaria. Punishment became more humane, generally taking the form of fines or imprisonment. Beccaria argued for only the sufficient amount of punishment needed to deter criminal behavior, but for him, it is clear that certain considerations should be applied to the manner in which punishment is administered. These include the following (1963):

1. *Certainty.* The criminal should be fairly certain that punishment will take place.
2. *Celerity* (speed). The punishment should occur relatively soon after the offense or apprehension for the offense.
3. *Severity.* Punishment should not be excessive, but it should still be sufficient to deter the behavior.

SPECIFIC DETERRENCE

Specific deterrence is the amount of deterrence required to discourage a given criminal from committing a crime he or she contemplates. In the example (Table 3.1 on page 34), Joe the cocaine dealer purchases a given amount of cocaine from his supplier for $10,000. He then sells it for $20,000 to users. If we imagine his sales process to be relatively pleasant and effortless, and we imagine Joe to have no moral qualms about his role in supplying an addictive drug, deterrence theory suggests that he is likely to repeat dealing the substance. He garners a $10,000 profit each time he buys and then sells the given amount of cocaine.

What can we do to alter the way Joe looks at his business? For one thing, we can change his chances of being arrested and punished. In the last paragraph, Joe behaved as though his chances of being caught were zero. Before we look at apprehension, however, we need to be able to calculate the effects of punishment. Let's say that Joe is likely to receive one

TABLE 3.1 **Joe's Cocaine Business**

	Costs		Revenue	Net Revenue
		Model 1		
Cocaine	$10,000	Sales	$20,000	
Total	$10,000		$20,000	
				$10,000
		Model 2		
Cocaine	$10,000	Sales	$20,000	
Incarceration	$100,000			
Arrest Probability	(0.05)			
	= $5,000			
Total	$15,000		$20,000	
				$5,000

year in prison if he's apprehended. We now need to do something difficult: assign a dollar amount to the punishment he'll receive if he's caught and convicted. We'll say that a year in jail would be worth $100,000 to Joe; that is, he would be willing to spend a year in jail for that amount. We then can turn this around and say that Joe would find a year in jail worth $100,000 of punishment. (Economics students will realize that we have just calculated his "opportunity cost" for the incarceration. This is true because Joe has already agreed that the lost opportunities and activities he misses by spending a year in jail are "worth" $100,000.) So now, Joe's enterprise costs $110,000 instead of $10,000.

But wait; it costs $110,000 if his chances of being apprehended are 100 percent. But they're not. In reality, Joe's chances of being caught actually range from 0.2 percent to 20 percent depending on which experts you believe (Akers 1990). Let's say that he has a 5 percent chance of being arrested. We can multiply the dollar amount ($100,000) connected with the punishment by the probability of being apprehended (0.05). We get $5,000, which can now be added to the cost of the cocaine. His total costs are now $15,000, and his revenues are $20,000, so he's still likely to remain in business.

What if we made Joe's likely prison stay three years rather than one? Now his total cost becomes $25,000 rather than $15,000, and deterrence theorists would predict that he would cease dealing cocaine. We could also change the chances of his being caught. If we triple the number of police on the streets, we can potentially raise this probability from 5 percent to 15 percent. Using our original prison sentence of one year, Joe's total costs are now $25,000, rather than $15,000.

One might well ask, do criminals really think this way? Chances are they don't, much of the time. In fact, interviews with petty criminals show that they are often superstitious and irrational in the ways they look at their chances of success and the likelihood of being punished (Katz 1990). Some criminals liken their careers to gambling, using phrases like "I was really hot that month" to describe streaks during which they were very successful. Also, it's likely many don't find incarceration to be as punishing as we think. Prison becomes one more location in the criminal lifestyle. For young, poor criminals, a prison term is often desired because it represents an upward change in social status and a chance to improve their skills in future criminal enterprises (Regoli and Hewitt 2000).

If a criminal enterprise is more professional or of long duration, however, it's likely that rational ways of thinking become more important. Professional criminals probably never calculate their opportunity costs and probable rewards in the formal way we have, but they do carefully consider likely payoffs and likely costs. To fail to do so would mean that they could not conduct operations over any extended period of time.

GENERAL DETERRENCE

General deterrence is the idea that the rational considerations that affect Joe can be generalized over the entire population. Rather than just personally deter Joe, punishment can deter criminals or potential criminals generally. Since general deterrence deals with the single-point rational decision making of a great number of individuals, it's harder to measure than specific deterrence. There is no doubt that most individuals react appropriately when laws and punishments change. For example, during Prohibition, many Americans stopped drinking just as the law required them to do (Behr 1997). Unfortunately, it may also be true that deterrence works least well for those who are inclined the most toward criminality. For these individuals, rationality may seldom come into play. So general deterrence may apply mainly to those individuals least in need of it.

INCAPACITATION

The deterrence argument, as we saw above, implies that punishments can promote law-abiding behavior because these will then act as deterrents on the illegal behavior of the rational criminal. As we also saw, deterrence does not always work. Thus, one reason that has been given for increasing prison sentences absent the effectiveness of deterrence has been the ability to **incapacitate** a criminal, at least for the period he or she is in custody. There is no doubt that incapacitation works, but also that it seems a poor strategy in many ways. In order for it to be effective, we probably have to confine more and more people for longer and longer periods. One reason for this is that many criminal enterprises, such as dealing drugs, represent "market niches." If one offender is incapacitated, another steps up to take his place. The new criminal is often younger, so excessive incapacitation may have the unintended consequence of expanding the criminal population across the board (Ekland-Olson, Kelly, and Eisenberg 1992). Arguments for the death penalty often incorporate incapacitation, because, if a criminal is dead, he or she can hardly commit crimes.

CONSIDERATIONS OF JUSTICE

When assessing deterrence and incapacitation, we also need to look at the idea of **justice**, which is actually somewhat unrelated to deterrence theory, although they seem similar at first glance. Justice revolves around the idea that criminals need to pay for their crimes according to a calculus in which the punishment they receive ultimately equals their injuries to others or to the community. Depictions of "Justice" as a figure usually show a woman holding scales. This idea is different from deterrence because it's not concerned with deterring the individual criminal, but with "balancing the books" in terms of crime. Justice derives from the idea that aggrieved parties historically had the right to take revenge on those who had perpetrated crimes against them. The payment for crime was frequently death at the hands of the victim or his or her relatives, or at least expropriation of the criminal's goods.

When the government began to monopolize the means of coercion—necessary to modern governmental administration—it implicitly had to promise that it would revenge itself on criminals, much as victims or their families had in earlier times. If the community as a whole feels victimized, the outcry for justice is even greater than it is if only a single victim were involved. For this reason, justice and deterrence are frequently confused. Often provoked by politicians calling for increased law-enforcement efforts (even when the crime rate is falling, as it has been for several years), the public frequently desires "more justice," by which it means more punishment. Deterrence, however, means tailoring punishment to just what is required to deter given criminals from committing crimes. In deterrence theory, judges should be given wide latitude to impose different levels of punishment for the same crime. In this way, the courts can match the appropriate amount of deterrence with given criminals. Movements for increasing justice, however, have stressed increasing punishment, implementing mandatory minimum sentences in which judges lose discretion over penalties and must apply certain amounts of punishment, irrespective of the facts of any individual case. Ironically, advocates of justice usually invoke a deterrence argument to support their position, often saying that it takes more punishment to get the requisite deterrent effect.

PUNISHMENT AND BRUTALIZATION

Critics of excessive punishment, frequently of the death penalty specifically, claim that it feeds a general culture of violence due to a general **brutalization effect** (Ehrlich 1975). If offenders see that society punishes them savagely, they may take their cue from this and, in turn, pursue their criminal trades savagely. Calls for increased justice, or assertions that criminals get off too lightly, can lead to situations where criminals and potential criminals believe that the legal system, and hence society, functions illegitimately. This perception is frequently enhanced by differential treatment of different races and ethnic groups. If one or more groups are regarded as likely to behave criminally, and if this perception is reflected in aggressive police treatment of individuals in ethnic communities, then brutalization is likely to produce both more criminals and justifications for criminal behavior. There can be no doubt that the general refusal of the African American community in Los Angeles to accept O.J. Simpson's responsibility for his wife's murder was prompted by years of inappropriately aggressive police work in ghetto neighborhoods. When the Simpson murders occurred, the community was simply not willing to believe the police version of anything. It had seen too many local young men shot dead by police when it turned out that the men were unarmed and were no threat to anyone. Around 50 percent of the people in jail are African American, a figure out of proportion to their presence in the population, which is about 16 percent. To the extent that blacks actually commit crimes at a higher rate than whites, which is not at all proven, the effect is likely to be one of poverty and brutalization.

RESTORATIVE JUSTICE

An alternative to deterrence (which in its time was extremely progressive), the **restorative justice** (also called **peacemaking criminology**) movement attempts to end cycles of victimization. Criminals, after all, usually have histories of having been victims themselves. Research on brutalization and on the effects of poverty has suggested that many criminals are not particularly deterred by the prospect of incarceration. As we saw, they may well consider it part of their lifestyle. Restorative justice has the goal of reuniting offenders and victims in supportive communities. It consists of the following elements (Colson 2001):

1. *Victim–offender mediation.* Victims and offenders are brought together with a mediator to resolve their differences. Participation is voluntary for both parties.
2. *Conferencing.* Once the offender has admitted guilt, community support networks for both victim and offender are brought into conference with

both parties. These can include their respective families, but also a variety of community groups.

3. *Circles.* If a penalty is to be given to the offender, a sentencing circle is often used. This is a large community council that affixes penalties.

4. *Victim assistance.* Material and psychological assistance may be given to the victim.

5. *Ex-offender assistance.* Similarly, material and psychological assistance may be given to the perpetrator.

6. *Restitution.* The perpetrator is expected to restore the victim to wholeness if it's possible to do so. This may mean restoring stolen property or paying the medical bills for an injured victim.

7. *Community service.* Offenders may be required to make restitution to the community at large as well.

The idea of restorative justice fits well with John Braithwaite's (1990) notion of **reintegrative shaming**. He proposes to deal with crime by publicly shaming offenders while at the same time offering them the necessary support to help them change their ways. If means can be found to actually help the offender integrate with society, this strategy is likely to be effective.

SUMMARY: CLASSICAL OR DETERRENCE THEORY

Classical and deterrence theories are based on the idea that criminals are rational, and that they take into account the likely consequences of their actions in deciding whether or not to commit crimes. By extension, we can postulate that deviant behavior, in general, can also be subject to rational calculation. The first proponent of classical theory was Cesare Beccaria, although the theory is similar in many ways to utilitarianism. The likely costs and benefits of criminal or deviant activity can be calculated. Law enforcement can alter the intensity of punishment or the probability of being apprehended to obtain a deterrent effect. Deterrence can be analyzed as either specific deterrence (what it takes to deter one particular criminal) or general deterrence (what it takes to deter criminals generally). An objection to deterrence theory is that brutalization may occur with excessive punishment, with more rather than less crime taking place because of a general negative social attitude fostered by this excess. A good alternative to deterrence theory is restorative justice, in which a process of mediation involving the victim, the criminal, and the community is used to reintegrate offenders.

4

The Age of Positivism

An Antisocial Personality?

Keith has always been an isolated boy. When he was seven, he was still wetting the bed at night. Later, he started some fires. When asked why, he could not give an explanation. The most disturbing trend has started now that he's turned 10. He's been keeping some neighborhood cats in the cellar—cats that he managed to trap—and he's been experimenting with various ways to hurt them. He's tied some of them up and hoisted them so that they slowly strangle. On others, he's used a stolen hunting knife. When his parents caught him last week, they took him for counseling. The social worker he's seeing tells them that these are very dangerous signs of possible future problems.

Positivism, the use of objective science to study deviance and crime, got off to a bad start. The term in this context refers to a system of scientific observations about people who break society's rules. It arose out of currents of disillusionment with "pure" rationality accompanying the Enlightenment. Perhaps there was more to human behavior than rational intentions of human actors. After all, classical theory could not explain times when people acted in ways not in their best interests. These instances, as we'll see, are all too common in deviant behavior.

Positivism also came directly from the Enlightenment itself. As society lost the superstitious bias of the Middle Ages, people became more interested in the science of Greece and Rome, such as it was, desiring to enhance this knowledge. The rise of business meant constant innovation in search of profits; this also directly fueled interest in science.

However, initial scientific interest in deviance and crime was lacking in credibility. Early positivists studied facial features and the shapes of criminals' heads (**phrenology**) looking for "traits" indicating criminal behavior. It wasn't until the dawn of the twentieth century that this science became at all respectable in today's terms. But just as modern chemistry arose from medieval alchemy (the "study" of transforming base metals into gold—an impossible goal), scientific criminology advanced from the superstitions of phrenologists to an accurate and serviceable body of theory and findings. Today, positivism informs a useful body of theory and has yielded helpful information enhancing our understanding of deviance.

BIOLOGICAL THEORIES

Biological theories of deviance and crime suggest that aberrant behavior stems from the body and is often heritable. These theories hold that this behavior is derived from problems with the brain or nervous system. In the beginning, many such ideas were spurious (without foundation). Today, however, it's probable that the modern versions of these theories may at least partly account for behavior.

Lombroso

Cesare Lombroso (another Cesare!) and his followers believed that heritable biological traits caused criminal behavior. Publishing in the late 1800s, Lombroso (1911), a medical doctor influenced by Charles Darwin, believed that some individuals were "atavistic"—that is, they were throwbacks to more primitive people who lived by predation and exploitation. Significantly, Lombroso thought these individuals could be identified by their atavistic appearances: heavy brow ridges, large jaws, apelike ears, and so on. Although he probably did not have this in mind as he carried out his research, his criminal types tended to look Mediterranean or African when rendered as drawings, reflecting a cultural bias toward northern European types. Subsequent research, of course, has proved that there is no foundation whatever to this theory.

Two of Lombroso's students, Ferri and Garofalo, went on to classify criminals according to a scheme not strictly biological. Ferri (1917) distinguished five types of criminal:

1. Insane criminals influenced by mental disease
2. Born criminals influenced by heredity

3. Habitual criminals influenced by moral weakness
4. Criminals of passion who have a momentary lapse in an otherwise moral life due to emotion
5. Occasional criminals who respond to opportunity

These categories are more useful than Lombroso's, actually resembling the ways modern criminologists see perpetrators. The lesson is that, given Lombroso's idea of classifying malefactors in terms of biological nature—a classification system without merit—others can go on to form a useful classification system.

The Phrenologists

Writing slightly before Lombroso, Franz Gall stated that he believed bumps in the skull indicated propensities toward different types of behavior, including criminal or deviant actions (Savitz, Turner, and Dickman 1977). This system of beliefs, called *phrenology*, was not new in the nineteenth century. The idea that the shape of one's body indicated his or her character had been around since ancient times. Palmistry was similar, stating, for example, that the length of someone's life was indicated by the length of his or her life line, the crease down the center of the hand. One's liking for erotic pursuits was said to be dictated by the "mount of Venus," the fleshy part of the palm at the base of the thumb. Various portions of the cranium were said to be laid out like the palm, and in fact to correspond to parts of the palm and to the planets in corresponding astrological analyses. Naturally, no scientific basis for this has ever been discovered, although it's interesting to note that acupuncture, based on the idea that the body has "meridian" lines of energy running in parallel array up and down its length, has been validated. Acupuncture has been used successfully in treating chemically dependent people and criminals in a variety of treatment settings. Clients report that it seems to calm them, making them less inclined to commit antisocial acts, use drugs, or harm themselves or others (Brumbaugh 1994).

The Jukes and The Kalikaks

The idea of "feeblemindedness," which often preoccupied late-nineteenth-century thinkers, coupled with the idea of heredity ushered in by Charles Darwin, gave rise to notions that antisocial behavior ran in families. The **Jukes and the Kalikaks** were two American families (the names are fictitious), characterized by intermarriage and isolation, studied retrospectively over several generations (cf. Dugdale 1910). In these particular families, there was a higher-than-average amount of criminality and insanity, although it has never been convincingly demonstrated that heredity was the sole cause. The reason could have just as convincingly been poverty or training in antisocial behavior from having grown up in a troubled family.

Sheldon's Somatypes

Physical attributes can sometimes be correlated with behavior, however. Shortly after World War II, Sheldon (1949) noted that there seemed to be three basic body morphologies (shapes). He called these **endomorph**, **mesomorph**, and **ectomorph**. The endomorphs were basically overweight people. They were, according to Sheldon, sociable and accepting in their relations with others. The mesomorphs were muscular and aggressive. They were somewhat more likely to use personal strength to get what they wanted in relationships. Ectomorphs were thin and cerebral. They basically were thinkers, and tended not to exploit others if left alone.

Researchers testing Sheldon's types have noticed a tendency for mesomorphs to get into more trouble with authorities and with society than other types (once differences in the total distribution of endomorphs, mesomorphs, and ectomorphs have been taken into account), so there may be some basis to this theory (Cortes and Gatti 1972). It's likely, however, that if physical characteristics have anything to do with behavior, this is just one of dozens of characteristics that influence deviant activity. We should thus be suspicious of single-point theories concerning why people do what they do, especially biological ones, because these imply that a criminal's antisocial behavior may be a "given."

Developmental Abnormalities

Another factor that might have an influence on behavior is clear mental retardation (Levine and Reed 1998). Problems such as **Down syndrome**, produced by an extra chromosome, may cause an individual to be mentally retarded, hence frustrated in his or her dealings with others. This frustration could conceivably be transformed into aggression. With Down syndrome, however, reality is very different from theory. Children with this problem, although of subnormal intelligence, are generally sunny and agreeable. There are quite a number of other mental retardation syndromes, however. In Kleinfelter's syndrome, for example, individuals have two X chromosomes and one Y chromosome, instead of the normal complement of one X and one Y in a male and two Xs in a female. Some of these syndromes result in subnormal intelligence, which may conceivably produce frustration. Turner's syndrome (single X), for example, can produce a retarded, stunted female.

A syndrome of interest, which, incidentally, does not produce mental retardation, is **Multiple Y**. The normal male has a single X and a single Y chromosome in each of his cells. A few males, however, have two, three, or even more Y chromosomes in each cell. Some researchers have believed that multiple Y males are super-masculine, having greater-than-average tendencies toward aggression and exploitation. The theory became popular when it was announced that massmurderer Richard Speck had XYY syndrome—not true, as subsequently proved to be the case. Speck had climbed into a student nurses' dormitory one night and murdered eight students, one after the other. It does turn out that (as a rough measure of antisocial behavior) the incidence of multiple Y males in prison is slightly greater than in the nonprison population. This difference was initially thought to be due to height (multiple Y males have a tendency to be tall, and tall men may act more exploitatively toward others), but subsequent research has indicated that height does not completely explain the prison–nonprison discrepancy, so there may be something to this theory. The incidence of multiple Y is probably no greater than one male in a thousand (Witkin 1976).

Another problem that can occur during development is **fetal alcoholism syndrome (FAS)**. If a mother drinks or uses drugs during pregnancy, her baby is likely to have physical or nervous system problems. Sometimes these problems are manifested in gross physical ways, but often they may be more subtle. Recent research on FAS has confirmed that victims may be inappropriately aggressive, lack a sense of conscience, lack insight, have low impulse control, and have a myriad of other problems that may prompt deviant behavior (Bracken and Weiner 1984). It's even possible that some intergenerational transmission of alcoholism may be due to exposure of the fetus to alcohol in the womb as much as to genetics, which probably also plays a key role. Education of prospective mothers on the dangers of drinking or drugging during pregnancy has probably decreased some of these problems.

Inherited Mental Illness

One likely cause of deviant behavior is inherited mental illness. We'll deal with this issue in greater detail in a later chapter, but certain mental disorders, such as schizophrenia and bipolar disorder, are almost certainly heritable (Lange 1931). **Schizophrenia** is characterized by hallucinations (seeing or hearing things not actually occurring) and sometimes paranoia—the false belief that people or other forces are "out to get" the schizophrenic. **Bipolar disorder** is characterized by either mania (overexcitement) or depression (feelings of lethargy and worthlessness). Mania, in particular, can lead to deviant behavior because manics have little insight as to how their behavior is affecting others, or control over it. Because these disorders are biologically driven, effective treatment is now available in the form of medication.

Sociobiology

We'll revisit **sociobiology** in the chapter on sexuality, but it's worth mentioning here. This body of theory is derived from studies on animals and insects, and says that humans follow deep patterns common to all animals, many of which account for deviant as well our normal behavior (Wilson 2000). Sociobiologists believe that much deviant behavior, especially that of men, is coupled with reproduction. Men try to fertilize as many women as they can, or at least they have the drive to do so. Women want men with resources, and so encourage men to get as many material possessions as they can. This situation gives rise to adulterous, acquisitive men, many of whom try to gain access to multiple women. Even if they do not have the high sex drive men do, women, too, can practice deviant behavior in this schema. They may "gold dig," encouraging men to be aggressive, deviant, or criminal to provide the gold-digger with wealth. According to sociobiologists, women are quite capable of being with one man for his resources and with another, secretly, because he seems to be better (more aggressive and dominant) "breeding stock," which women interpret as sexiness. Like many other theories, sociobiology may have some truth to it but is probably not the whole story.

PSYCHODYNAMIC THEORY

The end of the nineteenth century was rife with optimism about finding the source of human behavior. Many suspected that the all-pervasive rationality of the classical theorists was overstated. Philosophers like Friedrich Nietzsche began to emphasize the role of the irrational. At the same time, however, the more-or-less superstitious notions of Lombroso and the phrenologists were being discredited. It was clearly time for a more in-depth theory of human motivation to appear. **Sigmund Freud** was a Viennese medical doctor, originally trained in neurology, who was anxious to make a name for himself. Frustrated at not being given credit for discovering the use of cocaine as a topical (placed on the skin) anesthetic, he took courses in "animal magnetism" in Paris from Charcot, a hypnotist. Although Freud never used hypnosis in his subsequent practice as a psychiatrist, he gained valuable insights about the unconscious mind and about the use of suggestion in therapy. In the years around the turn of the twentieth century, he wrote a series of books on his theory of the personality (see Figure 4.1) and founded the psychoanalytic movement (Gay 1989).

Freud (1989) believed that the personality is essentially made up of three components: the **id**, the **superego**, and the **ego**. The id is the initial, animal, "desiring" part of the personality. Originating in the young child, it wants only to be fed at first. It's the part of personality experiencing uncontrolled rage if its desires are thwarted. At about the time of toilet training, Freud believed, a second personality component emerges, the superego. This is the image of the infant's disapproving parents, and this part of the personality derives specifically from being thwarted and directed in terms of toileting. The function of the superego is to make the

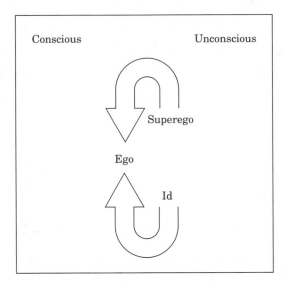

FIGURE 4.1   **Freud's Theory of the Personality**

child feel guilty whenever it does or is about to do something of which the parents might not approve. Both the id and the superego are largely unconscious—the child is not aware of their presence much of the time.

The last-evolving part of the personality, by contrast, is quite conscious. This is the ego, capable of rational calculation. Its purpose is to obtain for the id a small portion of what it desires, without offending the superego. Freud said, "Nothing can hide from the superego, not even thought," by which he meant that even contemplating doing something "wrong" can lead to lashings of guilt by one's conscience. But the ego, as a rational calculator, can attend to reality and devise ways to get some of the id's wishes fulfilled without running too far afoul of superego punishment.

Freud said that the id's wishes change as the individual goes through developmental stages (see Table 4.1 on page 46). At first, the infant only wants to be fed and to urinate and defecate on impulse. At this **oral stage**, he or she is "polymorphous perverse," able to derive sensual gratification from these basic functions. Later, as toilet training commences during the **anal stage**, he or she derives pleasure from withholding his or her bowel movement, exerting control over his or her body. At the **phallic stage**, which follows, he or she desires the parent of the opposite sex as the first stirrings of genital pleasure become apparent to the developing child. In boys, the issue of desiring their mothers (the **Oedipus complex**) is particularly pointed. They quickly become aware that mother is already taken—by father. According to Freud, this leads to "castration anxiety" (here, loss of the penis, not the testes) because (1) they are already probably aware that some people (women and girls) do not have penises and

TABLE 4.1   **Freud's Stages of Development**

Stage	Age
Oral	0–2
Anal	2–4
Phallic (Oedipus complex)	4–6
Latency	6–12
Adolescence	12–18

Source: Freud 1989a.

(2) they are afraid that their fathers will take away their genitals because of their desires toward their mothers. The sexuality of children at this age is not the full sexuality of a human adult, but it's sexuality nonetheless. Needless to say, this theory of infantile sexuality was very unpopular and involved Freud and the psychoanalytic movement in considerable controversy.

After the Oedipal period, children drift into a period of **latency** (ages 6 to 12), when their sexual desires for the opposite sex go away and they play mainly with children of the same sex. At the end of this period, sexuality reasserts itself at the beginning of adolescence.

It's easy to see how Freudian ideas can lend insights to deviance theory. The id is always scheming to be let out—to have its way in terms of pure, primitive desire. The later Freud imagined that humans have two instinctual poles, one of eroticism (sexual pleasure) and the other of the death (destructive) instinct. That is, they wish for destruction as much as for pleasure. Freud believed that it didn't much matter in terms of the death instinct whether pain and destruction happened to someone else or to the person in question. So, on a deep unconscious level, people were often inclined to be self-destructive as well as willing to destroy others.

All of this can prompt deviance, even criminality. The desires of the id, if insufficiently checked by the superego, can wreak havoc on the persons and property of others. The id gives rise to deep feelings of hostility, as well as to sexual urges likely to be antisocial because they are so primary and are by their nature likely to disregard others' social and sexual needs. When there is insufficient superego to limit us, or when the ego cannot be successful in planning for partial, appropriate fulfillment of desire, there is likely to be trouble.

Modern Applications of Psychodynamic Theory

An initial problem with Freud's theory of the individual psyche is how it's to be linked to social groups. Freud had posited that the individual pretty well has his or her personality fixed at an early age, and, absent a great deal of psychotherapy, is not likely to change. Others, like **Christopher Lasch**, offered a more social Freudian vision, however. Lasch (1991) posited that personality developed just as Freud had said it did. For an individual to be successful, however, he or she needs to experience socialization, in which realistic, supportive encounters with family members or people in the neighborhood temper his or her relations to authority. Absent those warm, but limiting, constraints, he or she will retain a savage, punishing superego, since this is the nature of the superego in young children, whom Freud believed to be irrationally terrified of their parents. With weak or harsh parenting, or weak or harsh adult authority experienced as a child, the superego will remain terrifying, and the young person may paradoxically decide to disregard it completely, turning into an antisocial or narcissistic (very self-important) personality, exploitative of others but periodically lashed by his or her conscience, which is always experienced as an angry, external force.

This helps to explain many things. Criminals, while behaving exploitatively toward others, are often very moralistic and punishing in their orientation toward others' behavior. Prisoners often beat up sexual offenders in jail. Poor people, who have frequently been subject to harsh child rearing, are frequently both more likely to offend in terms of society's rules or laws, and more anxious to punish those who do. Although there is no evidence that harsher punishments forestall crime, people who have been treated harshly as children are often those who call for these punishments. Some of these individuals are also very likely to have been perpetrators at one time or another (Mignon, Larson, and Holmes 2002).

Lasch's theory provides confirmation for a point scholars have made for some time. Intact families and intact neighborhoods make for better individuals, less likely to practice egregiously deviant behavior or to offend criminally. Although, as Freud noted, the superego gives us a sense of discomfort, developing a superego that has been realistically tempered by authority structures that are predictable and make sense to the ego (which must negotiate them) reinstates a sense of comfort and belonging. Lasch can reconcile the ideas of Freud, who emphasized a sense of discomfort living in society, and Durkheim, who emphasized (as we'll see in the next chapter) a sense of comfort living in society.

Another application of Freud's theory is through **object-relations theory** (Rubovitz-Seitz 1999). Unlike Freud, with his earlier emphasis on biological drives (the id), object-relations theorists believe that it's our relationships that shape our behavior from an early age. If we have a relationship with a mother who does not care for us, we may unconsciously react by trying to self-provide the nurturance she should have given us, developing a narcissistic personality. Narcissists may be more inclined to break society's rules because of their sense of entitlement. They may occasionally go into a rage when they see that society does not share their inflated notions of self-importance.

THE ANTISOCIAL PERSONALITY

Whatever the ultimate cause, a small percentage of individuals do not have the sense of conscience most people do. Given that people often desire more than they have, either in terms of pleasures or possessions, these individuals can be quite dangerous. **Antisocial personalities**, now also called *sociopathic personalities*, act without regard to the rights or feelings of others (American Psychiatric Association 2000). Many times, these traits lead the sociopathic individual to be a merciless competitor in business or sports. Coupled in some individuals with a hunger for physical stimulation, however, in some sociopaths these traits also lead to the desire to hurt or kill others for pleasure, resulting in serial murder or rape. Frequently charming, sociopaths use this attribute to get what they want from others or to set them up for victimization. Ted Bundy, a highly organized sexual serial killer, was quite charming, especially to women, who were his victims of choice.

Antisocial personalities previously were called "psychopathic personalities." This is probably misleading, since psychopathy connotes uncontrollable acting out, and many antisocial personalities are well-organized and very strategic in their exploitation of others. Probably no more than 1 or 2 percent of the population are antisocial personalities, but these people are capable of doing damage out of proportion to their numbers. Depending on the individual, these personalities are very difficult to treat. In some cases, psychotherapy with a skilled practitioner has been successful, but many remain resistant to treatment.

THE PLEASURES OF CRIME AND DEVIANCE

Although he is not speaking of antisocial personalities per se, **Jack Katz** (1990) writes about the pleasures of getting away with crime, robbery, and assault. Taking a phenomenological approach, he says that there is something enjoyable about crime and deviance, and that we do not pay enough attention to this factor when trying to explain why individuals are attracted to deviant behavior. Katz shows how shoplifters and stick-up men positively enjoy getting over on their victims. Unlike the Freudian approach, the emphasis here is on the construction of the criminal self for sensuously rewarding criminal pleasures, not on acting out the agendas of a pleasure-seeking unconscious id. As a game with pleasurable payoffs, and not just in money, the process of committing crime can be intrinsically rewarding. By extension, much deviant behavior in general works this way. Clearly, one does not have to have an antisocial personality to enjoy crime in part of his or her life. He or she could be very attentive to the needs of some significant others, yet victimize other persons outside of this circle.

A CRIMINAL PERSONALITY?

Attempts have been made to determine whether a distinct **criminal personality** actually exists. Some early studies claim to have found such a personality. Yochelson and Samenow (1976), for example, state that criminals behave in a sexually irresponsible manner in general and are characterized by the following personality issues:

1. *Afraid of put-downs or injury.* The criminal personality is touchy, always ready to attack.
2. *Angry.* There is a sense of pervasive rage about this personality.
3. *Inordinate self-pride.* This personality is prideful, perhaps in reaction to negative feelings about himself or herself.
4. *Interactions characterized by lying.* He or she exaggerates the truth or makes up lies out of whole cloth.
5. *Refusal to trust.* He or she does not trust others.
6. *Irresponsible.* He or she cannot be trusted to take care of the ordinary responsibilities of living: paying bills, taxes, and so on.

A number of other studies, however, have found no stable differences between criminals and the general population. Meta-analyses (studies that compare a number of individual studies at once) have in some cases found no differences and in other cases have found evidence of distinct differences (see, for example, Waldo and Dinitz 1967). So it's still not clear whether there is a personality difference between those we designate as criminals and those we do not.

SUMMARY: THE AGE OF POSITIVISM

Reacting against the concept of the rational deviant, positivism tried to study deviants and criminals objectively and scientifically, including, as with Freud, their unconscious motivations. Lombroso attempted to find criminality in the physical appearance or physiognomy of individuals, but failed. Phrenologists attempted something similar by analyzing the bumps on the skulls of individuals, but also failed. Others studied impoverished families intergenerationally, attempting to determine whether "feeblemindedness" was inherited, also failing to reach conclusive results. Sheldon determined, however, that bodytype may be correlated with aggressive forms of deviance.

Developmental disability may produce aberrant behavior, but it's not clear that it consistently does so. Certain mental diseases, such as schizophrenia and bipolar disorder, can produce deviant or criminal behavior, and it's possible that sociobiology, studying heritable sex differences in deviance, may describe an effect as well. Freud introduced psychodynamic theory, and it's likely that the unconscious plays a role in driving deviance. Refinements of Freud, such as Lasch's theory and object-relations theory, put more of an emphasis on the social environment. The relatively rare antisocial personality is likely to spawn deviant or criminal actions. Katz explained that criminality may have intrinsic rewards that make it pleasurable. It's not clear, however, that there is a distinct deviant or criminal personality that can be identified.

5

Modern Sociological Theories of Deviance, Part 1

Making His Own Way

Juan is a young man growing up in a poor urban neighborhood. Living at home with his mother and two younger sisters, he attends high school. He likes science and gets good grades in all subjects. Lately, however, acquaintances he knows in Los Locos, the local "set" (gang), have been pressuring him to join up. Juan goes out of his way to avoid them, sometimes taking a circuitous route home from school. In addition to his studies, Juan takes part in quite a few community activities. He is a member of singing groups at both his church and his school. He also studies Taekwondo at a dojang (studio) in a storefront on his block. Juan does not intend to go down the road he's seen so many other youth from the neighborhood go down. He cultivates the friendship and advice of the adults around him and occupies his time either doing homework or in activities. Almost all of his friends are either martial arts students or boys and girls from the science club at school.

In the previous two chapters, we've seen how deviance theories can be applied to individuals. In this chapter and the next one, we'll see how deviance can also be seen as a product of **groups** or **society**. In other words, deviance can be society's doing as much as an individual's. Key to many of these analyses is the idea of modernity. That is, does modern society produce tendencies for individuals to deviate, providing new opportunities for deviance and crime?

DURKHEIM'S THEORY OF ANOMIE

Emile Durkheim (1984), a sociologist writing in France at the turn of the twentieth century, held that society, broadly speaking, existed in one of two forms. In very primitive circumstances, it was in a state of **mechanical solidarity**, where people behaved well by imitating others. If they erred, they were publicly shamed or punished. Religion, government, and law were one, and woe betide him or her who deviated from the very public, well-known norms of behavior.

In Durkheim's view, modern society possesses **organic solidarity** (the whole depends on the existence of very different complementary parts). It introduces new problems compared with the rather stable existence in primitive society. For one thing, the division of labor now becomes a feature of social life. This means that people in one town can be occupied in one type of economic endeavor while those in another can be occupied in an entirely different one. The bonds between people in these two towns, although real, are based on faceless economic relations through markets, not on direct face-to-face social relations. Just as the people in two towns are separated from each other socially, people within a town can also be separated—economically dependent on one another, but separate in the sense of not having continuous face-to-face contact. Modern economics requires this increase in economic specialization. Individuals tend to be pulled apart more and more, even if they live relatively close to one another.

Durkheim's theory of deviance depends on the idea that people do best when they experience norms as close and constraining. In other words, people actually enjoy the feeling of control they get from others, and experience it not as having their freedom constrained, but more as warm support. (There is no doubt truth to this. Children frequently act out badly to see where parental limits on their behavior actually lie. Even if they get a spanking after "going too far," they're satisfied because they then have a greater sense of parental norms.)

Durkheim said that not knowing social norms is a problem he called **anomie** ("from away" + "law"). He believed that anomie is extremely depressing, and, in fact, is ultimately a major cause of suicide. It can also lead to a range of errant behavior other than suicide. Anomie occurs when people live separated from their primary group life by the division of labor in modern society. Durkheim (1976) based this on the finding that city-dwellers and Protestants had higher suicide rates than rural-dwellers and Catholics in the France of his day. He believed that the modern division of labor was a good thing, but that it tended to emerge in an "abnormal" or unbalanced way (Durkheim 1984). He thought the abnormal forms of the division of labor could be corrected by such measures as (1) more workingmen's associations, (2) trade associations for manufacturers, and (3) emphasis on joining primary groups, like hobby clubs, to restore a sense of normativeness. There should simultaneously be a strong business sector, a strong working people's system of associations (trade unions), and a strong government to constrain and control errant impulses. If these ideas seem distant from deviance theory, note that modernity in Europe or Japan generally has taken pretty much the shape Durkheim recommends, and that there is indeed less crime in those countries than in the United States, which is generally "wilder and woollier," perhaps because people living here are more individualistic, less subject to the control of groups.

An elitist, Durkheim believed that norms impinge differently on people of different social stations. For the educated or wealthy, the problem is not so much anomie, but egoism—willfulness (roughly equivalent to narcissism or exaggerated self-importance), where the individual fails to carry out obligations to society that should be acknowledged through *noblesse oblige* (the requirement that superiors have duties to inferiors). The polar opposite of anomie is an excessive sense of group loyalty. This results in excessive altruism, sometimes leading to suicide, as in Japan, where people occasionally kill themselves on behalf of a group, or because of a sense of shame at violating group norms. The opposite of egoism is fatalism, in which individuals give up all prospect of directing their lives and become totally passive.

Unlike Freud, Durkheim believed that integration with society gave individuals an increasing sense of comfort. Although he is often considered a conservative thinker, perhaps because of his celebration of a healthy business class, he would not qualify as one by contemporary American standards. After all, he calls for strong labor unions and a large state. The shape of modern social democracies in Europe or Japan (which might be considered excessively liberal in America) probably owes much to Durkheim's ideas. Although we might consider these societies more controlling than the one we are used to, they offer much in terms of security, health care, and reduction in crime.

MERTON'S THEORY OF STRAIN

Taking up Durkheim's project of explaining deviance in social terms, Robert Merton (1957) attempted to define tendencies to commit deviant actions or crime specifically by position in the social structure. Merton was fascinated by the influence of the overarching **goal** of success in America. Given this goal, he posited several different reactions to it, depending on whether a group accepted or rejected success and whether or not the group had the **means** (capability) to achieve a measure of it. It's important here to note that, as a sociologist, Merton wasn't discussing the attitudes of individuals but of different groups in the status structure. He believed that an incompatibility between goals and means yielded incongruency leading to anomie, which Merton defined in terms of **strain**, as opposed to Durkheim's normlessness.

Table 5.1 shows Merton's breakdown of the reactions to the intersection of goals and means. Note that **conformity** (a positive attitude toward success and sufficient means to achieve it) yields a condition of minimal strain. Society's goal (success) is acceptable. Moreover, members of certain groups have the means to attain it. Small wonder that they conform to the rules. They benefit if they do.

A second contingency, **innovation** (a positive attitude toward success but lack of means to achieve it), reflects strain. Here, groups want the fruits of a competitive society but find themselves without the means to garner them. Some then innovate—that is, they use illegitimate means to achieve these goals. This could mean poor young men dealing drugs on city streets rather than accepting counter jobs at McDonald's. As the young men might put it, you can't buy a flashy car and other desired accoutrements without big money. To get it right away, you must commit crimes.

Innovation also explains deviant behavior committed by groups in respectable positions, such as widespread business deviance. These groups may take the position that success cannot happen without bending the rules. Soon this becomes a self-fulfilling prophecy, and everyone commits the same transgressions, potentially putting those who don't transgress at a business disadvantage. Thus, innovation becomes a phenomenon that applies to the entire group, not just individuals.

What happens when groups forget the overall success goal in society, but continue to use "appropriate" means? Here, we get **ritualism**. We often see this phenomenon in bureaucracies, where office workers go though the motions—and require everyone else to do so as well—without their diligence and attention to detail being linked to success. When you go to the

TABLE 5.1   **Merton's Theory of Strain**

	Attitude toward Success Goal	Means Available?	Strain?
Conformity	Positive	Yes	No
Innovation	Positive	No	Yes
Ritualism	Negative	Yes	Yes
Rebellion	Negative	No	No
Retreatism	Negative	No	No

Source: Merton (1957).

Department of Motor Vehicles and stand in one line after another, this is an example of ritualism. The workers may seem to enjoy the fact that they can subject you to repeated inconvenience. Technically, it is deviant behavior because it expresses strain between diminished success goals and overactive means (which might in other settings achieve success).

If both goals and means are negative, we can get either **rebellion**, in which groups reject society's goals and actively try to change its nature (and its means and goals), or **retreatism**, in which groups drop out of society. Rebellion characterized many young people in the 1960s, who, appalled by racism and the Vietnam War, tried to change the political and economic rules. They were not successful in changing the rules, but their activism was a factor driving many reforms that are with us today. Retreatism characterized other young people—the hippies—who tried to "turn on, tune in, and drop out." The phrase referred to the use of substances like LSD, a drug that inclined them toward lives characterized by contemplation, not toward accomplishing goals. These groups rejected society's success goal; both used means not approved by society to create new agendas and lifestyles. Both indicate deviance, because, although there is a lack of strain within the groups, there is strain between their means and goals and those of society.

Merton's strain theory goes well with his prescription that sociologists eschew grand theories in favor of theories of "middle range." Rather than speak broadly about anomie, as Durkheim did, Merton devoted his studies to capturing the experiences of specific groups and strata and to accounting for possible causes of deviance affecting these groups. Because his theories are midrange, they lend themselves to verification by empirical research. By the same token, they are, at best, only probabilistic. Explaining deviance in terms of blocked opportunities is appealing, but this sociological theory does not do a good job of accounting for individual behavior. Why is it that some people from poor neighborhoods ultimately succeed while others go on to become criminals? Merton's broad theory, although much more specific than, say, Durkheim's, cannot explain this.

DIFFERENTIAL ASSOCIATION

Differential association takes the position that deviance is learned (Sutherland 1939). Moreover, what's learned as appropriate behavior and as deviance depends on one's specific group. Although this may sound fairly obvious, it was not always so. Part of the problem was researchers' tendency to see deviance and crime in the light of notions of good and bad. The implicit idea was that everyone shared the same norms. Actually, they probably don't. Differential association reasons that one's early primary groups, especially the family and one's childhood friends, heavily shape one's moral outlook and behavior.

Consider this. A Gypsy leader comes to the emergency room of a hospital. He subsequently dies, and the doctor explains to his two wives that there was nothing that the facility could have done to save him. The women throw themselves on the floor, crying and rending their clothing. Meanwhile, the hospital fills up with many Gypsy men, who wander the hallways restlessly. The county sheriff pulls up outside with 20 cars full of deputies, red "gumballs" on top of each car pulsing brightly. The hospital's crisis intervention counselor walks around serving the Gypsies refreshments, hoping to avoid a crisis in which they tear up the hospital or the sheriffs arrest them. Finally the huge crowd clears out without violence. When they do, it is clear that they have stolen bedpans, IV stands, and many other pieces of hospital equipment. The hospital had tried its best to save their leader—so why did they steal from it?

This isn't something as simple as Gypsies taking revenge on the emergency room, although this may have played a role. Basically, they stole from the hospital because they saw it as permissible to steal from non-Gypsies. In fact, such theft is a way to obtain status as much as material rewards in Gypsy communities. In differential association, one is socialized into patterns of deviance or nondeviance depending on one's specific upbringing. In some ways, the idea of differential association makes definitions of deviance problematic. Clearly, what works for one group may be anathema to another. On the other hand, there are probably some deep standards that pertain to most groups. For example, one is not usually permitted to kill members of one's own society or tribe without reason, although this rule has been broken in some societies. And it has frequently been the case that it has been permissible to kill or injure persons outside of one's society or tribe. Differential association also suffers from a problem in that it doesn't work in terms of defining deviance within a group as opposed to between groups. How do we explain someone who is obnoxious according to local norms, even though he or she has been socialized in the same way as everyone else in the group?

Differential identification (Glaser 1956) extends the idea of differential association. Here, what's emphasized is the deviant person selecting models from a variety of individuals he or she has known in the past. If the person is moving toward deviance, he or she will select deviant individuals as models. If the person is moving toward conventional behavior, he or she will select a conventional model or models. For Glaser, the reason a person may select one as opposed to the other has to do with whether that person encounters blocked opportunities for success and believes he or she must become deviant.

DIFFERENTIAL OPPORTUNITY THEORY

In spite of the idea that blocked opportunities tended to lead to deviance, Cloward and Ohlin (1960) believed that a key factor was missing from the other theories. This was a **differential access to opportunities** to commit deviance or crime. A group may experience blocked opportunities for conventional success but remain relatively quiescent because opportunities for aberrant behavior do not exist. These authors suggested that there must also be means available for deviant behavior. Thus when an immigrant group comes to the United States, its first generation, although relatively poor and oppressed, may remain relatively conservative and law-abiding. Its young people (who are more likely to innovate) have not, as yet, discovered opportunities for deviance or crime. They may not as yet have the cultural tools necessary to integrate themselves into crime markets. For later generations of young people, this may change as they find opportunities for conventional success relatively blocked and opportunities for criminal success relatively open. Their style of dress is likely to change from the conservative style of the older generation to styles reflecting thuggishness or "flash" wealth. They are likely to express contempt for the first generation's old-world ways.

Mizruchi (1983) described the enculturation of strain and differential opportunity for deviance, and provides a bridge between these theories and differential association. For him, experience with differing legitimate and illegitimate opportunities gives groups the impetus to form ideas about ends and means to get what they desire. These lead to differing sets of values depending on a given group's experiences. He recapitulates Durkheim's concepts of egoism and anomie respectively in terms of boundlessness and bondlessness, since these dimensions are most likely to lead to problems. Messner and Rosenfeld apply strain theory specifically to American society, arguing in *Crime and the American Dream* (2000) that our society intensely conditions the likelihood of crime because it both elevates the goals of material and monetary success and strongly de-emphasizes ethical means for achieving them.

COHEN'S DELINQUENT BOYS

Albert Cohen (1955) became among the first to apply strain theory to real situations. According to him, school emphasizes certain **middle-class values** that are difficult for boys from lower-class families to live up to. These include (1) ambitiousness, (2) responsibility, (3) developing economically oriented skills, (4) postponing gratification, (5) rational planning, (6) manners and courtesy, (7) de-emphasizing physical aggression, (8) constructive play, and (9) respecting others' property rights. If boys fail to meet these criteria, they may be subject to punishment or ridicule. They consequently suffer a loss of self-esteem. In order to restore this loss, they may form groups—gangs actually—that have norms pretty much the opposite of those of the school and its successful children. In this way, Cohen artfully blends insights from both strain and differential association theory. Strain sets the stage for rejection of middle-class values.

Differential association explains the ways in which the boys create new groups that socialize them in new antisocial ways.

THE ISSUE OF NEUTRALIZATION

Cohen says that there is tension between the social norms and norms of delinquent or deviant groups. As we've seen, the deviant person may feel a loss of self-esteem experiencing the difference between his or her behavior and society's expectations. If he or she joins or forms a group organized around deviant activities, he or she may feel more comfortable. Members of deviant groups may generate explanations concerning reasons their behavior is "not really deviant" in the light of society's actual or potential disapproval. This process is called **neutralization** and entails distancing from stigmatization and feelings of guilt by offering excuses for the deviant behavior. According to Sykes and Matza (1957), these excuses tend to fall into the following categories:

1. *Denial of responsibility.* The act was beyond his or her control.
2. *Denial of injury.* No one was really hurt or adversely affected by the act.
3. *Denial of victim.* The victim "had it coming."
4. *Condemning the condemners.* "Everybody does it. Why are they picking on me?"
5. *Appeal to higher loyalties.* He or she was serving a higher cause.

Thus, poor people in urban centers who fraudulently claim to have been in bus accidents in order to get insurance settlements (when they were not even on the bus to begin with) may use all of these excuses. They may say that, when they heard about the accident on the radio, they couldn't resist the opportunity to put in a false claim. They may state that, because of insurance, no one was injured by their actions. They may say that the bus or insurance companies "had it coming" for being rich, powerful organizations. They may say that everyone would try this scam if they had a chance. Finally, they may argue that they tried to get the insurance money for their family, a higher loyalty than obeying the law.

Although the techniques of neutralization may seem appalling, they point up the fact that deviant or criminal behavior troubles perpetrators, who have to invent rationalizations for their behavior. Otherwise, they would just take a "go to hell" position with regard to their actions. This indicates that perpetrators are often "of two minds" in regard to destructive behavior (or at least that they are aware of society's likely response), and that treatment may be possible if the part of the mind that wants to do (or is aware of) the right thing is put in control.

AGNEW'S GENERAL THEORY OF CRIME

Robert Agnew (1992) revised strain theory, which he believed properly emphasized the role of negative events in shaping deviant behavior, by distinguishing three different ways strain is experienced. The first (following Merton) is the failure to achieve positively valued goals. The second is the removal of positively valued life events; being fired from a job is an example. The third is experiencing negative events. Being victimized oneself can lead to one's own criminal activity. Since these are individual as opposed to group experiences, Agnew accounts for differences in the individual production of crime by discussing the coping strategies the individual uses to deal with them.

SOCIAL DISORGANIZATION THEORY

A more **geographical** theory of deviance came from the University of Chicago school of sociology. Classical Chicago sociologists wrote between 1910 and 1940. Most were qualitative, devoting themselves to interviews and observations, but some were quantitative. Some Chicago theorists (Shaw and McKay 1942) took the position that urban geography had much to do with the production of crime and deviance. As a city grows, immigrants are brought in to staff its industries. Soon the city is separated into concentric zones, like an archery target (see Figure 5.1). At the core is the central business district. Around that is an industrial zone. Next comes worker housing. Then there are the more affluent suburbs. Clearly this twentieth-century city could not have developed without the streetcar to get suburban dwellers downtown to their office jobs.

Key to production of deviance is a **transitional zone** where the industrial zone meets worker housing. Large numbers of poor workers are brought in to occupy marginal positions in the city's economy. Many are unemployed. Called a "slum" in classical literature, this zone consists of the affluent housing of yesteryear that has become "blighted," that is, run down and decayed. Stately homes may be carved up into several apartments, all containing large families. Marginal shops and businesses may hang on by their fingernails on the trash-ridden, poorly maintained streets. Some buildings in the transitional zone may have originally been built as worker housing—tenements. If the city continues to expand, the zone moves outward. Due to overcrowding, poverty, and lack of opportunity, rates of deviance and crime become far greater than in other parts of the city.

Other Chicago theorists refined this theory to make it less geographically deterministic. Krohn (1986) found that social disorganization was valid, but only if the neighborhood in question lacked groups and associations. It's easy to see that this theory combines elements of both Durkheim and

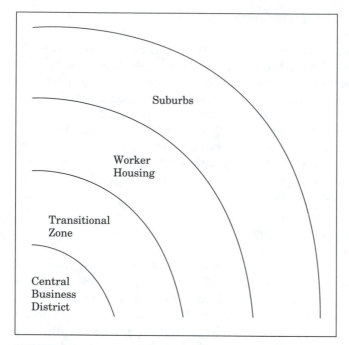

FIGURE 5.1   Concentric Zone Theory

strain, because it deals with the controlling/supporting effect of groups and varying opportunities for success. Like other macro theories, it is incapable of dealing with individual variation in various group contexts, except as a statistical matter. Another issue is that cities now evolve according to a polynuclear model (Los Angeles is an example). In these cities, affluent and poor areas are likely to be chock-a-block with one another. Social disorganization could still be used to analyze these cities, but the concept of transitional zones might have to be revised to accommodate this new urban model.

STARK'S DANGEROUS PLACES

A more innovative micro-application of detailed geographical models of crime and deviance is Rodney Stark's (2002) social ecological theory. Stark wanted to know why the same run-down neighborhoods produced higher rates of crime, even when different cultural groups cycled through them at different points in their history. His explanation based itself on density—which exposed members to more deviance; poverty—which added to the density and crowding; mixed use, which puts housing and commercial enterprises together, creating both establishments to steal from and a variety of gathering places for deviant activities; transience—which breaks down decent institutions; and dilapidation—which makes crime and deviance seem appropriate to the environment. All of these factors build an atmosphere characterized by moral cynicism (residents know too much about each other's misdeeds), increased opportunities for crime and deviance, increased motivation to deviate (its rewards can be seen), and diminished social control—due to the weakening of institutions.

The troubled atmosphere created by these factors amplifies deviance by (1) attracting crime-prone individuals and activities, (2) driving out the least deviant, and (3) further reducing social control. Some of the successful reforms under Rudolph Giuliani that made New York City a more pleasant place to live take account of Stark's theory. The "broken windows" theory—the idea that crime flows from unattractive environments—and the proactive policing of high-crime locations that has been so successful there are essentially derived from social ecology.

ASSESSING ANOMIE, STRAIN, DIFFERENTIAL ASSOCIATION, AND GEOGRAPHICAL THEORIES

Both Durkheim and Merton can perhaps be faulted for overgeneralization. Their theories can explain contexts or circumstances in which persons become deviant, but cannot explain which individuals will do so and which will not. Merton is sometimes criticized for failing to explain upper-class deviance, since his theory of innovation explicitly discusses lower-class peoples' blocked means for achieving success. That said, these theories do seem fruitful ways to examine these contexts. Although individuals do not respond to issues of social structure uniformly, theories can help explain propensities for many individuals to respond in deviant or criminal ways depending on their location in the social structure. By discussing the effects of individual life events and individual responses to them, Agnew creates a way to adapt strain theory to a general theory of crime.

Differential association can also be critiqued on grounds of overgeneralization. In some neighborhoods, many young people join gangs, but many do not. Here, the notion is that one often has a choice, even though the choice may be difficult. As with other macro-type theories of deviance or crime, social structure can be seen as providing environments for learning deviance; but not everyone elects to participate in these specific contexts. The idea of learning deviance as normal behavior in group contexts seems sensible, but not everyone in these environments becomes a deviant group member. Geographical theories offer much useful detail, but, again, only explain contexts and tendencies—not every person follows the deviant pattern in his/her neighborhood.

SUMMARY: MODERN SOCIOLOGICAL THEORIES
OF DEVIANCE, PART I

Durkheim opened the door to modern analyses of deviance with his concept of anomie—decreased contact with social norms. In his view, anomie could lead to depression, even suicide. He also introduced the concepts of egoism, fatalism, and altruism, each of which in too great a quantity could have negative consequences. According to Durkheim, the modern division of labor made group life problematic, increasing anomie, but society could remedy this by providing overlapping associations and group memberships. Merton added the idea of group reactions to strain regarding the success goal in society and whether groups had the means to attain it. Conformity was a state of no strain because groups believed in success and possessed means to achieve it. Innovation involved believing in success but feeling that legitimate means were blocked; group members might turn to crime. Ritualism meant abandoning of success goals but going through appropriate motions nonetheless; groups following this model might become obsessive bureaucrats. Rebellion and retreatism each meant that groups rejected both society's success goals and appropriate means to attain them. In rebellion, groups strove to change the rules in general; in retreatism, they dropped out, abandoning both appropriate goals and means.

Differential opportunity theory states that not only must structural strains be present, but opportunities for deviance or crime must also exist. If not, deviance and crime will be minimized. Differential association emphasizes deviance as learned from members of one's group, particularly groups in which one experiences early socialization. Cohen emphasized the ways in which gangs provided an alternative for poor boys who felt that they could not live up to the middle-class success goals emphasized in school. Sykes's and Matza's neutralization techniques discuss ways in which people breaking society's rules justify themselves to self and others. Agnew accounts for differences in individual experiences and responses in his general theory of crime. Finally, social disorganization theory discusses the city as a device for producing deviance and crime by successively moving a troubled zone of impoverishment out from the city center.

6

Modern Sociological Theories of Deviance, Part 2

The Effects of Labeling

Sam is just 10 years old. His mother and father are of the old school, and they believe in strong discipline. When Sam does something wrong, his mother slaps him and tells him what a bad boy he is. Usually, his father also gives him a whipping when he gets home from work. His parents have told him that they think children are naturally bad and need to have it beaten out of them. The result is that Sam's behavior around them has become pretty careful. He knows what will happen if he is caught doing something they disapprove of. When he's out in the neighborhood, however, it's just the opposite. Sam, big for his age, is getting to be quite a bully. The other children are scared of him, and some go out of their way to avoid him at all costs. Although he has not been caught yet, Sam has begun stealing from stores. He figures, in a strange way, that this is what he has been meant to do all along.

Previously, we saw that deviance is sometimes a reaction to social structure or social circumstances. In this chapter, we'll extend this theme, examining more critical theories of deviance. First we'll examine Marxian and conflict theories (including feminism); then we'll take up labeling theory. We'll inspect control theory, which turns the issue of deviance on its head, asking how it's possible that people behave appropriately at all. Finally, we'll examine Donald Black's theory of social control.

MARX

Karl Marx is not commonly thought of as a theorist of deviance, but his work has implications for deviance nonetheless. A critic of emerging capitalist society, he's usually considered a student of the effects of large-scale economic forces, particularly on the working class or proletariat. He believed that **capitalism**—Western industrial society—was characterized by conflict between the owners of the means of production (factories) and the workers who provided labor (Marx and Engels 1965). Capitalism had "freed" these workers from feudalism, under which they were bound to a lord's lands as serfs. But such freedom was an illusion, as Marx saw it. Workers were free only to try to sell their labor power to capitalists. There were always more workers available than there were jobs, so workers in general were paid a subsistence wage. Surplus workers constituted a "reserve army of labor." Marx believed that capitalism was unstable due to crises of boom and bust, and that it tended to produce fewer profits over time, dumping more and more previous owners into the working class (proletariat). These crises, plus the swelling, underemployed working class, would ultimately produce a revolution, ushering in socialism. The proletariat would be disciplined and organized by the capitalist production process, as well as by the labor unions it evolved to deal with injustices and low wages. Hence it would be prepared to take power. However, before this happened, society would exist in a state of delusion, in which the ideas of the ruling class (the owners) would be in control. The workers would thus have "false consciousness." They would not see that it would be in their interest to change society from capitalist to socialist unless crises became extreme, or unless they learned Marxist theory.

Although Marx seems to have little to say about deviance, it's possible to build deviance theory based on classical Marxism in two senses:

1. *Capitalism, if Marx is correct, creates **"criminogenic"** cultures, where everyone attempts to profit at the expense of others.* The economic system, after all, is based on just such principles. The tendency to exploit others affects everyone, as owners compete against each other and exploit workers, and workers compete with each other to sell labor power.
2. *Capitalism also creates a permanent underclass, the **lumpenproletariat**, below the working class.* This class is not capable of being organized in

the same sense as the proletariat (which is disciplined by the workplace). Marx believed that this criminal class was susceptible to recruitment as thugs who could be used to attack workers' movements—a prediction that came true when fascism became a world phenomenon during the period of the 1920s through the 1940s. The lumpenproletariat has no desire to work or to organize, and is interested in a life of crime and indolent hedonism. Because of this, it's a dangerous class.

Admittedly, these are very macro propositions. Like other macro theories, they have the disadvantage that they cannot really predict individual behavior or specify which individuals are likely to commit deviant actions. They're also very general. Not everyone is rapaciously competitive in business. Only a small percentage of the very poor are criminals. Still, many might agree that Marx is on to something. A competitive business society probably makes it more likely that competition, even some exploitive or criminal competition, characterizes commercial and interpersonal dealings. The continued existence of the very poor, even in modern societies, makes it more likely that some will lead lives of crime.

BONGER'S MARXIST CRIMINOLOGY

Bonger, a Dutch criminologist writing in the early twentieth century, refined Marx's inchoate notions of crime causation even further. Bonger (1969) believed that crime is socially constructed; that is, it changes from period to period and place to place. Having said this, he stated that behavior isn't likely to be considered criminal unless it threatens upper-class interests. Even though laws may be written to protect rich and poor alike, they are mainly targeted against members of the poorer classes. The essence of the capitalist system is to rule by force; social relations are colored by this. Human nature is hedonistic (pleasure oriented). Because pleasures must be paid for under capitalism, selfishness becomes the order of the day. People focus on acquiring money and abandon the fellow-feeling they might otherwise have. Superiority is demonstrated by the possession of money. Poverty engendered by capitalism creates tremendous need, and this, also, leads to crime. Crime frequently occurs when there is an opportunity not available through other means.

Like Marx, Bonger is a macro theorist. Because he is specifically interested in deviance and crime, however, he's capable of specifying the general effect of capitalism more precisely. Bonger introduces a dimension largely missing from Marx—the possible demoralizing effect of a **strong state**, which comes into being to support capitalism. Marx preferred to concentrate on the alienating effect of production, and did not say much about the nature of government. For Bonger, the oppressive effect of government insures that laws are enforced differentially, against the poor, not the rich.

QUINNEY'S CRITICAL CRIMINOLOGY

Refining older radical criminologists, contemporary **critical criminolo-gists** such as Richard Quinney were instrumental in creating a radical criminology school at the University of California at Berkeley. Like previous radical criminologists, they were faced with the simultaneous problem of specifying how behavior comes to be defined as criminal and accounting for the production of criminality. They take a critical view of these problems, adopting a Marxian point of view, but, like Bonger, specifying the issues more precisely. Quinney (1974) delineates his critical criminology theory in six propositions:

1. *Official definition of crime.* Crime is defined by agents of the dominant class, the ruling class.
2. *Formulation of definitions of crime.* Crime is that behavior conflicting with ruling-class interests.
3. *Application of definitions of crime.* These definitions are applied by the class having the power to control law administration and enforcement.
4. *Development of behavior patterns in relation to these definitions.* Those not in the ruling class react to pervasive definitions of crime by, in many cases, behaving criminally.
5. *Construction of conceptions of crime.* Concepts dealing with crime are disseminated by the powerful (according to their interests). Both concern about crime and the criminal behavior itself increase as a result.
6. *Construction of the social reality of crime.* All of the above factors taken together produce what we think of as "crime."

Note that Quinney accounts for both the definition of crime and the production of crime by saying that capitalism broadly defines this form of deviance, then makes it more likely to happen. Although he shows in detail the mechanisms by which joint definition and production of deviance are likely to occur, there is no doubt that crime flows from the social order in general.

VOLD'S THEORY OF CULTURAL CONFLICT

George Vold (1958) took a more variegated position than Quinney. Vold said it was not so much class conflict that set the stage for the definition and production of crime, but the norms and behaviors of various specific groups in conflict. Thus immigrant groups might form gangs after coming into conflict with norms stemming from majority groups in the larger society. These groups might put forth an alternate set of norms and behaviors in keeping with the minority groups' expectations of what was correct behavior. This, in turn, was likely to be experienced as crime by majority groups. Thus it was normal and reasonable for Sicilian immigrants in America to revere local strongmen who provided neighborhood government. It seemed natural that these strongmen should be able to exact tribute from the people who lived in the neighborhood in return for the governance they provided. Of course, we know these neighborhood strongmen of the early 1900s as the founders of the American Mafia. Teenagers, also, may form minority groups whose behavior may be experienced as crime by the majority. They may form youth gangs in reaction to the fact that they and their interests are devalued by society and defined as outside the pale of normal behavior.

SPITZER'S THEORY OF DANGEROUS POPULATIONS

Spitzer (1999) says that the key problem for capitalist societies is managing dangerous populations. He agrees with other Marxist criminologists that the overarching ethic of exploitation covertly legitimizes the poor trying to steal from the rich or change the conditions under which they live and labor, so the task for social control is putting a lid on groups he refers to as (1) "social junk" [*sic*] (those members of the reserve army of labor cast aside by capital and (2) "social dynamite" (those members of society who might act against capital) either in large or small ways—for example, through crime or through revolutionary activity). For him, society might choose to try to normalize these populations, for example by decriminalizing certain types of drug use; to convert them, for example by turning militant gang members into social work paraprofessionals; to contain them, for example by creating ghettos; or to covertly support criminal enterprises like organized crime, which, in turn, control "problem populations."

FEMINIST APPROACHES

Feminist approaches stress how **patriarchy**, a system by which men have taken preeminence for the last 5,000 years or so, has emphasized aggression and selfishness. According to these analyses, men have used the natural vulnerability women experience during childbirth and child rearing to take over. Some feminist approaches cite the development of agriculture as key (Gimbutas 1991). During its development, societies for the first time had surpluses worth stealing. Also, agriculture meant that some could work but others would be free to govern, make war, and devise hierarchical religions to justify these behaviors. War-making ability gave men, for the first time, the ability to capture slaves, but it also emphasized men's large physical stature and greater aggressiveness. All this gave rise to societies in which women were the lesser sex. Men's well-documented predilections for greater criminality and deviance than women may spring from these cultural roots, as well as from some of the sociobiological factors we have already examined.

Another way in which feminism has critiqued the study of deviance and crime has been in drawing attention to the neglect of women as objects of study. Men have traditionally been seen as of greater interest to researchers. Additionally, the criminal justice system has responded to women by taking either a (1) chivalrous or (2) paternal attitude toward them. This has meant, for example, that young women have historically been confined for longer periods of time for less serious offenses, probably because the state believed that it had a duty to protect them, but also probably because it believed that women had deficiencies of character (Bartol and Bartol 1998).

Not surprisingly, as women have gained greater equality with men as a result of the feminist movement and society's greater demand for skilled workers, their tendencies to engage in deviance and crime have grown. The rates of women committing crimes and engaging in deviant activities, although still not as great as those of men, have increased substantially (Hill and Atkinson 1988).

POSTMODERN THEORIES

Another set of theories stems from culture. Often called **postmodern** theories, these focus at least as much on how society defines deviance as on any deviant activity. Here, sets of ideas about deviance and, significantly, about its "treatment" are called "discourses." For postmodernists, criminality and mental illness are constructions of language. Emphasizing these types of behavior brings forth treatment bureaucracies that "define" these behaviors and find cases, because it's their nature to do so. Critics should **deconstruct** the ideologies (false systems of belief) that posit deviance and its treatment in the first place. In postmodern analysis, humans are seen as duped by systems of **discourse** unless they dispute these rather seamless cultures of arbitrary belief by arguing or disagreeing with them. Most postmodernists would radically reject the notion of deviance, and many would also reject the idea of crime. Although these ideas might not seem useful as theories of crime and deviance, some students of these fields do call themselves postmodernists. Many are as fascinated by society's beliefs about poor behavior as by the behavior itself. Foucault (1995), to choose one author, makes a convincing case for changes in the ways crime has been seen and enacted in society between premodern times and the present. He does the same for mental illness in another work (1988). Forms of deviance become opportunities for systems of meaning that unfold behind humans' backs, creating bureaucracy, control, and oppression. Rather than gaining knowledge with the passage of time, humans become more and more befuddled. Premodern societies made the conflict with authority quite clear; modern societies obfuscate this conflict and establish outposts in people's heads, controlling them through "mental health," case management, and probation. Postmodernists might call for intervening with troubled people at the level of family or close community, but eschewing the more global definitions and bureaucratic structures contained in professional, bureaucratic, or state responses.

ASSESSING MARXIAN, CONFLICT, FEMINIST, AND POSTMODERN THEORIES

Although there is something persuasive about the idea that the rich have much to do with defining crime and may frequently escape arrest for misbehavior, points of view held by radical and critical criminologists may be too much all-of-a-piece. Most Americans, rich or poor, agree that criminal activities are wrong. Most victims of crime, moreover, are members of the poor and working classes. So, although the market economy may have much to do with why people commit crimes, victims are usually poor people, not rich people. Therefore, poor and working-class people want perpetrators caught, prosecuted, and punished, perhaps even more so than the wealthy do. Like other macro theories, conflict theories also don't explain why some people from poor circumstances (or rich circumstances, for that matter) commit crimes while others do not.

Feminist theory may help to explain why men, in particular, behave aggressively. Postmodern theory, although it would seem to have few uses as a theory of deviance, may have some value as a corrective set of ideas when we find ourselves feeling excessively smug about behavior, and about our beliefs about the causes of certain types of behavior.

SOCIETAL REACTION THEORY

Imagine this. You are an intellectual man in your mid-twenties with few social skills. You don't have a girlfriend. You've taken a series of dead-end jobs, ranging from security guard to fry cook, since graduating from college with a history degree. You have a passion for Japanese and German military equipment and are something of an expert in the field. One of the main pleasures in your isolated life is talking to yourself about what you've lately read on these subjects. Having absolutely no fashion sense, you dress funny. One night, you are walking down the street talking to yourself about Me109s, when a police cruiser pulls up. The police get out and interview you. They've had complaints from some of your neighbors about the shabby, dirty condition of your tiny apartment—something that's of no concern to you. Reflexively, you mumble to yourself. The officers decide to take you to the hospital for a psychiatric evaluation.

When you get to the crisis unit, you're angry, and you refuse to speak to the admitting nurse or to the on-call psychiatrist who interviews you later. They each write in your progress notes that you are "mute," but that, according to the officers, you appeared to be responding to unseen stimuli earlier. The doctor places you on oral Haldol, and when you refuse to take this medicine, three male psychiatric technicians forcibly inject you, and then put you in restraints on a bed for several hours. The medicine depresses you, so that you can hardly speak. The nurses and technicians write in your progress notes that you have a "flat affect." You're totally cut off from your usual pursuits, and you don't feel like talking to the other patients, who seem either very depressed or floridly crazy. When you meet with your physician, he says that he wants to keep you "for observation." He implies that there is something wrong with you. After a few days, it occurs to you that you are crazy. Following this, you begin obsessively sharing your knowledge of World War II with the other patients, even when they don't seem interested. You announce that Japan and Germany are about to declare war against the United States a second time.

This shows the essence of **societal reaction theory** (Becker 1963) (See Figure 6.1). The idea is that we all, even the most conventional of us, display strange behavior from time to time. If we do this sufficiently, and if the agents of social control become aware of these behaviors, we may be seen as "having a problem." If a **prestige figure**, in this case a doctor, **labels** us as belonging to a deviant category, we may "buy" his or her definition of the situation and begin to act accordingly. The normal strange behavior all of us engage in is called *residual deviance*. The theory is called *societal reaction* because it emphasizes deviance produced by society as a reaction to behavior. Deviance is essentially a construction, not real. It's also called *labeling theory* because it depends on a label being applied to the proposed deviant person. For labeling to fully take place, the individual targeted must internalize the label and produce deviant behavior. Labeling theories generally hold that deviant behavior increases subsequent to labeling.

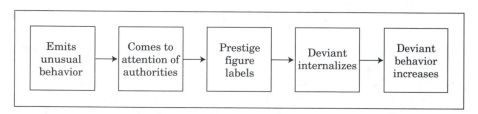

FIGURE 6.1   **Societal Reaction (Labeling) Theory**
Source: Becker 1963.

BROADER NOTIONS OF SOCIETAL REACTION

Lest anyone think that labeling pertains only to issues of mental illness, it's important to note that it has much to do with how we live in general. When a parent scolds a child, saying "You're a nasty little boy (or girl); you'll never amount to anything," the result is likely to be an increase in poor behavior, not a diminution. The same can happen in court. Well-meaning judges may believe that a stern talking-to, where the criminal is told exactly what sort of a person he or she has become, may be just the ticket to elicit changed behavior. But there is a chance that it may have the opposite effect. The perpetrator is likely to experience this as a degradation ceremonial (see Chapter 8), in which he or she internalizes the label and subsequently acts it out. Tannenbaum (1938) was one of the first to point out the function that a "dramaturgical" (playlike) enactment of "good" suppressing "bad" seemed to serve, and the tendency for those designated as being on the wrong side of these enactments to internalize the negative label and reproduce it in their behavior later. Anticipating Cohen's application of social strain to gangs, he said that logical behavior for young people who had been shaped into bad behavior through labeling was to form groups with others who had the same experience.

Becker (1996) extended the idea of societal reaction to encompass the idea of a deviant "career." Here, he cited the tendency for a person's involvement in a known deviant lifestyle to become a **master status**—the fixed role in which others think of that person first. Thus, if one is homosexual, others may think of one first as "gay," even though, as a full human being, one plays many, many other roles, most of them having nothing to do with being homosexual. Such people are then treated as though they are generally, as opposed to specifically, deviant, and are often shunned. They then tend to form groups based on the deviant master status, which becomes a basis for solidarity. This explains much about why deviant subcultures often exaggerate stereotypical aspects of the labels applied to them— as with drag culture in the gay world. They are both mocking their labels and achieving a sense of group integration from them.

ASSESSING SOCIETAL REACTION THEORIES

As with radical theories, there is doubtless some truth to labeling. At the same time, these theories, at times, have been overused. In the 1970s, some labeling theorists believed that virtually all psychosis (seeing and hearing things) was created by labeling. Now we are fairly sure that schizophrenia is biological and inherited. But we shouldn't throw the baby out with the bathwater. Even if major psychoses are biological, there is no doubt that other people's expectations and utterances have much to do with fitting targets of labeling into deviant social roles. In all likelihood, minor psychiatric disorders are at least partly created by labeling, in spite of the current fashion of seeing most psychiatric problems as stemming from biology.

Families, teachers, police, and the courts, however well-meaning, may apply labels that have tremendous consequences in encouraging future negative behavior. So labels must be carefully assessed by those who use them, if they really want society to improve. At times, it's true, labels may be self-imposed therapeutically, as in Alcoholics Anonymous, where alcoholics self-label to overcome the denial that's part of the disease, but these uses are deliberate and have been shown to work over time.

CONTROL THEORY

Theories of deviance usually take the position that deviant or atavistic behavior is the exception, rather than the rule. That is, we expect that people will behave agreeably, unless there is some reason for them to do otherwise. **Control theory**, by contrast, says that people tend to behave badly or selfishly by nature, and that it's the task of deviance theory to explain why people behave well at all. Foremost among control theorists is Travis Hirschi (1969), who takes the position that, absent a strong bond to society, deviance or crime is likely to occur. He says that this bond has four components:

1. *Attachment.* One needs close ties to others, especially one's parents and close friends. When these ties are present, one tends to behave in accordance with society's rules.
2. *Commitment.* If one aspires to put time and effort into legitimate activities, one tends to behave in accordance with society's rules.
3. *Involvement.* If one actually spends time and effort in legitimate activities, one tends to behave in accordance with society's rules.
4. *Belief.* If one attaches moral validity to society's rules, one is likely to obey them.

These propositions imply that strong socialization and child rearing lead to conforming, law-abiding citizens. Gottfredson and Hirschi (1990) later expand this into a general theory of crime, attributing all criminal behavior to a lack of control resulting from having been reared poorly.

Another well-known control theorist, Reckless (1961), suggests that it's **containment** of errant impulses that is important. This comes in two forms; inner containment, dealing with ways through which individuals evolve techniques to control themselves; and outer containment, dealing with the forces that control them from outside.

However, if it's now tempting to think that "more is better" in terms of discipline, one should be aware of a significant body of psychological research showing that parents with *assertive* but neither overly punitive nor overly lackadaisical child-rearing styles do best in terms of results. So the middle ground here, as in many other behavioral issues, turns out to be best (Sprengkle and Russell 1979).

DONALD BLACK'S PURE SOCIOLOGY OF DEVIANCE

In another approach, Black (1998) suggests that it's not so much deviance that's important. It's the issue of **social control**, an empirical phenomenon that can be measured, yielding a pure sociology. Here, he means that most of our approaches to deviance are ideological because they smuggle in our preconceptions about right and wrong without saying so. If we measure social control as the consequences of behavior people find unacceptable, we get a much more interesting and accurate set of problems and conclusions, according to Black. Many supposedly deviant or criminal activities are really manifestations of social control. If someone is murdered, for example, it's likely that the murderer believed himself or herself to have been victimized by the one who was murdered. Robbery is likely to be committed for similar reasons, if not against those who have directly aggrieved the robber, then against a group of people against whom the robber has a grudge. Black extends his analysis to social norms and the law, showing how the likelihood of sanctions and punishments is related to a variety of causal factors, but not really to issues of "justice" or right or wrong. Although many scholars have problems with his abandonment of deviance and crime as social problems, he provides a very interesting and potentially very fruitful set of questions and issues.

SUMMARY: MODERN SOCIOLOGICAL THEORIES OF DEVIANCE, PART 2

In this chapter, we've seen how the ideas of Marx, Bonger, Quinney, and Spitzer lead to radical and critical criminologies, in which the emphasis is on the ways a social class system leads to the production of crime, either by promoting excess competition or by creating a permanent underclass. Vold creates a cultural conflict theory of deviance, in which immigrant groups generate behavior unacceptable to majority groups in society. Feminist theory emphasizes patriarchy, a system of male domination in society featuring aggression and exploitiveness as cultural values leading to bad behavior. Postmodernists cite the definitions of deviance as arbitrary and as leading to the creation of systems of meaning and bureaucracies having their own autonomous agendas of expansion.

Societal reaction theory emphasizes people becoming deviant in response to labels—attributions from authority figures. Control theory states that the emphasis in deviance and crime should be on why people behave at all, not why they misbehave, and studies the factors that make for acceptable behavior. Donald Black's sociology of deviance studies human behavior as social control, including forms of deviance. For him, what is interesting is what factors make punishment more or less likely, whether the punisher is an individual or a social group.

PART II

PERSONAL DEVIANCE

7

Drug and Alcohol Abuse

Enter Addiction

Jeff is a college student who is attending his first "rave" on a Friday night. Given instructions by some friends, he arrives at an unused warehouse where a doorman collects $15 from each person seeking admittance. The room, packed solid with standing young adults, booms with prerecorded music played through giant speakers. Jeff sees a few people from school and many others who dress in more extreme styles. He recognizes them as lifestylers from town.

Linking up with friends, Jeff is shown how to buy "X"—Ecstasy—for another $15. Excited to try this, Jeff buys a hit and swallows it. After a bit, he feels energized. His whole world comes alive with interesting, exciting sensations. He stands, pulsating to the music, totally swept away with these new, fascinating perceptions.

After a few hours of standing, Jeff notices he is coming down. His jaw hurts where he has been grinding his teeth, a by-product of X intoxication. He feels slightly depressed. After saying good-bye to his friends, he drives home. The next two days, Jeff feels quite depressed. It is as though the chemical has taken something out of him. He feels listless during the first part of the school week, but is "getting it together" again by Wednesday. He resolves to catch up on some of the reading he failed to do when he was feeling crummy.

On Thursday night, a friend asks him, "Do you want to hit the rave again on Friday?"
Jeff thinks for a moment, and says, "Sure."

Drug and alcohol abuse is a central problem in American society. Around 14 percent of Americans are thought to be **alcoholics** (Cockerham 2000), who have a mental and physical compulsion to drink. A smaller, but still significant, percentage of Americans are addicted to drugs. Drinking and drug use have become common among high school students. During any given month, around 30 percent of high school students have become intoxicated from alcohol use (U.S. Department of Health and Human Services 2002). The percentage of students intoxicated by drugs is smaller but still represents a significant problem.

USE, ABUSE, AND ADDICTION

Use, **abuse**, and **addiction** are not the same. With alcohol, for example, there's a continuum that ranges from appropriate use (one or two drinks, glasses of wine, or glasses of beer in an evening) to abuse (binge drinking to drunkenness) to addiction (mental and/or physical dependence on alcohol). So not all alcohol or drug abusers are addicts. For simplicity, however, we'll mainly focus on addiction as the end point of drug and alcohol abuse. At the end of the chapter we'll deal with treatment for drug and alcohol abusers who are not yet addicts.

MODELS OF ADDICTION

Physiological Addiction

Many, but not all drugs (it's not commonly acknowledged, but alcohol is a drug also) cause **physiological addiction** when overused. This physical addiction is characterized by:

1. *Tolerance.* Used over a period of time, it takes more of a drug to give the same physical or psychological effect as before. An experienced drinker can thus drink others "under the table." Because of this increasing tolerance, the intensity of addiction tends to be **progressive**—it gets worse over time.
2. *Withdrawal.* The addicted individual suffers unpleasant and/or harmful physical effects at the end of a period of use. The common "hangover" is a mild example, but the withdrawal from some drugs can be life-threatening.
3. *Craving.* The addicted individual craves the substance, especially during periods of withdrawal. These cravings are often felt as physical sensations—for example, by a roiling tightening of the stomach muscles.

Physiological addiction takes place in the **nervous system**, which consists of the brain, the spinal cord, and nerves radiating away from the brain and spinal cord. These nerves gather sensations and report them to the brain. They also convey instructions away from the brain, telling other parts of the body what to do. The system has millions of nerve cells, which send messages to one another through **synapses**—places where nerve cells come together. At the synapses, the nerves communicate with each other through neurotransmitters—chemicals that carry signals from one nerve to the next. Much of the action from addictive drugs happens in the synapse. (Alcohol is an exception. Much of its effect is in the cells themselves.) Generally speaking, the depressants, including opiates and benzodiazepines, decrease transmission of sensations across these synapses. The stimulants do the opposite; they increase sensations. The hallucinogens increase the sensitivity of nerve cells to their connections with other cells, providing an overload of perceived sensations. We'll cover these classifications of drugs in more detail below.

Addiction can then be explained physiologically by the body's natural tendency to restore **homeostasis**, a balance. When action in a pain nerve synapse has been blocked (as with heroin), for example, the body naturally tries to increase the synapse's sensitivity by adding neurotransmitter sites. This leads to the body experiencing pain if the addictive substance is withdrawn. The pain disappears when the body reabsorbs the new sites.

Psychological Addiction

However, addiction can also be seen as a phenomenon occurring in the personality system of the individual, which changes the personality to an **addiction system** (illustrated in Figure 7.1 on page 80). This is **psychological addiction**. Here, if an addiction is present, the individual is (1) **cognitively preoccupied** with the specific drug or other addictive substance much of the time. He or she almost always has **excuses** for using the drug ("My job is too hard"; "My wife nags me, so I have to drink"), and **denial**, in which the addict gives himself or herself (or others) reasons for why he or she does not really have a problem with addiction ("I can't be an alcoholic because alcoholics drink in the morning, and I wait until nighttime to get drunk").

If an addiction is present, the individual then suffers (2) **negative behavioral or physical consequences** from use of the addictive substance. These can range from being arrested for "driving under the influence" to damage to one's body from repeated use. These then set the addict up for the next stage of the addiction system.

As a result of these negative consequences, the addict then experiences (3) **negative emotions**, such as depression, fear, or anger. In non-addicts, these emotions would probably work as negative feedback, signaling to the drinker or drug user that he or she should stop the behavior. In addicts,

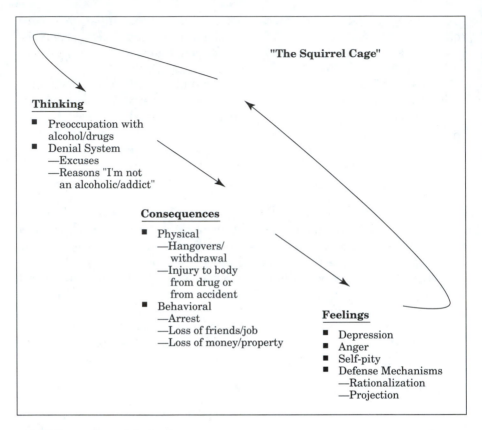

FIGURE 7.1 The Addiction System

however, they work differently. In spite of negative consequences and negative emotions, the addict "knows" that drinking or drug use will make him or her feel better, if only temporarily. He or she then repeats the specific thinking that allows drinking or drug use (step 1). The addict is thus in a "squirrel cage." His or her drinking or drug use results in progressively worse consequences and progressively more negative emotions, but he or she feels able to turn only to the addictive substance itself for relief.

A tremendous advantage to seeing addiction from this psychological perspective is that one need not depend on the addictive properties of the drugs themselves to assess whether an addiction is present. And the addictive systems model can thus be extended to other behaviors that are not even drug or alcohol related. These can include gambling, overeating, compulsive sexuality, and a host of other problems. The ability to present addiction as a psychological system is of use in working with addicts, who almost always have well-developed denial. These clients or patients are likely to confront counselors with such statements as "Marijuana isn't really addictive" or "Gambling isn't really as bad as taking drugs" during treatment. Positing addiction as a psychological as much as a physical system allows us to confront these portions of clients' denial systems, making it more likely that they can recover.

Social Aspects of Addiction

Some authorities have also discussed the idea that addiction has a group or **social** basis (Beattie 1987). Although this is not entirely persuasive, the notion here is that addicts cannot function without systems of **enablers**—persons who facilitate the addictive process by covering up for, or supporting, the alcoholic or addict in his or her addiction. Classic examples include the wife who calls in sick for a husband who is too hungover to go to work on Monday morning, or the liquor store owner or drug dealer who allows the alcoholic or addict to "run a tab." Loved ones who "nag" the alcoholic or addict are paradoxically also enablers, because they provide excuses that are used to justify the drug use or drinking. According to this school of thought, the key process in treating addicts is to get control of the enablers (or to remove the addict from access to them). Robbed of their social support, the addict becomes easier to treat.

Related to enabling is **co-dependency** (Beattie 1987). Here, the enabling is regarded as a primary addiction, itself. Co-dependents typically grow up in a family where addiction is present. As adults, they unconsciously seek out addicts with whom to form relationships. The co-dependent is "addicted" to the poor behavior of the addict, even though he or she may have no classical addictions himself or herself. The addict provides the co-dependent with payoffs in the form of opportunities to feel morally superior, martyred, or "in control" of an immature partner. When the addict enters treatment, it is essential that the co-dependent learn what his or her role has been in supporting the addiction, in order not to continue the behavior when the addict returns home. This behavior may tend to push the addict back toward drinking, using drugs, or other addictive behavior.

ASSESSING MODELS OF ADDICTION

There can be no question that addiction is real (and sometimes this can be true for people who use substances or engage in behaviors that, in themselves, have no intrinsic addictive properties). While it is extremely valuable to be aware of the addictive properties of drugs, it is useful to be aware of the psychological or behavioral systems through which addiction plays itself out. It is also useful to be aware of the social level of addiction. Although it may be questionable to say an addiction absolutely requires the participation of others, there can be no argument that removing an addict's social supports hastens the day when the addiction can be treated. Visualizing addiction as a phenomenon related to all three levels (physical–psychological–social) probably serves us well in understanding and intervening in this condition.

CHARACTERISTICS OF DRUGS

Beginning in the 1980s, researchers began to believe that addicts generally have preferences for a **drug group of choice** (Inaba and Cohen 1993). Hence, even if an addict tends to be drawn toward a variety of addictive substances and behaviors, he or she usually prefers one type of experience to another. Researchers have suggested that addicts prefer either depressant (calm, comforting, nurturing), stimulant (powerful, energetic, alert), or hallucinogenic (novel, magical, hallucinatory) sorts of experiences depending on their specific personality characteristics. But this is not to say that addicts and other users do not cross over into other categories if the supply of their favorite substance dries up. In the late 1960s, the United States government persuaded the Mexican government to spray many of its illegal marijuana fields with Paraquat, a herbicide. Marijuana users, previously disparaging alcohol use, quickly switched to alcohol when the price of marijuana—which was now in short supply—climbed to prohibitive heights. Hippies who had previously reviled "juicers"—drinkers—found themselves drinking to excess when their supply of pot was cut off. In the next section we'll review the three major categories of drugs (illustrated in Table 7.1), along with examples from each category.

Depressants

Depressants generally reduce stimulation through the nervous system. They do this either in a general way (opiates, barbiturates, alcohol), or in more specific ways (benzodiazepines, for example, which act on the hypothalamus in the brain). The site of action is usually the synapse (the connection between nerve cells), although, with alcohol, the inhibition takes place in the body of the nerve cell. By decreasing irritating or painful stimuli, and, at least in the case of alcohol, relaxing inhibitions, the user experiences a sense of **euphoria**—intense well-being and pleasure. Because the overall depressing effect can threaten breathing if an excessive amount of the drug is consumed, or if the drug is consumed in combination with other depressants, these drugs are extremely dangerous. Without exception, they are also dangerous when withdrawn after chronic use.

Alcohol.   Alcohol has been used since human beings have existed. It's a result of the natural fermentation process through which plant material decays, aided by microorganisms. All forms of alcohol are poisonous in quantity, but ethanol, the type we drink, is less so than the others. Driven by addiction, alcoholics occasionally drink more poisonous alcohols, such

TABLE 7.1 **Drugs of Abuse**

Drugs	Duration/hours	Detoxification
Depressants		
Alcohol	Liver detoxifies 1 oz./hr.	Give descending doses of benzodiazepine
Opiates		
Heroin	6–8	Methadone/Clonidine
Morphine	4	Methadone/Clonidine
Codeine	2–4	Methadone/Clonidine
Barbiturates		
Seconal	1–2	Barbiturate
Nembutal	1–2	Barbiturate
Tuinal	1–2	Barbiturate
Benzodiazepines		
Valium	3–4	Benzodiazepine
Ativan	3–4	Benzodiazepine
Xanax	3–4	Benzodiazepine
PCP	3–4	Cranberry juice/antipsychotics
Stimulants		
Cocaine	1 min. to 1 hr., depending on route	None, benzodiazepine/ antidepressants for comfort
Amphetamines		
Methamphetamine	6	None, benzodiazepine/ antidepressants for comfort
Benzedrine	6	None, benzodiazepine/ antidepressants for comfort
Hallucinogens		
LSD	6–8	None, antipsychotic may be used for agitation
Ecstasy	3–4	None, antipsychotic may be used for agitation
Marijuana	1–2	None, antipsychotic may be used for agitation

as rubbing or isoprophyl alcohol, but this practice can cause damage to the body. Problems with alcohol occur in two forms. There is **acute alcohol poisoning**, in which a large dose of alcohol overwhelms the brain and the victim suffers life-threatening symptoms due to depression of the respiratory (breathing) center on the brain stem. Each year, several individuals—usually young men undergoing fraternity or military elite unit initiations—die as a result of these poisonings. Such initiations are usually marked by around-the-clock drinking with a major emphasis on drinking a large quantity in a short time. It is important to note that these victims of alcohol poisoning are typically not alcoholics—persons with long-term addictions to alcohol. In fact, because of lessened tolerance to alcohol, they may well tend to be nonalcoholics.

In the second form, **alcoholism**, the damage is more long-term in nature. Alcohol can cause brain and nerve cell loss, leading ultimately to dementia (confusion), and peripheral neuropathy—numbness in the extremities. It can also contribute to gastritis (inflammation of the stomach), which can lead to ulcers. Alcohol attacks heart tissue and can contribute to a heart attack. It can also attack the pancreas, the organ that makes insulin. One of the key organs affected is the liver. Here, alcohol eliminates some of the clotting factors the liver produces, allowing blood to leak out of blood vessels. This accounts for the red faces and red facial lines chronic alcoholics sometimes have. Alcohol also turns liver tissue to fat. Given enough time, the fat turns to scar tissue (**cirrhosis**), in which the damage is irreversible.

In chronic alcoholics, care must be taken to carefully supervise the withdrawal period—the time during which drinking ceases and the alcoholic's body returns to normal. This is called **detoxification**. During this period, it is possible for the alcoholic to develop epileptic seizures (shaking fits with unconsciousness) or delirium tremens ("DTs"), where the victim becomes completely disoriented due to withdrawal-induced problems in the brain. Another class of depressant (benzodiazepines) is therefore frequently used to match the previously consumed amount of alcohol. The benzodiazepine is then slowly withdrawn over a period of a week or so. Hence, a doctor in a hospital-based detoxification program might administer 40 to 80 mg of Valium (a benzodiazepine) to a patient during days 1 and 2 of his or her admission, 20 to 40 mg during days 3 and 4, and 10 to 20 mg during days 5 and 6. The patient would be drug free on day 7, and likely would not have suffered life-threatening symptoms during the detoxification period.

Benzodiazepines. During the 1960s, effective minor tranquilizers were invented. These are the **benzodiazepines**. Common types include Valium, Librium, and Xanax. Other short-acting forms such as Halcyon are used as sleeping medications. (Rohypnol, another short-acting benzodiazepine, has been used as a date-rape drug because it has the capacity to cause unconsciousness quickly, possibly with amnesiac [forgetfulness] effects when the victim wakes up.) They are effective in alleviating anxiety and for a long time were thought to be safe and nonaddictive. During the 1970s and 1980s, however, it became clear that many individuals were abusing these medications for recreational purposes. From the abuser's point of view, an advantage to these drugs is that they work on one specific part of the brain. Hence, unlike with alcohol, there is no obvious body and behavioral effect in low to moderate doses. Thus, others are not as likely to perceive that the individual is under the influence. But to the surprise of doctors, many individuals began experiencing such withdrawal symptoms as epileptic seizures as late as a month after the medications were discontinued. This makes it imperative that detoxification take place under medical supervision, using descending doses of a benzodiazepine, as with alcohol. Unfortunately, many individuals who abuse benzodiazepines use them in conjunction with alcohol, creating a dangerous synergy that puts the individual at much greater risk for respiratory arrest than he or she would be on either substance alone.

Opiates. **Opiates** have been used since ancient times. Natural opiates are products of the sap of the opium poppy and have many uses as painkillers. The natural opiates include morphine, heroin (now illegal), and codeine. In the last century, a number of synthetic opiates have also been produced. These include Demorol, Dilaudid, and a host of others, most of which are used as painkillers following trauma (injury) or surgery. As drugs of abuse, opiates are very seductive. When the user is not in a great deal of pain, the drugs produce a strong feeling of euphoria, which, depending on which substance is used, can last anywhere from 4 to 12 hours. While benzodiazepines are almost always taken by mouth, opiates are usually abused by snorting (inhaling into the nose), smoking (smoking a vapor of the opiate), skin popping (injecting under the skin), or mainlining (intravenously injecting in order to experience a "rush" when the drug hits the brain).

The opiates are all highly addicting because they cause changes at the synaptic level from which it takes the body several days to recover following cessation of the drug. The opiates present a more immediate problem, as well. They all have powerful abilities to depress respiration. For this reason, emergency services must be called immediately if a person is found who has **overdosed** on an opiate. Emergency rooms and emergency personnel have narcotic antagonists, which, when administered to an overdosed patient, can immediately counteract the effects of the opiate.

Although withdrawal from opiates such as heroin is highly unpleasant, it is usually not life-threatening. Addicts report feelings of pain, agitation, tiredness, chilling, and inability to sleep. Withdrawal can also cause diarrhea, and patients must be monitored to ensure that they are not losing an excess of fluids and electrolytes (minerals and salts) because of this. In some cases, methadone, a long-acting artificial opiate, is used in descending doses to detoxify addicts. The methadone must be carefully accounted for since it is more addictive than heroin. (Other programs use methadone indefinitely in order to satisfy the cravings for heroin. This is called **methadone maintenance**. Oral methadone does not produce the same rush or as much euphoria as injected heroin.) In some cases, nonaddictive Clonidine, a blood pressure medication, is given during opiate withdrawal. It makes the addict dizzy and sleepy for a number of days while it is being administered but alleviates the pain and cravings of detoxification.

Barbiturates. Like benzodiazepines, **barbiturates** were invented for legitimate clinical reasons. The barbiturates include pentothal (short-acting), Seconal, Nembutal, and Tuinal (medium), and phenobarbital (long-acting). Stemming from the early twentieth century, these drugs are beneficial as sleeping medications, induction (initial) anesthetics for surgery, and anti-epilepsy medications. Like the benzodiazepines, the key difference between drugs in this class is the duration of action. But like alcohol, the barbiturates have profound effects on the entire nervous system, not just particular parts of the brain. Hence, the risk of accidental death from respiratory arrest (particularly if the barbiturate is combined with alcohol) is high. As with the benzodiazepines and alcohol, there is also a danger from epileptic seizures during withdrawal. Because of this, detoxification must occur under medical supervision, and must involve descending doses of a barbiturate.

PCP. Pencyclidene, or **PCP**, was originally invented as an animal anesthetic. It was quickly found to have intoxicating properties when used by humans. It is usually taken orally or by smoking. A depressant, PCP also has some hallucinatory properties and is very cheap to manufacture. Persons on PCP sometimes can have violent behavioral reactions, and there is some anecdotal evidence of increased strength shown by people under its influence. Persons on PCP should be placed under a doctor's care, and should be detoxified in quiet, pleasant settings. Users are offered large amounts of cranberry juice to leach the PCP out of the fat tissues, where it tends to accumulate. Ketamine ("Special K"), another animal anesthetic similar to PCP, has similar effects and is a favorite of younger drug users.

Stimulants

Stimulants temporarily increase the sense of energy, power, control, and mastery. They generally do this by increasing the sensitivity of the sympathetic nervous system—the part of the nervous system that controls the fight-or-flight reaction people have toward threats in their environment. The nerves in this system use epinephrine (adrenalin) or norepinephrine as neurotransmitters. When users take these drugs in the absence of a real threat, the resulting feeling of excitement often leads to a sense of euphoria. The body, however, regards the drug experience as an episode of overstimulation and allocates resources as though the individual were truly in a fight-or-flight emergency. This explains why stimulants as a group are probably the most debilitating to the user's body. They exhaust chemicals and nutrients the body needs for normal functioning. When used chronically, they can injure the body, sometimes irreparably.

Cocaine. **Cocaine** is a substance that occurs naturally in the Andean regions of South America. In its natural form (leaf material), it can be chewed or brewed in a tea. Like many other natural plant substances, it has beneficial effects in low doses. Andean natives use it to improve circulation at oxygen-poor high altitudes. When refined, however, cocaine turns into a potent and very addictive substance. It is usually refined into a stable form, cocaine hydrochloride, for transport. As such, it can be snorted or injected into a vein. Both of these methods ensure that the cocaine will be quickly felt in the brain. After the blood from the nasal mucous membranes or an arm vein is returned to the heart, it is quickly sent to the brain.

Many users, however, want to feel the effects of cocaine even more immediately. Smoking a drug allows it to enter the brain immediately following inhalation. The cocaine is essentially delivered all at once, allowing a more potent but shorter "high." For this reason, users obtain smokable cocaine, which must be processed to remove the hydrochloride portion of the compound. (Smoking cocaine hydrochloride leaves only an unusable charred residue.) To do this, they must obtain **freebase**—cocaine processed using chemicals—or **crack**, which uses a cheap and inefficient baking soda process. The freebase process is especially dangerous, because it involves highly flammable chemicals that are subjected to heat by the user before smoking.

Smoking is a particularly addictive way to use cocaine. Because the drug is delivered all at once, it wears off almost immediately. Consequently, the user desires another dose as soon as possible. In addition, tolerance is achieved very quickly. Thus it takes more and more to yield any sort of high at all. Cocaine smokers thus go from user to addict faster than any other group of drug abusers.

Cocaine, like the opiates, occasionally kills in one use. Unlike the opiates, however, the dose need not be greater than that which is usually consumed. Here, death occurs from overstimulation of the heart, followed by heart failure. When used over time, cocaine can leach the calcium out of one's bones and teeth and debilitate the condition of one's skin and hair. Cocaine, because it uses up the nervous system's resources and because it tends to keep users awake for long periods of time, often produces psychosis (hallucinations—seeing or hearing things that are not there; or delusions—believing things that are not true, particularly paranoid fantasies that others are "out to get" the user). Fortunately, the detoxification for cocaine is not usually life-threatening, although it should occur under medical supervision. Users are usually able to feel somewhat normal after a week or ten days, although the period is marked by tiredness, over- or undersleeping, and depression. Frequently, benzodiazepines are given during this period to alleviate agitation. It is common for cocaine addicts to feel marked cravings for the drug three weeks to a month after discontinuance of use, and antidepressants as well as therapy are advised to get the addict through this period.

Amphetamines. Similar to cocaine are the **amphetamines**. Drugs in this class include benzedrine, biphetamine, and methamphetamine. These drugs all have similar effects. They have been available both legally and illegally since the early 1920s and may be used as "wake-up" drugs by students or truck drivers, for the treatment of narcolepsy (chronic sleeping), or for weight control. Like cocaine, they are extremely addictive, and because tolerance is quickly achieved, they are relatively ineffective for legitimate use over any extended period of time. They differ from cocaine in that they persist longer in the body; thus, dosing does not have to be repeated as frequently. But like cocaine, they can be snorted, injected, mainlined (injected into a vein), or smoked. They can be easily manufactured from materials readily available from drug and industrial chemical supply houses.

Ritalin, which is used for hyperactivity in children, is similar to the amphetamines in its effects and methods of use, and is becoming a current problem because prescriptions for its use are fairly common. Children have been known to take Ritalin away from other students at school, and, in some cases, children have sold portions of their prescribed supply.

Because of their ease of manufacture and because they sharply elevate mood (at least for a time), amphetamines are a popular drug among poor people. Secret amphetamine cookeries are a common feature of poor rural areas, especially in the West. These cookeries (or "meth labs") are found in nonurban areas because the process uses volatile chemicals and smells bad. In some cases, cheap rooms in motels have been used as temporary meth labs. Sometimes, these labs have exploded, killing the "cook" and occasionally innocent bystanders as well. The manufacture and sale of amphetamines, particularly methamphetamine, has been a favorite of motorcycle gangs because they (1) are often located rurally, (2) enjoy amphetamine use themselves, and (3) have distribution networks based on "runs" (mass trips to distant locations) and contacts with other motorcycle gangs.

As with cocaine, the use of amphetamines can be life-threatening in its acute phase (following use), but tends to be far less life-threatening on withdrawal. An amphetamine overdose could cause a crisis from high blood pressure, heart failure, or an epileptic seizure. Withdrawal may be characterized by tiredness, agitation, or both. In some cases, benzodiazepines are given to alleviate nervousness or agitation. Nevertheless, detoxification should occur under medical supervision due to the degree of injury the body usually suffers from extended amphetamine abuse.

Hallucinogens

Hallucinogens are drugs that enable users to perceive reality differently. They include relatively high-powered variants, such as LSD or mescaline, and relatively innocuous ones, such as marijuana. When these drugs are ingested, users feel that they are in a magic world, intrinsically more interesting than the mundane one in which they ordinarily live. In high doses, many hallucinogens enable one to see or hear things that are not actually there (hence the name hallucinogens). But in low or moderate doses, these drugs may merely enhance perception, making sight, hearing, sound, or touch more sensitive. Hence, users of LSD or marijuana may spend hours listening to music or looking through a kaleidoscope. Marijuana probably functions like a low-grade aphrodisiac for many, because of the enhanced sense of touch it offers.

There is little real evidence that hallucinogens are debilitating to the body. It is likely, however, that chronic use can impair a person's faculties for reasoning and decrease his or her ambition to pursue conventional goals. Used chronically, hallucinogens can disorganize one's thinking, leading to impaired living and adaptation skills. These drugs may or may not be "**gateway drugs**," drugs that may lead to harder drug use. The ambiguity reflected here is because hallucinogen use has been a political football. Interest groups that favor hallucinogen use emphasize the ways marijuana, in particular, can provide a sense of increased appreciation, increased relaxation, and increased sociability. Conservative groups may emphasize marijuana use as a common precursor of heroin or other hard drug use. It is actually likely, however, that other variables, such as social class, have much to do with whether a substance functions as a gateway drug or not.

LSD. Lysergic acid diethylamide (**LSD**) is a hallucinogen originally synthesized in the 1940s. It has strong hallucinogenic properties. A person ingesting LSD (almost always orally) is subjected to a six-to-eight hour "**trip**" characterized by unusual perceptions, which may or may not include hallucinations. The user is not generally at any physical risk during this time, but his or her thinking may be very impaired. Under the influence of LSD, a very few people have participated in suicidal behavior, such as jumping off roofs, believing that they could fly. Others have suffered from grave psychological episodes ("**bad trips**") during which they have undergone paranoid episodes or frightening hallucinations. During a bad trip, a user may be given antipsychotic medication.

LSD was a favorite drug of the **hippies** during the 1960s. The hippies were young people who believed in wearing unusual clothing, growing their hair long, and using LSD and marijuana to counter the conformist values that had characterized the United States during the 1950s. The hippy movement also developed out of the civil rights movement and opposition to the Vietnam War. Young people declared that they could not conform to the norms of a society that remained racist and that pursued aggressive policies overseas. A leader during this period, Timothy Leary, a former Harvard psychology professor, advocated using LSD to "turn on, tune in, and drop out," suggesting that youth should abandon conformist American values in favor of a more tribal ethic. LSD and marijuana had popularity because they focused the user in a magical here and now and tended to preclude future-oriented and abstract thinking.

Marijuana. **Marijuana**, which grows wild in many parts of the world, has been used since time immemorial, and is still one of the most commonly abused substances. It is usually smoked, but can also be ingested in food, and yields a milder hallucinogenic effect than LSD. Usually, users do not experience the frank hallucinations possible with LSD, but marijuana can still confer an effect of profound unreality. In chronic use, it can irritate the lungs, much as tobacco can, and may pose some risk for lung cancer. Although physiological addiction to marijuana is unlikely, an addictive relationship to the substance can sometimes develop. It is not uncommon for addicts to chain-smoke **"joints"** (marijuana cigarettes). Heavy use can require something like detoxification, because the user is likely to be somewhat disoriented for periods of up to a month. During this time caregivers may give the patient cranberry juice, because, like PCP, cannabis (the active ingredient) is fat-soluble.

Ecstasy. **Ecstasy**, or MDMA, is a short-acting hallucinogen with some of the characteristics of the amphetamines. It provides a **psychedelic** (hallucinatory) high that lasts for four or so hours. It has become a favorite of **ravers**, young people who attend live or recorded music sessions where large amounts of ecstasy and other drugs (such as inhalants) are consumed by attendees who generally stand during the entire event. The combination of the psychedelic effect and the stimulant effect gives users a euphoric feeling that greatly magnifies their enjoyment of the "rave." Ecstasy has also been used as a psychotherapy aid, although this practice is now illegal. During the 1980s, a number of therapists reported that ecstasy seemed to lower patients' defenses during therapy so that they could discuss their problems without excessive shame or guilt.

MODELS OF TREATMENT

Before the nineteenth century, there were few attempts to treat addiction. The behavior, when it was taken into account at all, was generally assessed as sinfulness. During the 1800s, however, a new movement attempting to achieve human perfection using religion, science, and a new sense of high-mindedness in society was introduced as part of the Progressive movement. The first attempts to reform alcoholics were generally revival movements in which individuals **"took the pledge"** to become **teetotalers** (nondrinkers for life). A vivid account of such treatment is given in Mark Twain's *Huckleberry Finn*. Huck's dad (an alcoholic) attends a revival meeting where he takes the pledge. He is adopted by two spinsters, who take him into their home and pray over him. After a few weeks, he develops a "powerful thirst," sneaks out a window, sells the clothes they have provided him, and buys whiskey. This vignette introduces one of the problems with the nineteenth-century religious cure. It was likely to be of short duration.

Addiction treatment made little progress until the twentieth century. During the early 1900s, a movement toward spiritual self-help began developing in England and, later, in the United States. This was called the Oxford Movement. It made use of a series of steps for spiritual self-improvement, and it would prove to be one of the foundations for Alcoholics Anonymous, the first successful means of treating alcoholism.

Alcoholics Anonymous

Alcoholics Anonymous (AA) probably owes most to Bill Wilson, its principal founder (Thomsen 1999). An army lieutenant in World War I, he abstained from alcohol during his childhood and army years. When he started drinking during the celebrations that marked the end of the war, he quickly found that he was a severe alcoholic. Bill's 1920s were marked by constant drunkenness, sometimes punctuated by brief attempts to sober up. A traveling investors' representative, he frequently awoke in distant cities, unaware of having made the train trips that had brought him there. Alarmed by his own drinking, Bill checked into early "dry-out" hospital wards on several occasions. These were places where an alcoholic could detoxify, usually through the offices of orderlies who brought the patient bottles purchased outside the hospital, which they could use to bring their drinking down to a lower level or to nothing during their stays.

During one such hospitalization in the early 1930s, Bill, alone and sick and tired from his repeated struggles with alcoholism, said, "If there is a God, let him reveal himself to me now." According to him, the entire room lit up with light. Bill never took another drink in his life after that day. Upon discharge, Bill was anxious to share the spiritual experience he had with other alcoholics. He brought several of them into his home, but at first he was unsuccessful in imparting his experience to them, and they inevitably returned to drinking. During this period, however, he met a physician named Dr. Bob. (The use of first names alone is the usual practice in AA.)

Dr. Bob had been a member of the Oxford Groups. He was also an alcoholic, and was quickly cured through Bill's offices. As their association deepened, the two men found that combining the steps of the Oxford Groups with Bill's spiritual experience led to the first effective program for treatment of alcoholism. As the program grew, AA added steps, bringing the total to twelve. The first four steps are as follows:

1. Admitted we were powerless over alcohol, and that our lives had become unmanageable.
2. Came to believe that a power greater than ourselves could restore us to sanity.

3. Made a decision to turn our lives over to the care of God, as we understood him.

4. Made a searching and fearless moral inventory of ourselves (Alcoholics Anonymous 1997).

In essence, AA uses a paradoxical method to treat alcoholism (and later, drug addiction, through Narcotics Anonymous [NA], Cocaine Anonymous and the like). The alcoholic usually perceives himself or herself to be locked in a struggle with the addiction. He or she frequently tries to quit, but fails. AA suggests that alcoholics "turn over" this struggle to a "higher power." This has the effect of removing the tension between drinking and not drinking. If the alcoholic has urges to drink, he or she is asked to put off taking a drink until the next day. If he has the urge to drink the next day, he delays drinking another day, and so on. At some point, the cravings for alcohol generally disappear. At the same time, the alcoholic is encouraged to attend an AA meeting at least once a day. Here, he or she begins to hear members' stories relating to how they overcame their addictions. He or she is usually introduced to the 12 steps, and it is suggested the he or she begin work on the first three. Often, the alcoholic chooses a sponsor—a member of the group with substantial sobriety time, who functions as a mentor and guide in the AA program. Meetings are absolutely free (although contributions are requested) and can be found in virtually every community in North America and in many other parts of the world, frequently on a daily basis.

Using these methods, AA claims an ultimate cure rate of 50 percent (Alcoholics Anonymous 1997). Methods of estimating this rate are imprecise, however, because it is based on surveys of members. There is no way to capture data from members who have dropped out and stopped coming to meetings.

Hospital Programs

The earliest hospital programs were simply dry-out wards, with no counseling available. With the great success of AA, however, hospitals became interested in providing AA meetings or AA sorts of counseling within the hospital. A problem, existed, however, in that AA's written traditions prohibited being paid for its services. Gradually, however, portions of the program were installed in hospitals, either in the form of AAs bringing meetings to the hospital on an uncompensated basis, or by hiring members who used their knowledge of alcoholism in an informal way to work with patients. In the 1980s, the hospitals devised ways to add programmatic elements to AA–type counseling. One of the first improvements was intensive scheduling. Once he or she finishes detoxification, the alcoholic or addict enters a three-week-to-one-month reeducation program that frequently lasts from early in the morning until late at night. A patient's schedule might start with a 6:30 A.M. spirituality group led by nurses, followed by an exercise walk, followed by breakfast, followed by a two-hour group led by a counselor. The object of the two-hour group is to continue to work with the patient's denial system, which tends to reassert itself even if the patient has initially requested treatment. Here, the counselor calls on other group members to confront patients who offer excuses or other types of denial. After several days in the group, alcoholics generally are in less denial, and are willing to confront newcomers about their own denial systems. Characteristically, also, alcoholics open up emotionally. As conceived by Vernon Johnson (1990), they pass through four stages while attending the group:

1. *Admission*—willing to say that a problem exists
2. *Compliance*—willing to go through the motions of treatment, even if not completely accepting it
3. *Acceptance*—seeing the truth of alcoholism and treatment rationally, even if not as yet emotionally internalizing it
4. *Surrender*—emotionally accepting alcoholism and its necessary treatment

The balance of the treatment day is consumed in other groups and classes. Patients usually have a one-and-a-half-hour AA meeting each day. They have a class with a professional, such as a physician or dietitian, about the physical effects of alcohol or drugs. They meet with a counselor to do specialized work with journals on one or more of the AA steps. They may go on a recreational outing. In the evening, they generally go to an external AA meeting and have a late-night spirituality group run by the nursing staff. The effect of all of this programming is to fill up the alcoholic's or addict's experience with new perceptions and meanings that substitute for his or her previous lifestyle. Most of the patient's stay in the hospital program is spent in Johnson's compliance stage. That is, the patient may still have private reservations about the value of the program, or private plans to return to drinking or using drugs, but the continuous experience of verbalizing positive things about the program and intervening with other patients gradually reorganizes the patient's thinking to support recovery. At the end of the program, if all goes well, the patient intellectually and emotionally supports recovery, and intends to follow through. This usually consists of ongoing attendance at AA meetings once he or she has returned home.

Hard-core Programs

The in-hospital programs, which are almost always voluntary, were designed to work with patients who had something to lose if they continued to drink or use drugs. As drug treatment evolved, it became clear that many patients, typically those addicted to such hard drugs as heroin or amphetamines, or who came from disadvantaged social classes, did not respond well to such programs. The genteel atmosphere of hospital treatment did not jibe with their previous experience of life as a series of "hard-knock" encounters. Accordingly, more hard-core **social model** programs began to evolve to deal with these patients. Frequently, these programs did not use medical detoxification. The experience of withdrawal symptoms, if not too life-threatening, was felt to be therapeutic because it reminded the addict of the consequences of his or her drug use. Physicians and nurses were seen as undesirable as workers because of perceived tendencies to "coddle" the clients (they were never referred to as patients). Almost all of the counselors in hard-core programs were recovering drug addicts, frequently graduates of the very facilities where they now worked. Accordingly, they were willing and able to confront clients in extremely forceful ways based on their own experiences as addicts or street people.

Clients were frequently forced to shave their heads on admission. In many programs, clients who failed to show progress, who made excuses, or who showed denial were forced to wear signs that said "I'm a baby" and the like. Counselors frequently roused patients from bed and held group sessions in the wee hours of the morning in order to catch them with their denial systems down. There is no doubt that some of these programs were extremely effective in the short run, strongly resocializing the clients as they did, but it is not clear how well the treatment generalized to life following discharge. Some programs (such as Synanon) finessed this question by keeping the clients for years. Synanon had the philosophy that the world outside was too corrupt to sustain a nonaddicted lifestyle; thus residents needed to commit to it for life. Others, like Delancy Street in San Francisco, transitioned clients back to productive independent lives following several years of residency, during which they progressed from constant supervision to being able to work outside the facility while residing in apartments that were maintained by the program.

ASSESSING MODELS OF TREATMENT

Addiction, by most accounts, is a lifelong condition. Because of this, it is probably not realistic to insist that all persons treated make an immediate recovery and practice complete abstinence for the remainder of their days. The majority of alcoholics and addicts relapse one or multiple times following initial treatment. These individuals benefit from treatment in the long run, even if they temporarily return to drinking or using drugs. What seems to be key to ultimate and continuing abstinence is aftercare—continuing to have a relationship with a program or structured set of practices after leaving the intensive phase of treatment. For many, AA or NA provides just such aftercare. For others, continuing to attend structured group therapies one or more times a week provided by their program does the trick.

In terms of the controversy surrounding the approach most appropriate for alcohol or drug abuse clients, AA/NA, hospital programs, and social model programs all have their place in the treatment continuum. Clearly, clients who have as yet suffered few of the effects of their addiction and continue to maintain a comfortable lifestyle may respond well to AA/NA or hospital treatment. Those, however, who come from very deprived circumstances, or who have lived a drug-addicted lifestyle for years, may need the intense confrontation and support a long-term social model program can offer.

THE ISSUE OF DRUG LEGALIZATION

Unfortunately, Americans' philosophy toward drug policy seems to be one of extremes. On one hand, the "war on drugs" approach suggests cracking down on drug abuse at all levels: supplying, dealing, and use. Here a deterrence approach is expected to yield results by raising the "costs" to those involved in the trafficking of illegal substances. On the other hand, many Americans, both liberal and conservative, favor legalization of the manufacture, sale, and possession of drugs in line with the legalization of alcohol following Prohibition. (Many of these individuals would argue, however, that sale to minors should be banned, or that advertising of drugs should be prohibited or regulated, much as with alcohol.) It is likely, however, that each of these approaches is excessively one-sided. Cracking down has filled our country's jails with poor and minority men, creating huge social expenses, both monetary and in terms of the damage to poor communities. Legalizing drugs, on the other hand, would open the floodgates to greater rates of addiction, much as legalizing gambling has done.

A third path is available, however. Drugs can be decriminalized, much as they are in parts of Europe. Sentences, especially for users or small dealers, can be set at minor misdemeanor levels, rather than as felonies, as is too often currently the case. This strategy has worked well in parts of The Netherlands. A key part of this system would be expanded treatment resources, including **education programs** for people who, although they may not have an addiction problem with drugs or alcohol, have gotten into trouble with substances. These programs, which are currently in use in some communities and in the military, furnish a limited amount of instruction (often about 10 hours), not treatment, to people who have, for example, driven under the influence of drugs or alcohol. They are designed to educate the user and offer him or her alternatives or choices about drug or alcohol use. The user is compelled to attend the classes because the alternative is jail or a fine.

SUMMARY: DRUG AND ALCOHOL ABUSE

In this chapter we have discussed alcohol and drug abuse as possibly leading to addiction, and discussed its characteristics. We learned the addiction systems model and explored several types of drug preferences addicts are likely to have. We discussed several types of drugs found within each of these classifications, including some of their physiological characteristics and special dangers. We discussed the evolution of treatment and the treatment models currently available. After assessing these models, we examined the question of legalization and looked at short-term informational programs for non-addicts with abuse problems.

8

Mental Illness

A Mental Patient's "Career"

Jerry is a 40-year-old man who has been diagnosed schizophrenic for many years. His first psychotic break occurred when he was 18, and he was sent to a private hospital for a few months. When his dad's health insurance ran out, Jerry was discharged to home, but quickly wound up in the state hospital when he had a relapse after he stopped taking his medications, which he said made him "tired."

The family has refused to have Jerry live at home for years because he becomes angry and accuses his mother of conspiring against him with the voices he hears. He has threatened her violently on several occasions. Usually he lives in one of a number of board-and-care homes located in poor neighborhoods in the downtown area. Jerry likes these homes because supervision is fairly minimal. If he wants to fake taking his medications, he can. On some occasions, Jerry has even bought drugs in the neighborhood, and on two occasions, these uses of marijuana and amphetamines have landed him back in the hospital when his psychotic symptoms flared up.

Jerry usually goes from a board-and-care home to the county clinic to the state hospital back to the board-and-care home three or four times a year. He gets few services when he is not in the hospital. When asked about his case, his social worker case manager says that, with her 120 clients, she does not have time to pay attention to Jerry, except in the most general ways.

The study of mental illness as an area of deviance is fascinating and complex. Defining what is "insane" can be key to what is seen as sane. Because of this, social control depends to some extent on social definitions of what is seen as pathological ("sick") in human thought and behavior. Here, we study how insanity may be at least partly socially constructed; we examine the classification and treatment of mental disorders; and we give some attention to such other important phenomena as the institutions, organizations, and practitioners that care for the mentally ill. We also examine the history of mental treatment systems and the epidemiology (spread) of mental problems.

SOCIETAL REACTION REVISITED

In Chapter 6, we saw how some forms of deviance were encouraged by the prestige figures who labeled problem persons as belonging to deviant categories. Deviant behavior increased if the "deviant" accepted the prestige figure's definition of the situation. Unsurprisingly, psychiatric deviance is often thought to be the area where **labeling theory** (Scheff 1975) can be most appropriately applied. Here, the classic example occurs when a person who appears to be confused, and is talking to himself or herself, is legally taken into custody by the police or by **mental health workers** (psychiatrists, psychologists, social workers, or nurses) for a 72-hour observation period. If the examining physician communicates or strongly implies to this patient, who in classical labeling theory may not actually be mentally ill at all, that he or she believes the patient to be "schizophrenic" or "mentally ill," the patient may then exaggerate the unusual behavior in conformance with the "diagnosis" imposed by the labeler.

Currently, however, more and more extreme psychiatric problems are thought to stem from biological causes; hence it's doubtful that many of today's schizophrenic (seeing or hearing things), bipolar (going through extreme mood swings), or depressed patients are diagnosed or confined to mental hospitals as a result of issues of labeling alone. But it's also likely that labeling helps drive the "careers" of quite a number of patients who suffer from less extreme conditions. One example is **multiple personality disorder (MPD)** (also called *dissociative disorder*). Here, the personality is thought to fragment into many different sub-personalities, some of which are not conscious of the others. If this condition exists at all, it's extremely rare (Spanos 1996). Nevertheless, quite a number of hospitals and physicians have long traded in treating these supposed patients. Because the condition is thought to require long-term treatment, hospitals can keep patients for months, often for as much as $1,500 per day. Labeling was probably involved at the outset because many patients went along with therapists' suggestions that they had MPD, and often that they had been chronically molested by satanic cults as children. There is little real evidence that many such group molestations ever took place, but psychiatric hospitals have admitted hundreds and hundreds of these patients nonetheless. Psychiatrists labeled the patients, who then believed the label and manufactured the memories to match it. Similar examples include unruly teenagers' being confined to mental hospitals on such non-diagnoses as "adjustment reaction of adolescence," "conduct disorder," or "oppositional-defiant disorder." Since some rebellion is part of normal adolescent development, it's not clear that confinement for periods typically ranging from one to six months or longer was the appropriate treatment in these cases. These hospitalizations were popular with doctors and hospitals, since patients or their insurance companies could be charged for the care. Insurance companies usually did not resist suggestions for extending adolescent treatment as much as they would have that of adults. Here, it's unlikely that patients would buy the exact label involved, but it's clear that many ultimately subscribed to the implicit label "mental patient," because their behavior often worsened following hospitalization (Vandenburgh 1999; Luske and Vandenburgh 1995).

CLASSIFICATION OF MENTAL DISORDERS

For brevity, we'll classify mental disorders in the following way as shown in Table 8.1. First, there are major disorders derived from inheritable

TABLE 8.1 **Mental Problems**

Mental Problems	*Treatment*
Major Problems (Acute or Chronic)	
Schizophrenia	Hospitalization, Haldol, Thorazine, reality-based therapy
Bipolar disorder	Hospitalization, lithium carbonate, psychotherapy
Major Depression	Hospitalization, antidepressants, psychotherapy
Minor Problems (Less Acute)	
Selected personality disorders	
Narcissistic personality	Psychotherapy
Antisocial personality	Psychotherapy
Borderline personality	Psychotherapy
Histrionic personality	Psychotherapy
Anxiety disorder	Benzodiazepines, psychotherapy

traits. Chief among these are schizophrenia (occurring in 1 percent of the general population), biopolar disorder (manic-depressive disorder—1 percent of the general population), and major depression (may affect from 10 to 20 percent of the general population) (Cockerham 2000). Second are disorders likely to occur as a result of life events, especially events occurring in childhood. These include, among other conditions, personality disorders and anxiety disorders. The current "bible" of psychiatric disorders, ***Diagnostic and Statistical Manual IV*** (**DSM-IV**), forgoes this basic system of classification because its authors want to keep the door open to the notion that some of these more mundane conditions, like anxiety, are inheritable, but this is unproven. In any case, even the inheritable disorders, like schizophrenia, are probably partly caused by **stress** (Cockerham 2000; Thoits 1995). In studies of identical twins reared separately, if one becomes schizophrenic, the other has a 50 percent chance of also doing so (Heston 1977). This says that schizophrenia is probably inherited (since only 1 percent of the population gets the disorder), but it also says that something else must be helping to cause the disorder, since only one in two twins gets it. Researchers think that this "missing" factor is probably stress. In the following sections, we'll deal with the different types of disorders and the medications currently used to treat them.

Schizophrenia

Schizophrenia is a condition usually emerging in adolescence. It's characterized by seeing things, hearing things, having paranoid delusions, and being apathetic toward normal cares and concerns. Schizophrenics are frequently confused and ambivalent (can't make choices in the most trivial of situations). Psychiatrists have historically divided schizophrenia into four general types, although the specific names change every few years. These are (1) paranoid type (fearful, believes someone is "out to get" him/her); (2) disorganized type (childlike, "spacey"); (3) catatonic (frozen, statue-like); and (4) undifferentiated type (long-standing schizophrenic who has settled, less intense long-term symptoms). Many schizophrenics originate as paranoid types (although they may turn into less intense undifferentiated types later) and are probably somewhat more dangerous than average members of the population because of the intense fear they experience (Zitrin et al. 1976).

Persons having their first **psychotic break** (onset of schizophrenia) are typically initially cared for in hospitals, because their medications and behavior must be carefully monitored. They are often started on **Haldol**, a butyrophenone tranquilizer, which usually makes the psychotic symptoms disappear, although the patient may also feel as though much of his or her energy is sapped by the drug. Other medications that are used include Thorazine (the original major antipsychotic) and Mellaril (often used with children or older people). These last two medications are phenothiazines. All of these drugs have the unfortunate side effect of temporarily causing some degree of Parkinson's disease, characterized by a tremor of the arms and hands, which can be offset by administering anti-Parkinson's medications. In some cases, patients who took the original phenothiazines for years developed an extreme type of permanent Parkinson's called tardive dyskinesia. After two or three weeks on the medications, the patient is typically ready to return to a less intensive level of care than intensive inpatient treatment (Maxmen and Ward 1995).

Once developing schizophrenia, a patient usually retains the condition for life, although it may go into remission. Schizophrenics comprise a large portion of the mentally ill who need supervised living arrangements, whether these be hospitals, intermediate care facilities, or board-and-care homes.

Bipolar Disorder

Persons with **bipolar disorder** are subject to large mood swings. The patient may spend weeks or even months on a "high." During this time, he or she may feel very euphoric, talk incessantly, get little sleep, pace up and down constantly, and become absurdly generous, often giving away his or her car or other possessions. Patients may "act out" in an inappropriate way sexually because they have little insight into the effects of their behavior. During the "crash" that usually follows this **manic** high, the patient may become deeply depressed, both because of a depletion of neurotransmitters and because of realizing the extent of his or her inappropriate behavior during the high.

Bipolar disorder is treated with **lithium carbonate**, a naturally occurring mineral salt. Lithium, however, is mainly an anti-mania drug, so it's often started when the patient is experiencing a high, not during the depressed phase. Also, lithium is quite toxic in low doses. Unlike most medications, the therapeutic dose and the lethal dose are quite close together. Because of this, patients are always started on lithium under a doctor's close supervision. The patient is asked to have his or her blood drawn several times a week during the first few weeks of treatment in order to ascertain his or her lithium level to make sure it's not a toxic one. Bipolar patients are frequently hospitalized as inpatients because of their destructive behavior in the manic phase and their self-destructive behavior in the depressed phase.

Major Depression

Major depression is a condition that affects at least 20 percent of Americans at some point (Cockerham 2000). Although everyone gets a little "bluesy" at times, persons with major depression experience a debilitating disease that can be life-threatening. Depressives feel worthless, without purpose; they feel that their lives are pointless. They frequently get too little sleep due to anxiety (or they sleep too much), lose interest in food (or eat too much), and are plagued by negative thoughts. People with major depression can be at great risk for **suicide**. Because of this, caregivers should be alert to changes in the thoughts the depressed person is experiencing. People at very great risk for suicide may generally have a plan (how they propose to carry out killing themselves), the means (way), and the motivation (intent) to do so. When a person has decided to take his or her own life, he or she frequently improves in mood, so favorable changes in depressed patients do not always signal real improvements. They can indicate that the patient is at greater risk.

Depression can be treated with a variety of antidepressant medications. These include such older **tricyclic** medicines as Elavil and Tofranil, which are effective but may cause the patient to lose fluids. They are generally given at bedtime because they tend to put the patient to sleep. A new generation of drugs, called **selective serotonin reuptake inhibitors (SSRIs)**, is also available, and is said to be even more effective than the tricyclics. The SSRIs have been controversial, however, because they cause a more energizing effect than the tricyclics. A very few patients have been reported to fly into rages on them, or even to commit suicide after starting them. Because of the risk of suicide, particularly if a suicidal act has already taken place, depressed patients are frequently started as inpatients in a psychiatric unit, at least until their medications have been stabilized. In the next sections, we'll consider the minor problems.

Selected Personality Disorders

The **personality disorders** are more controversial than the more major problems presented directly above. They are probably caused by childhood experiences. If one's mother shunned one as an infant, the theory states, one might develop a narcissistic personality to make up for this early rejection. According to the DSM-IV (American Psychiatric Association 2000), there are 11 personality disorders. Here, we'll look at the more major ones.

Narcissistic personality is a condition in which the individual has an exaggerated sense of self-importance not justified by his or her accomplishments. All of us have met people who could fit into this category, but in order for it to be a personality disorder, individuals must experience this as a deep, pervasive feature of their personality, over which they have little control without psychotherapy. People who choose to act self-important as a tactic for success don't count. (These individuals may have antisocial personalities instead.) Narcissists sometimes experience "narcissistic rage" when it becomes clear to them that they are not as successful or important as they previously thought.

Antisocial personality is a condition in which the individual appears to lack a conscience in the conventional sense. As far as this person is concerned, others' rights really don't matter. These individuals can be dangerous if their personality disorder is coupled with a need for excitement and with sadistic tendencies. In these cases, the antisocial person can turn into someone who obtains pleasure by doing damage to others. **Serial killers** represent an endpoint on a continuum of antisocial personalities. Early signs of an extreme antisocial personality are hurting animals or starting fires as a child, or late bedwetting. There is some evidence that mild to moderate antisocial personalities can be treated with psychotherapy.

Borderline personality is one of the most interesting personality disorders. Here, the individual, capable of putting on a charming front much of the time, has a problem relating to others in a realistic way. Borderlines have been characterized as being "**psychotic about relationships**." They frequently assume that strong ties already exist with a new friend or therapist when the relationship is just starting, and proceed according to these erroneous assumptions. A person with this condition might, for example, stalk a therapist, camping in the bushes outside the therapist's house because the stalker "just knows" the therapist is in love with him or her. Borderlines are thus dangerous as human services clients because they can be very seductive to unwary workers. Glenn Close plays a borderline very effectively in the now-classic thriller *Fatal Attraction*.

Histrionic personality is a condition in which the individual feels the need to dramatize his or her life to the maximum extent possible. The person's cares and concerns become overwhelmingly important, and he or she gives voice to them—loudly. Histrionic (dramatic) persons care deeply for others, so, in this sense, they are unlike narcissists or antisocial persons, but their emotional responses are "**over the top**." Histrionics can be treated with psychotherapy.

Anxiety Disorder

It's now thought that **anxiety disorder** has some physical, inheritable components to it. As Freud conceived of it, however, anxiety flows from the traumatic way in which we are socialized (Chapter 4). He called this the "uneasiness in culture." Extreme cases of this uneasiness result in a pervasive condition of fear. In some patients, this sense of dread can loom so large that they refuse to leave their homes (**agoraphobia**). In other cases the fear may attach itself more specifically to an object. Medications such as benzodiazepines work well with anxiety disorder, but the most successful approaches incorporate psychotherapy as well.

INSTITUTIONS AND ORGANIZATIONS

Americans have slowly embraced mental health as an institution. The amount of change that occurs in a dynamic economy necessarily makes for a great deal of insecurity, leading to increased stress. As religious participation has become somewhat less than universal in America, a variety of mental health services have evolved to deal with this insecurity, or with much more frank psychiatric symptoms. Currently, the types of organizations that treat mental disorders include state hospitals, Veterans Administration (VA) hospitals, freestanding private hospitals, and psychiatric units of general hospitals. Frequently, counties operate their own psychiatric units, either as subunits of the county hospital or as freestanding facilities. Outpatient clinics also exist. These may be operated by the VA, counties, religious organizations, or groups of practitioners.

State Hospitals

Erving Goffman (1961) characterized these facilities as **total institutions**. In them, patients were treated with great disregard for their humanness or individuality. They were closely supervised 24 hours a day by a staff whose members had complete authority over each patient. Admission to the hospital was a **degradation ceremonial**, in which patients learned that they were to behave in a subservient manner at all times. The staff underlined this by forcing patients to give up their street clothes, making each patient take a delousing bath, and so on. State hospitals have been on the decline since the 1950s, as alternatives for treating patients have emerged. However, most states still use them to care for the criminally insane, or as overflow for their county facilities. They are generally huge physical plants with ward after ward occupying building after building. These organizations generally serve the indigent (people without health insurance or the means to pay). Large portions of most of the state hospitals that remain in operation are now closed.

Freestanding Private Hospitals

A large number of these hospitals were constructed in the 1980s (the number peaked at 404 in 1998) (Center for Mental Health Services 1992), but many have been closed or converted to nursing homes following shifts in insurance reimbursement that have made it harder to collect reimbursement for psychiatric patients. They generally serve middle-class or wealthy patients who have health insurance.

Psychiatric Units of General Hospitals

Many hospitals have these units. Like the freestanding facilities, they serve people with the means to pay. They generally keep patients for shorter periods of time than freestanding facilities, however, because the general hospital has more of an "emergency" character than the freestanding hospital.

County Units

These units may be located in the county general hospital, if there is one. Occasionally, they are freestanding units. They generally serve indigent patients on an emergency basis. Hospitalization tends to be short-term in nature. It's to these facilities that individuals on involuntary holds are generally delivered.

Community Mental Health Centers

These organizations were specifically authorized by the Community Mental Health Centers Act of 1963. They are publicly operated clinics that see outpatients on a sliding fee basis. That is, the fee for services is adjusted on an ability-to-pay basis. Similar organizations are operated on a private basis by nonprofit or religious service organizations.

Critical Research on Settings

Goffman's research on total institutions, mentioned above, was the most influential exploration of the ways hospitals helped prevent patients from getting back to anything like normalcy. Another key study was Rosenhan's (1999) research in which he and a team of researchers lived as "pseudopatients" on a mental ward: All faked just enough symptoms to obtain admission, then acted perfectly normally. Rosenhan documents the fact that the staff deeply depersonalized the patients. Some staff were verbally abusive, others simply minimized contact with patients, seeing them only through their "master status" (Chapter 6) as patients. The staff could not identify the fact that the pseudopatients were normal, although the legitimate patients became aware of this quickly. Along with Goffman's study, Rosenhan's research fueled the drive to reform inpatient mental health settings (see below) in the late 1960s and early 1970s.

PRACTITIONERS

Practitioners who assist persons with psychiatric problems include psychiatrists, psychologists, social workers, licensed counselors, and nurses, all of whom may conduct psychotherapy if they have had the appropriate training and have been licensed or certified to do so, depending on the state involved. Paraprofessionals, such as psychiatric technicians, are also used to care for patients in outpatient and inpatient settings.

Psychiatrists

Psychiatrists are medical doctors who have followed up their internship with a three-year residency (specialized training period) in psychiatry.

This training usually occurs at a specialized facility, such as a state or VA hospital. They are the only practitioners who can write prescriptions for medications. They also conduct psychotherapy.

Psychologists

Psychologists are behavioral scientists who have specialized training in psychological testing. They are the only practitioners who can administer and interpret tests. They also conduct psychotherapy.

Social Workers

Social workers have special expertise in the interaction of patients with social systems outside of the hospital. They also conduct psychotherapy. They are responsible for placing the patient on discharge from the hospital.

Licensed Counselors

In many states, **licensed counselors** function as therapists on a less expert level than psychiatrists or psychologists. Not many hospitals employ them, but they are frequently employed in the outpatient portions of mental health systems.

Registered Nurses

Registered nurses (RNs) are responsible for supervising day-to-day inpatient care. At the master's degree level (most nurses have bachelor's or associate's degrees), a very few conduct psychotherapy in much the same manner as social workers or licensed counselors.

Psychiatric Technicians

Psychiatric technicians actually administer day-to-day care to inpatients, and sometimes to outpatients such as those in day treatment settings. Their training varies widely. In some states, they possess the equivalent of practical nurse licenses and must attend a calendar year of community college to qualify to work with mental patients. In others, they receive no formal training whatsoever.

HISTORY OF UNITED STATES MENTAL HEALTH SYSTEMS

Although we don't always think of the different activities of organizations and practitioners in mental health as a "system," it has turned into one over the years. Patients now typically access various types of organizations and practitioners to receive care. This system is complex, and, one can argue, rather unworkable in many ways. In order to understand it, we need to examine the history of its various parts.

Birth of the State Hospitals

The early 1800s were marked by humane tendencies, one of which was the **Medical Superintendents Movement**. The medical superintendents, who were by no means psychiatrists (the field had not been invented yet) established the first asylums—attractive facilities located in the country where mental patients would be able to farm and would regain their health. They began receiving patients from urban centers. These facilities quickly became overloaded with patients, however, as urban authorities sought to clear their streets of not only the mentally ill, but of anyone who looked as though he or she would become disruptive to good order. When these facilities became overcrowded, they became "snake pits" where all types of patient abuses occurred.

The situation of mental patients changed little over the course of the nineteenth century. During the later 1800s, physical treatments were introduced that involved giving agitated patients hot or cold baths or packing them in wet sheets. During this period, many more wards were constructed at these hospitals, which were, by now, almost always operated by the individual states. The majority of living units became "back wards," which housed chronic patients who were expected to remain there for life.

The early 1900s ushered in the use of **electroconvulsive therapy (ECT)** ("shock treatment"), in which an electric current is passed through a patient's brain. ECT has limited clinical uses, among them alleviating depression in patients who cannot be helped by antidepressants. However, in its early days, it tended to be given to virtually any patient for any reason, because it stunned the patient for several days, thus making agitated patients appear less so. This era also introduced **lobotomy**, an even more shameful chapter in American psychiatry. Here, surgery was used to separate the prefrontal lobes of the cerebral cortex from the rest of the brain. The operation was relatively simple, consisting of driving a tome (a stiletto-like tool) past the eye, through a thin spot in the skull, and waving the instrument from side to side, cutting the nerve tracts. This calmed the patient down, but he or she also lost the capacity for sophisticated thinking. This practice disappeared after World War II, as new medications were introduced. As late as the 1970s, however, cryogenic (extreme cold needle) **psychosurgery** was still used to burn the hypothalami (parts of the brain dealing with excitation) of extremely violent mentally ill offenders who volunteered for the program in return for a chance at parole (Cockerham 2000).

The Deinstitutionalization Era

The major revolution in mental illness treatment was the invention of Thorazine in 1953. This drug not only functioned as a major tranquilizer (anti-agitation drug), but it also alleviated the hallucinations and delusions that accompanied schizophrenia. As with ECT, psychiatrists used Thorazine for too many problems at first, and in excessively high doses. Many patients from this era became physically ill from infection because the drug tended to kill white blood cells. Others contracted permanent Parkinson's symptoms (tardive dyskinesia). By and large, however, chlorpromazine (the generic term for the drug) was effective in preparing many patients for discharge from the large state hospitals in which they had typically been poorly cared for. In 1953, the population of the state hospitals was around 500,000. Fifteen years later, it was less than 100,000 (Cockerham 2000).

The emergence of a new class of medications was not the only reason for the mass discharge of patients from state hospitals. During the 1950s and 1960s, the public became aroused at the horror stories—many of which were true—coming out of these institutions. Not only was there forced shock therapy, but patients might be put into restraints for days if their behavior was at all disruptive. In some state hospitals, attendants secretly overmedicated unruly patients, since there were no controls placed on the actual doses given, even if the written order was for a reasonable dose. During the 1950s and 1960s, planners had also been studying community efforts to care for the mentally ill, particularly in such cities as Gheel, Belgium, where mental patients had been humanely cared for in private homes for centuries.

In 1963, President Kennedy signed the Community Mental Health Centers Act, which accelerated the process of **deinstitutionalization**. Soon, many previous state hospital patients were living in board-and-care homes in the community. In many of these homes, however, there was only a moderate amount of programming (daily therapeutic and recreational activities). In others, there was none. In addition, most of the homes were located in poor, crime-ridden areas of cities, so the integrative community atmosphere that the planners had hoped for did not always exist. Still other patients were sent to locked nursing homes in the community. These patients, previously confined to back wards at the state hospitals, were now essentially cared for at back wards in the community, by workers who typically had less professional training than the state hospital workers.

The biggest tragedy, however, was that a large number of patients were discharged from the state hospital to welfare hotels, or worse were simply given a check each month and told to fend for themselves. Many of these individuals became the **homeless mentally ill** of today.

The Revolving Door

While frequently beneficial, community care for the mentally ill has other problems besides the ones cited above. Many of the patients treated in community mental health systems are schizophrenic. The most effective treatment for that condition is major antipsychotic drugs. When these patients are transferred from the hospital to board-and-care homes, they are expected to continue taking their medications. But patients often say that they don't like the feeling of being sapped of energy that butyrophenones and phenothiazines give them. Thus they stop taking their medications in these community facilities, where supervision is much more lax and where the patient cannot legally be compelled to take medications. Some days or weeks after they cease taking the medicines they need to remain sane, these patients decompensate (become mentally ill again), and are typically placed back in an acute hospital setting, where they spend at least two weeks having their medications readjusted. They are then likely to be discharged back to the board-and-care home, where the process is likely to repeat itself once again.

While the patient may enjoy the "change of scene" this process provides, it's a very expensive one for society. Each hospital admission typically costs thousands of dollars. Even if the patient has been in the hospital during the previous week or month, the same tests and evaluations must be ordered on admission. Each of these is expensive, and typically society is handed the bill, since chronic mental patients generally don't have health insurance.

Under some circumstances, mental patients who refuse to take their medications have proved a danger in the community. In 1999, a chronic schizophrenic man suffering delusions pushed a woman off a New York City subway platform to her death. He had failed to take his medications, and it was not clear if he was even receiving any case management from the community mental health system that should have been overseeing his case.

SOCIAL EPIDEMIOLOGY

Another concern has been the charting of the distribution of mental disorders by such factors as geography or social class. Faris and Dunham's (1939) early study of social class and mental disorder in Chicago showed that more psychiatric admissions took place for patients who lived in the inner city as opposed to the suburbs. These inner-city areas were characterized by more individuals living in poverty than in the more affluent outer areas of the city. Later, Hollingshead and Redlich (1953) showed that, if the population were divided into five classes from rich to poor, a far greater percentage of those from the lowest classes would be admitted to psychiatric hospitals than those from the highest classes.

In analyzing the studies, a key issue is whether **stress** or **drift** is the main factor. A stress hypothesis suggests that the unpleasant vicissitudes of lower-class life cause mental problems. A drift hypothesis suggests that individuals who have mental problems gravitate toward the lower classes, perhaps intergenerationally. This debate has not been completely resolved, but researchers are generally inclined to support drift as more decisive, implying that genes play a key role in severe mental problems.

Another watershed in epidemiology was the Midtown Manhattan Study (Srole et al. 1962). Rather than examine treated cases alone, this study attempted to ascertain the **true prevalence** of mental disorders in a section of New York City. It also confirmed that lower-class membership was a correlate of mental problems, and it speculated that stress played a central role in contributing to these problems.

SUMMARY: MENTAL ILLNESS

Mental illness is a key area in deviance. The societal reaction perspective suggests that many patients are labeled into being mentally ill, but, if this is a problem at all, it's probably much more common with people receiving fashionable diagnoses like multiple personality disorder or other personality disorders. Many mental diseases are real, and the more devastating ones are probably inherited. Key diseases include schizophrenia, bipolar disorder, and major depression. A number of other problems exist, including the personality disorders and anxiety. Key organizations treating the mentally ill include hospitals and mental health clinics. Practitioners include psychiatrists, psychologists, social workers, professional counselors, nurses, and psychiatric technicians.

The history of treatment involves the creation of the state hospitals, followed by the devolution to community mental health after Thorazine was introduced in 1953. Currently there are problems with the system because placing patients in the community allows many patients to fall through the cracks. Still others are caught up in the revolving-door syndrome in which they move from hospitals to community placements and back repeatedly. Social-epidemiological studies have shown that poverty is a correlate of mental illness, due either to stress from the lifestyle, or to the fact that the mentally ill drift toward the lower classes.

9

Sexual Deviance

Sexual Addiction

Charles has a sales job. But Charles also has a problem. Whenever he sees an ATM machine, he stops, gets $100 out, and goes to a massage parlor. Once there, he usually pays for fellatio, followed by lubricated masturbation to orgasm. This wouldn't be so bad if Charles wasn't married, but he is—with children. Because of his frequent ATM withdrawals, he's having to juggle the bills from month to month. Not only does he have the ATM–massage parlor habit, but he's having affairs with two of the secretaries he's met on his sales rounds. Neither has found out he's married or about the secretary at the other firm, but he knows they suspect something. He juggles them, too—just like the bills. Afternoons often find Charles sitting in an X-rated movie theatre instead of making his rounds. His salary has started to suffer. His wife wants to know where he goes late at night two or three nights a week, and he puts her off with lame excuses. He knows it's only a matter of time before his house of cards comes crashing down, but so far he's been able to continue his pattern. Charles doesn't look good these days. He's tired and jittery from all the strain, but he just can't seem to stop.

Sexuality is an area full of significance. It's by no means our most primary interest (food, shelter, and group membership are more primary), and individual sexual interest varies, but it's certainly one of our more fascinating preoccupations. Because of its charged nature and because a great deal of sexuality is social, involving other people, it's an area that functions under much direct repression in childhood and is subject to much informal and formal regulation later in life. Some students of sexuality, among them Herbert Marcuse (1990), have argued that sexual repression sets the stage for control over individuals in areas of life having nothing to do with sexuality. They believe that feelings of surplus shame and guilt from repressing the sex drive make people more controllable in other areas. Others, like Christopher Lasch (1991), believe that appropriate repression of unbridled sexuality is useful, and that this appropriate repression, occurring when culture and institutions are intact and functioning well, leads to orderly and fulfilling family life.

Because modern society is complicated, sexuality cannot develop solely in ways suggested by the nature of our bodies. Freud (1989a) was correct in stating that even young children have sexual interests, although these interests are more diffuse than those of adults. Humans have long childhoods before reaching actual puberty and probably experience vestigial behaviors from our primate ancestors, who reached adulthood much more quickly than we do. We see signs of this when young boys say things like, "Mommy, can I marry you when I grow up?" Freud thought that repression of child sexuality, occurring for boys at the Oedipal stage (4 to 5 years), marked the beginning of adult character development. For Lasch, however, repression must be matched by realistic encounters with social institutions that continue to shape behavior in firm, kindly ways, or the child is liable to throw early repression aside as unreasonable or overbearing and turn antisocial. Early socialization seems irrational and frightening unless complemented by positive, realistic encounters with social institutions.

The 1960s were characterized by an ethic that said that all sexual repression was misguided. Indeed, it was beneficial to dispense with some of the puritanical Victorianism characterizing nineteenth-century society. In retrospect, however, it seems clear that *some* repression is necessary to maintain trust between adults (for example, in marriage) or to protect children, who are almost always psychologically injured by sexual contact with adults.

In primitive society, a person becomes an adult at puberty, and extra, internalized sexual repression is often minimized (although poor behavior in respect to sexual norms is usually punished by public shaming, if discovered). In our social system, however, young people train an extra 6 to 12 years following puberty to work gainfully and to become citizens. Because of this, opportunities for adult sexuality (especially respectable married sexuality) as well as other stable, respectable types of adult participation are pushed forward in time. Adolescence, which does not actually exist in primitive societies, is a result of this "putting off" of adulthood. That the drive toward sexuality is strong, but is repressed and delayed, opens the door to idiosyncratic behavior, some of it harmless, some of it quite destructive.

SOCIOBIOLOGY AND SEXUAL DEVIANCE

Although by no means a proven theory, sociobiology (also called evolutionary psychology) lends interesting perspective to analyzing sexual deviance. This theory holds that men and women have different genetically conditioned reproductive strategies (Wilson 2000). Each individual acts in ways intended by nature (actually his or her genetic programming) to reproduce his or her genetic material in future generations. Absent social control, men follow an implicit strategy of attempting to fertilize more than one woman. This is facilitated by men's higher testosterone levels, which tend to make them more aggressive. Even in this age of birth control, our genes are still set up to prompt this behavior.

Women, on the other hand, are engineered to protect their reproductive investment by nurturing and raising a limited number of children. Because of this, they may favor men who earn a good living, or who seem interested in helping with child care. At the same time, however, many women may be interested in men who seem dangerous, or "sexy," even if the sexiness includes an interest in other women. This occurs because these women are also genetically conditioned toward selecting dominant men (dominant in caveman terms!) as mates. Studies have shown (Wilson 2000) that up to 10 percent of children are offspring of men whom women are not married to or paired up with, even when a woman is in a formal relationship. Thus some women are capable of simultaneously selecting one man for his providing and nurturing capabilities, and secretly selecting another for his aggressiveness.

Although at first it seems an exception to the theory (and is a "stretch"), even homosexual behavior can be explained by sociobiology. According to sociobiologists, the occasional occurrence of gay relatives in one's family tree means that a niece or nephew of the gay person stands an improved chance of getting a double monetary inheritance—one from his or her parents, one from his or her gay relative, who is more likely to be childless. Since the heir has *some* of the uncle's or aunt's genes, the niece or nephew presumably benefit from any material inheritance.

It must be stressed that sociobiology is completely unproven. It's likely that some of the behavior sociobiology explains can also be accurately analyzed by other theories. Male and female promiscuity, for example, can be explained by social critics who can point out the ways love and sex have become "commodified." In a market society replete with advertising, they claim, people become more and more attracted to the "surface" or "flash" aspects of things, including relationships. Both men and women may become anxious to trade off partners when the first flush of attraction is over. Thus there is a possibility that sociobiology does not interpret complex human culture as well as its proponents think it does.

MODELS OF SEXUAL VARIATION

Sexual variation can be classified by differentiating between tolerated sexual variation and proscribed sexual variation (Kornblum and Julian 2000). Neither of these is a natural category; each is based on society's reaction to types of sexual "deviance." Tolerated sexual variation is that which, although it may be taboo (forbidden) in polite discourse, is generally tolerated. Proscribed sexual variation is that which is subject to criminal penalties. It should come as no surprise that there's a continuing debate about which behavior will be classified in which category. The 1920s and the 1960s were marked by attempts, often quite successful, to move behavior from the proscribed area to the tolerated area. The 1930s and 1980s were marked by attempts, also often quite successful, to move behavior from the tolerated area to the proscribed area. As in any other area of deviance, moral entrepreneurs play major roles in defining what is tolerated and what is proscribed.

TYPES OF SEXUAL ACTIVITIES

Overt sexual activities can include vaginal intercourse, where a man places his penis in the vagina of a female partner, or anal intercourse, where a man places his penis in the anus of a male or female partner. It can also involve fellatio, where a male or female partner takes a man's penis in his or her mouth, typically stimulating it with the lips, tongue, and/or back of the throat; or cunnilingus, where a male or female partner stimulates a woman's clitoris, labiae, or outer vagina with his or her lips and/or tongue. "Sixty-nine" describes mutual fellatio and/or cunnilingus, with either a same or different sex partner. Anilingus is stimulation of the partner's anus by tongue. Not everyone enjoys all, or even many, of these activities, and it's incumbent on more "sophisticated" partners to respect the wishes of a partner who does not wish to participate in some or all of these activities. Failure to respect a partner's wishes in this respect, even during sexual activity that has already started, is like date rape, in that one partner has set limits and the other partner is ignoring them. For this reason, verbally "checking out" the acceptability of proposed activities needs to continue during initial sexual encounters, just as it does as a prelude to sexuality.

"Foreplay," probably a misnomer since it can be incorporated into sex at any point, including after orgasm, might include stroking the partner's back, face, arms, hands, neck, chest or breasts and kissing either the mouth or other parts of the partner's body. Orgasm following stimulation is ejaculation for a male or a series of pleasurable pulsations through the vulva and vaginal area for a female. Both sexes also typically feel great sensations of pleasure and relaxation throughout the whole body during and following orgasm.

SEXUALLY TRANSMITTED DISEASES

Because sexuality often involves penetration and/or exchange of body fluids, a number of diseases can be transmitted sexually. (Diseases transmitted this way are also called **venereal diseases**.) The most significant is Acquired Immune Deficiency Syndrome (**AIDS**), involving a virus that devastates the immune system, usually killing its untreated victims (Stine 2002). AIDS may take months or years to appear. During this time, the victim is infected and capable of transmitting the disease to others. It's generally transferred by blood–blood or blood–semen contact, but may also be transmitted through contact with vaginal secretions or possibly saliva. Because the rectum is highly vascular (provided with blood vessels) and lacks natural lubrication, unprotected anal intercourse is dangerous in this age of AIDS because of the potential for blood–semen contact. This may partly explain why AIDS initially spread more rapidly through the male gay community in the United States than the straight community, and why AIDS is pandemic (very common) among poor people in Africa, where anal intercourse is used for birth control. The symptoms of AIDS can be delayed for years by an expensive and inconvenient regimen of oral medications. Some authorities believe that treated victims remain certain to develop the disease if they live long enough, in spite of medications, due to the capacity of the disease to mutate (change) over time.

Syphilis is a bacterial disease that, if left untreated, can be devastating. It usually shows itself as a sore on or near the genitals within a few days of infection (which may be accompanied by a rash or fever), but then disappears to enter a latent (unseen) stage for months or years. Syphilis may then attack the nervous system, creating "gummae," which are lesions (injuries) directly on the victim's nerve or brain cells. A late-stage syphilis victim often hallucinates and has delusions much like those of a schizophrenic or long-time alcohol abuser. By this time, it's too late for antibiotics, the appropriate treatment for earlier stages. Ultimately, long-term syphilis kills its victims. In the Tuskeegee experiment, the United States government funded research in which a group of black men who contracted syphilis were allowed to go untreated for years, even after the development of effective antibiotic medications. Many died. This racist series of incidents is a hallmark of how experimentation should not be conducted.

Gonorrhea is another bacterial disease, also transmitted by genital–genital, mouth–genital, mouth–mouth, genital–anus, or mouth–anus contact. It shows itself as an early rash and/or fever, followed by a localized infection characterized by the production of pus. The local infection can be in the urethra in the penis (the central tube), the vagina, the rectum, or even the throat. Women are often not aware of vaginal gonorrheal infections, but the disease usually causes acute pain on urination in men who have urethral infections. Like syphilis, gonorrhea can usually be treated with antibiotics.

Many if not all venereal diseases can be prevented by condom use during vaginal or anal sex with a new partner. Because condoms break on occasion, experts counsel the use of spermicidal jellies, which also kill venereal disease organisms, in conjunction with condom use. Use of a condom or dental dam (a thin plastic shield) during fellatio or cunnilingus is also advised (McPhee, Lingappa, and Rosen 1999).

TOLERATED SEXUAL VARIATION

Masturbation—When Deviance Is Nearly Universal

In 1996, President Clinton fired Surgeon General of the United States Joycelyn Elders. Her appointment had been a stunning public relations coup. A competent, well-respected physician, she was the first woman and the first African American to become surgeon general. Why then did the president discharge her? The reason was simple: Dr. Elders had become an embarrassment. Specifically, she had called for classes teaching adolescents to masturbate. Even though it's nearly universal and likely very helpful in developing an adult sexuality (Masters and Johnson 1966), publicly calling for training in masturbation is taboo. This is an instance where the two definitions of deviance (Chapter 1) are in contradiction. Nearly everyone masturbates, and one definition of deviance is based on whether the behavior is unusual, so by this definition masturbation is *not* deviant. But masturbation is taboo and thus qualifies as deviance under the other definition—the one based on social opprobrium.

Pornography

Pornography (from the Greek, translated as "whore's writing") is the use of graphic images or text to sexually stimulate and arouse. Contemporary forms include films, videos, computer games, pictures, Internet films and images, and stories. Like alcohol, pornography has been with humans since the beginning of human speech and writing, although it's not clear that it has always played the same role in every society. In ancient India, for example, pornographic temple carvings sometimes played a religious role because Tantric practitioners believed that sexual activity could bring on an altered state of consciousness, a way to draw closer to the gods. For contemporary proponents, pornography focuses a healthy interest on sexuality. Consumers may discover new pleasurable techniques, or may use pornographic materials to invigorate the sexual parts of a relationship. For these reasons, defenders believe that much if not all pornography should be seen as "erotica"—materials used for legitimate stimulation, even aesthetic purposes. A number of studies show that no great harm results from pornography, and some anecdotal evidence indicates that some individuals or couples may benefit from using erotica as a substitute for, or adjunct to, sexuality with another person.

Detractors believe pornography (perhaps like "gateway drugs") can disinhibit individuals likely to use their sexuality in addictive or asocial ways (cf. MacKinnon and Dworkin 1997). They argue that this form of tolerated sexual variation should again be proscribed as it was before the mid-1960s. Feminists often see pornography as implying that men should see women's bodies solely as sexual objects, and as causing men to feel empowered to treat women in degrading ways. Antipornography advocates Catherine MacKinnon and Andrea Dworkin have argued that "pornography is the theory, and rape is the practice," referring to the idea that pornography provides models for men to abuse women. Although feminist critics focus on the issues of pornography featuring simulated violence or involving children, the overwhelming majority of pornographic materials feature adult sexuality between actors portrayed as consensual participants.

There can be no question, however, that the sexual world portrayed by pornography is one in which most women and men would not always feel comfortable. Sex and relationships are portrayed as highly commodified; physical attributes such as breast or penis size are represented as of great importance. Relationships are shown superficially, based on immediate attraction, not entailing loyalty. Sexuality is portrayed as the supreme desideratum in any interaction. Some 1970s and 1980s pornography featured simulated incest, although this is generally missing from 1990s pornography due to agreements between the adult industry and law enforcement.

Significantly, there is a general lack of equity between men and women in pornography. Even when the director is female, the film is shot from a male point of view because of the overwhelmingly male customer base. Sexuality occurs without formation of friendships or relationships based on trust, negating what most people consider a healthy approach to intimacy. Women are usually required to stimulate men for much longer periods than men are required to stimulate women prior to intercourse. Two or more women are often made available for a man's pleasure. They often stimulate each other, saving him the trouble while he looks on.

Pornography may "provoke, but then deaden" sexuality. Both men and women may react with physical arousal to pornographic materials (Kinsey 1948), but most women do not seek them out, and usually deny arousal (Rue 1983). (Although there is a very small group of women who consume pornographic materials independent of men, most consumers are either men or couples who use erotica as an adjunct to sex.) Because the relationships portrayed are based on sexual encounters alone, they may tend to lose their ability to fascinate over time. Hence there is probably a need to "ratchet up" stimulation. Pornography of the 1990s and early 2000s often features anal intercourse or "gang bangs" where multiple men penetrate a woman in order to introduce "something new." Similarly, interracial encounters are sometimes featured, implying they are another form of "kinkiness."

Because of this stimulating-then-deadening phenomenon, pornography contains a propensity to "addict" individuals who consume it. And, as we'll see below, pornography is a common ingredient in sexual addiction.

Affairs and Swinging

Although researchers are not in agreement as to the frequency of affairs, many married people stray from their relationships on one or more occasions. Some estimate the number of married men who have had sexual relations outside of marriage to be as high as 60 percent (Gould 2000). The same authorities believe that as many as 40 percent of women have had at least one affair. With men, these encounters can include casual sex, such as in the Clinton-Lewinsky scandal, where the parties used the excuse that the affair was not fully consummated because it was "only oral sex," a popular way of disputing that full sexual encounters have taken place. If Ms. Lewinsky's apparent feelings are an indication, however, one or both parties to an affair are likely to experience it as emotionally meaningful, even if the feeling is not shared. For this reason, affairs are dangerous. They can threaten long-term marriages or relationships because excitement tends to overshadow the staid older relationship, which may seem pale by comparison. In addition, trust between married partners is diminished because, even if the spouse never finds out about an affair, the adulterous spouse carries the secret with him or her. This can make the guilty spouse more guarded, less forthcoming. Another danger is that members of the married couple's social circle discover the affair and gossip about them behind their backs, lowering their social status.

"**Swinging**" is mate swapping (Gould 2000). Very few couples practice it, because most people regard sex as highly intimate, requiring a level of trust not accorded relative strangers. Sex calls for emotional openness because enjoyment probably depends for most people on the ability to be unguarded and "in the moment." In addition, members of most couples may have trouble trusting each other following mate swapping, even if their intention is for swinging to lead only to superficial relationships with outsiders. Like pornography, however, mate exchange has probably had different meanings in different cultures. Some groups of Inuits (Eskimos) have practiced mate exchange as a form of hospitality, for example. Some areas of the world with a tradition of "carnival" preceding Lent have had traditions that allow for occasional mate exchange. For example— and this is by no means widespread—in the 1960s one could attend pre-Lenten parties in Bavaria where house keys were thrown into a pile and people went home for one night only with the opposite-sex person whose key they had drawn.

One common form of swinging is the "closed" swing, in which two couples meet, exchange partners, and then go off to separate bedrooms, houses, or hotel rooms. An "open" swing occurs when two or more couples exchange partners and make love in the same room. During an open swing, partners may be re-exchanged, and two individuals may make love with a third at the same time. Because these temporary relationships are based on such superficial criteria as physical attractiveness, however, they tend to be commodified relationships, where only surface attributes are taken into account. One of the ironies is that swinging usually begins at the behest of men, who, if what sociobiologists say is true, have more desire for multiple partners. Once female partners become involved, however, it's often *they* who desire to continue. The men involved are more prone to become jealous of their partner's making love with another man (and/or woman). Women, who have better social skills, may enjoy social membership in the swinging group more than the men do.

Prostitution

Prostitution is defined as engaging in sexual relations for money or other considerations. Although it's probably not the world's oldest profession (tribal shamans, hunters, and food gatherers are no doubt older), its practice stretches into antiquity. Like many other forms of sexual deviance, its meaning and practice has varied across cultures. In the ancient Near East, for example, one could visit priestesses at temples, have sex with them, and leave an offering. In some communities, each young woman was expected to spend at least one day as a temple priestess, although she might not actually engage in sex, depending on whether or not she was chosen. Although this practice seems one-sided in terms of sexual discrimination, it was part of the religious beliefs of those societies. (Similar societies made selected young men fertility kings for a year, plied them with maidens, then executed them) (Tannahill 1982).

In modern America, female prostitutes range from streetwalkers, who accost cars in our nation's cities; to bar girls, who pick up men in bars; to call girls, who are dispatched to homes and hotels. Some prostitutes work in brothels, which tend to be either massage parlors offering services ranging from lubricated masturbation to fellatio, or houses catering to men of a specific ethnic group, such as Mexicans or Chinese, who work in the United States without women. Men occasionally also work as prostitutes, usually as streetwalkers serving gay clients.

Prostitutes have generally had troubled early lives. Some of the factors prompting participation include:

1. *Frequent history of abuse or neglect in the home.* Women who have been sexually abused, beaten, or ignored as children are more likely to become prostitutes. The abuse and/or neglect act as a "push" factor impelling them out of the home to the streets, frequently in a distant city. Once there, they become aware, or are made aware by a pimp (procurer), that they can support themselves through prostitution. Some types of sex work (see below) and prostitution pay very well (a "pull" factor), especially when contrasted with the types of service jobs or factory labor available to relatively uneducated women.

2. *Early, promiscuous sexual experience.* This, often prompted by sexual abuse, inclines women to define themselves primarily in sexual terms, even if past abuse was unwelcome. It's a fairly easy jump to prostitution from intense promiscuity.

3. *Drug addiction.* The most important issue in an addict's life becomes procuring the drug. (Like prostitution, drug addiction in women tends to result from early abuse.) Prostitution becomes a relatively easy means to get money for drugs and survival. (McCaghy and Capron 1997)

There is a difference in status between the lowest rung (streetwalkers) and the highest (call girls). Streetwalkers are more likely to be assaulted, even killed, since prostitutes are favorite targets of serial killers. They are also much more likely to have pimps—males who organize their lives in return for appropriating their money. Pimps provide services (bailing arrested streetwalkers out of jail, keeping other pimps at bay), but are chiefly involved because they provide the type of abusive control prostitutes are used to from growing up in families where there were similar patterns. The pimp becomes the man in a prostitute's life, for whom she must compete with each of his other prostitutes. Although competitors, these women also become friends and peers; access to them is available only if she is part of the "stable." She (paradoxically) also gains status among other pimps and prostitutes by having a pimp (Milner and Milner 1972).

Higher status prostitutes are often connected with their "tricks" through "escort" agencies, which take a fee (often 50 percent). Many prostitutes in this group have more normal backgrounds and are not as likely to have pimps. During the last several years, a new phenomenon of "sex workers" has emerged. Sex workers (at the most lucrative level) are women who combine dancing in "gentlemen's clubs" (strip joints) with

acting in pornographic movies with occasional "tricking" (sexually servic-
ing men). They make much of their money through dancing, and pornographic films act as advertisements for these "gigs," which customers can
locate through national Websites. Although these women make upwards
of $100,000 annually, their careers are likely to be short-lived because
success depends on youthful appearance. Many sex workers have a series
of breast augmentations because large breasts are especially desired by a
sizable percentage of the gentlemen's club clientele. A large proportion of
dancers' income comes from tips. Below this elite level are sex workers
who dance only, who lap dance (combine dancing with sitting on men's
laps and rubbing against them), who appear in peep shows, and who staff
phone sex lines. Many dancers provide such services as oral sex off site to
customers for an additional fee. Many sex workers now also staff Internet
Websites, where they post pictures of themselves with a variety of partners, provide live feeds to their homes or apartments (including bedrooms
and bathrooms), and run periodic live chats, interacting with clients in
real time.

Homosexuality

Freud (1989) believed that everyone was essentially "polymorphous
perverse," capable of sexual relations with both males and females, but
that our socialization channeled us toward the opposite sex. In his path-
breaking research in the late 1940s, Alfred Kinsey posited that humans
ranged on a continuum between completely heterosexual and completely
homosexual. Kinsey *et al* (1948) found that while as many as 37 percent of
adult men had experienced at least one homosexual act to orgasm between
puberty and old age, only about 3 percent of the population was exclusively homosexual. Some researchers believe that homosexuality may be related to genetics; but none of these theories have been conclusively proven.
Many gay people are convinced that homosexuality is as natural for them
as being "straight" is for heterosexuals. For Plummer (1975), individuals
who become homosexual are likely to pass through four stages. The first
stage, sensitization, implies a growing awareness that one may be gay. The
next, signification, incorporates becoming aware of society's condemnation
of homosexuality. The third stage, coming out, involves embracing a homosexual identity in the face of social disapproval. The last stage, stabiliza-
tion, involves accepting being gay and rejecting straight society.

Reactions to homosexuality are more problematic than homosexuality
itself. Many instances of discrimination against homosexuals have been
documented. These can range from not hiring persons perceived to be
homosexual, to actively harassing homosexuals on the job, even to assault
on homosexuals in work or other contexts. In one case, the Cracker Barrel
chain of restaurants tried to purge its employee rolls of all persons it

perceived to be homosexuals. In spite of demonstrations by the gay community, Cracker Barrel stuck to this policy. Since the discharges took place in "employment at will" states, where employers do not have to provide justification for firing employees, they held legally. In another incident, a male stockbroker perceived to be homosexual was harassed in the fraternity-house atmosphere of his firm. Senior managers made mocking films attesting to the idea that he was gay and distributed them throughout the company. When he was out of town on a business trip, the same managers repainted his car, decorating it with such epithets as "fudge packer" (referring to anal intercourse). The stockbroker was fired, but was ultimately able to collect an undisclosed settlement.

Many gays have been assaulted or even murdered by straight men with a special interest in homosexuals. Evidence shows that many individuals reporting that they hate gays are, at the same time, among those who indicate a high latent interest in homosexuality on psychological tests (Adams, Wright, and Lohr 2001). Still others, like certain small-town Texas high school football players, may have local traditions of periodically driving into the gay area of Houston to "bash" homosexual men. Some assaults have led to the deaths of victims. A number of assaults and deaths have also occurred in the military, and the creation of the "don't ask; don't tell" policy under President Clinton has not alleviated discrimination. In fact, as though to assert independence from presidential control, several branches of the military have increased their scrutiny of gays, discharging them when homosexuality is discovered. The individual does not have to actually engage in gay behavior. A very successful Annapolis midshipman (a naval officer cadet) was expelled for stating he considered himself gay, even though he'd never engaged in any homosexual activities.

PROSCRIBED SEXUAL VARIATION

Rape—A Sex Crime As Well As an Assault

Rape is defined as forcing sexual activity on an unwilling partner. This activity can consist of penetration of the victim's body by a penis, finger, or other object. Such penetration can be anal or oral as well as vaginal. Victims can be both female and male, and, as critics of the idea that rape is sexual frequently state, it's frequently carried out in order to humiliate or intimidate. But there can be no question that rape is a sexual crime as well as an assault. Most rapists report being in a state of sexual arousal. Rape can run the gamut from stranger rape to rape of an acquaintance to date rape, where the perpetrator typically thinks that he has done nothing wrong because of the belief that the victim wanted or deserved to be raped.

Because only about 50 percent of forcible rapes (and an even smaller percentage of date rapes) are reported (McGaghy and Capron 1997), the incidence of rape is probably greater than people imagine. Surveys (Koss 1989) reveal that 3.8 percent of college women have had sex forced on them at one point or another. But the true incidence is likely to be much greater than surveys indicate. At the same time, the legal system has not always been sensitive to the special plight of victims. Law enforcement has sometimes been quick to discount their assertions, and defense lawyers have frequently brought up the victim's sexual history as a defense, although this practice is less common now. Because of this, it's necessary to develop high consciousness regarding this crime and ways to deal with it. Persons engaging in consensual sex should ask each other frequently whether it's permissible to continue. Rape information should be widely disseminated, and advocacy units, which send workers—usually female— to work with victims during their medical treatment and encounters with the legal system, should be established.

Pedophilism

Pedophilism is sexual desire for children. Sexual activities with adults almost invariably cause children psychological injury and inability to adapt well (Barnett, Miller-Perrin, and Perrin 1997), absent extensive later therapy. Even when a child enjoys the experience, or feels especially favored by the adult singling him or her out for attention, he or she is almost sure to begin feeling that the relationship has been an abuse of trust. Not being able to trust adults (or family members in cases of incest) creates pervasive depression, putting the victim at great risk for failure in adult roles, and, as we've seen with sex workers, great risk for possible repeat victimization. Not all pedophiles actually practice molestation, but if they do, these practices are destructive to children's well-being. It's not always clear where normal sexuality stops and pedophilism starts, because the age of consent varies from state to state. In some, it's as young as 14; in others, as old as 18. In many states (New York is an example) the degree of "sex with a child" also depends on the spread in ages between the perpetrator and the minor. Thus a 19-year-old boy sleeping with a 16-year-old girl is treated more leniently than a 30-year-old having sex with a 13-year-old.

Child pornography, at least in the United States, consists of photographic images of children portrayed in a sexual manner. It's illegal to own child pornography because (1) these images represent the actual victimization of the child-models in the pictures; therefore purchasers and exchangers are abetting a crime; and (2) the images may actually encourage crimes against children, although this has not been proven. In other countries, Australia for example, it's also illegal to own drawn images or even written accounts of sex with children.

SEXUAL ADDICTION

Because of the success of the chemical dependency movement in identifying and treating addiction, and because sexuality itself can seem an addictive substance to some people, addiction models (Chapter 7) seem to work for compulsive sexuality. Patrick Carnes (2001), a pioneer in this field, classifies **sexual addiction** on three levels, depending on intensity (see Table 9.1):

1. *Level 1.* Here the harm incurred likely accrues to the addict himself or herself. Level 1 behavior includes compulsive masturbation, often with pornography; compulsive affairs; and repeatedly visiting prostitutes. All of these activities begin to separate the addict from his or her healthy relationships, confining him or her to a "self-made hell," where the only thing that gives pleasure is sexual addiction. Most sexual addiction is Level 1, and this behavior may characterize as much as 10 percent of the population.

2. *Level 2.* Here the harm to others is increased. Level 2 behavior includes **voyeurism**, in which addicted individuals attempt to view others in a state of undress (some voyeurs, however, may just "cruise" for fully dressed people, circling a block over and over to get a glimpse of someone who attracts them); **flashers**, (exhibitionists) who display their genitals, then run off; and obscene phone callers, who make aggressive sexual calls and then hang up. All of this behavior can have an extremely negative effect on others, who are likely to be frightened. These obsessions can also have a profoundly life-wrecking effect on the perpetrator, who can spend all of his or her productive life pursuing them. Voyeurs have been injured after falling out of trees, where they have spent the night hoping for a glimpse of a naked body. Flashers have been beaten by passersby when following their obsession.

TABLE 9.1   Carnes's Levels of Sexual Addiction

	Behavior	*Degree of Harm*
Level 1	Pornography Affairs Excessive masturbation	Moderate
Level 2	Voyeurism Exhibitionism Obscene phone calls	High
Level 3	Rape Molestation	Very High

Source: Carnes (2001).

3. *Level 3*. Here the harm to others is extreme. Level 3 behavior includes rape, incest, and child molestation. Rape frequently includes physical as well as sexual assault. Although critics of the addiction approach have disputed its value, charging that these behaviors are essentially "violence," there is no question that it's frequently valuable to use this approach in treating all three levels of addiction.

As with drug and alcohol abuse, treatment can consist of 12-step outpatient programs, other outpatient programs, and residential programs. In many states, residential programs for sexual offenders are part of the state prison system. There may be provision for individuals to be detained past their prison release dates, if treatment staff believe the perpetrator remains a danger. Although relatively infrequent, the occasional sexual murder of children or adults points up the fact that rapists are capable of doing more than merely sexually assaulting their victims.

SUMMARY: SEXUAL DEVIANCE

Sexual deviance is fascinating. Because of the necessarily conflicted nature of sexuality in society, it remains one of the most problematic areas as far as the average person is concerned. Most people have a sexual life. Because of the strong social controls on sexuality, very "normal" people are likely to experience ambivalence around sexuality. In addition, the specific content of sexual behavior is interesting and subject to endless conflict and negotiation with others. What sexual behavior should be winked at? What sexual behavior should be proscribed? Is masturbation tacitly permissible? What about prostitution, pornography, or homosexuality? When does sexual behavior constitute an addiction? All of these are questions for which there is probably no clear-cut answer that can be applied in all times and places.

PART III

SOCIAL DEVIANCE

10

Organizational and Vocational Deviance and Crime

A Case of Organizational Deviance

Joan works for a training company that conducts many seminars across the country at all times of the year. A recent English-major graduate of a major university, she is delighted to have gotten a job as a program planner with the firm. Her group leader teaches her how to plan seminars, from researching the topics, to hiring speakers, to doing market research to get suitable mailing lists for addressees to send brochures to. When she is planning her first seminar in computer technology, her group leader, Jim, mentions that she should order a certain interest-group mailing list through a nonprofit association—an association secretly set up by Joan's firm. "They won't rent it to us if they know we're for-profit," he says. When the list arrives, Joan is told to "scrub" it. "You have to remove the 'seeds,' the obvious plants (officers of the interest group), so that they won't be able to tell if we use the list again." Joan then learns that her firm has a special large Xerox machine to copy mailing lists, even those that are rented for one-time use, as this one is. She feels some ethical qualms, but is told that this is company policy. "They charge so much, we feel like we've bought the names," Jim says. Over the next few months, Joan learns about the dark side of seminars in other ways. At Jim's instructions, she pretends to accidentally stumble through an exit door in a hotel conference room rented by another seminar company so she can quickly count the house. She copies the other company's brochure and changes it enough so that it doesn't seem exactly the same when she does her mailing. For one seminar, she teams up with a nonprofit university for a nominal fee to them, so as to be able to use their nonprofit mailing rates, which cut her substantial mailing costs in half. After a year on the job, she has no ethical questions. In fact, she is now training an assistant, Marie, to help her.

The study of deviance and crime in work life is fascinating. Authorities estimate that economic losses from white-collar crime are 10 to 30 times as great as from street crime. Losses are on the order of $40 billion per year, whereas street crime may only represent $4 billion (Friedrichs 1996). But because of the drama and fear associated with street crime, most law-enforcement efforts are directed toward that area. Another factor governing the comparative lack of interest in white-collar crime is the fact that it is usually not discovered. When it is reported, victims frequently find that there is little law-enforcement budget set aside for prosecution, or that (because many frauds take place across state lines) there are questions of jurisdiction. Police and prosecutors may have no idea which governmental entity should take action, and referral to law enforcement may fall through the cracks. And perpetrators often have much higher social status than street criminals. Hence, they have more resources and are therefore more difficult to discover and prosecute.

ORGANIZATIONAL DEVIANCE

Organizational deviance is broader than simple white-collar crime—crime committed as part of working life. Studying organizational deviance is useful because much unethical behavior committed by organizations is not technically white-collar crime. If we must discuss only white-collar crime in assessing unethical business behavior, we miss a dimension of organizational behavior that is harmful to the public but that hasn't technically broken any law. Also, studying organizational deviance allows us to concentrate on organizations instead of individuals. Although some experts have charged that only individuals are ultimately responsible for behavior, it's clear for many others that organizations have great power to shape the perceptions and behavior of individuals who work in them. For this reason, many authorities believe that organizational deviance is a valuable concept.

For Ermann and Lundman (1987), organizational deviance is characterized by the following factors (see Figure 10.1):

1. Some of the organization's behavior is contrary to social norms the public holds for such organizations.

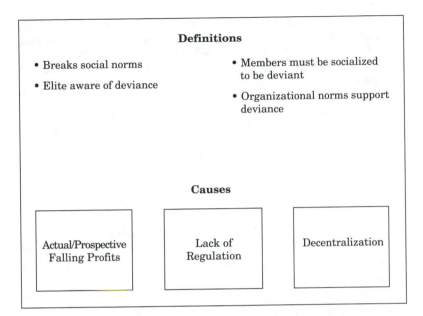

FIGURE 10.1   **Definitions and Causes of Organizational Deviance**
Sources: Ermann and Lundman 1987 and Vaughan 1983.

2. Top management is aware of the norm violations, permits them, and possibly encourages them.
3. The norms of at least some section(s) of the organization are deviant to broader social norms.
4. There is a socialization process taking place in deviant sections of the organization to bring people up to speed in willingness and ability to commit norm violations.

There is a difference between organizational deviance (perhaps even crime) and ordinary white-collar deviance or crime. In white-collar deviance or crime, the activity can involve as few as one or two people. Here, an entire organization is involved. The deviant activity usually helps the entire organization, rather than only one or a small number of people, which is why top management allows it to continue and perhaps promotes it.

What sorts of factors promote organizational deviance? After all, American business prides itself on the appearance of correct moral behavior. We usually say that we are an especially moral country. So why does this sort of deviance occur? Diane Vaughan (1983) proposes three causal factors (see Figure 10.1):

1. *Perception that profits are falling or about to fall.* Here, the organization sees its competition winning out and resolves to do anything necessary to survive. This frequently involves deviant activities.

2. *Lack of regulation exists*. If the industry is not well regulated—either by laws, regulations, or both—deviant activity may occur. Many businesses obey regulations when they are in place, but may feel "all bets are off" if none exist. Many modern businesses are "legalistic," tending to follow the letter of the law, not its spirit. So they may engage in unethical organizational behavior if no regulations yet apply.

3. *Certain organizational factors exist*. For Vaughan, one such is decentralization. The separation of corporate headquarters from "line" (operational) parts of the organization may mean that persons in line areas begin to use unethical practices, since close management oversight does not exist.

CASE STUDY: THE TEXAS PSYCHIATRIC HOSPITAL SCANDAL

In late 1991, a psychiatrist, Dr. Duard Bok, reported the private, free-standing psychiatric hospital where he was on staff, Psychiatric Institute of Fort Worth, for a variety of corrupt activities, among them large monthly "medical director stipends" awarded to psychiatrists hospitalizing large numbers of patients (Vandenburgh 1999). Direct kickbacks are always illegal in health care. Physician stipends, however—paying for a hospital ward's medical director—are technically legal. In this hospital, these stipends were sometimes more than $20,000 per month. Physicians often spent five hours a week or less at the hospital, performing case reviews, and were often also compensated by their patients' insurance policies for these tasks. The real purpose of the high stipends ($1,000 an hour) was to incentivize the physicians to place their patients in the hospital, which would bill their insurance companies at $1,500 a day. Adult patients often stayed in the hospital for 30 to 45 days, frequently discharged only when their insurance benefits were exhausted. Adolescents and children often stayed for 3 to 6 months. The diagnoses for the adolescents, in particular, were flimsy. In most cases, these young people could have been treated as outpatients.

As investigations took place, other shady practices came to light. Psychiatric Institute of Fort Worth hired a patient-finding firm, Recovery Line, at $120,000 per month to recruit patients directly. Its workers went to Alcoholics Anonymous meetings to find chemical dependency patients, and also staffed the hospital's "crisis hotline." When someone with a problem called, the counselor invariably attempted to hospitalize the prospective patient, if he or she had "good" insurance. This particular hospital also used billboards giving the phone number of Recovery Line, inviting prospective patients to call. In addition, all employed clinical staff—psychologists, social workers, and nurses—were required to contact fellow professionals to recommend the hospital for patients these community colleagues might turn up. Eight or ten of these "marketing calls" were required each week from each staff member. Staff not making calls were in danger of being fired.

As the scandal unraveled through news accounts, it became clear that the situation at Psychiatric Institute of Fort Worth was not isolated. Many psychiatric hospitals throughout the state used the same methods. Some also used television ads suggesting that depressed persons or out-of-control teenagers should present themselves at these hospitals for psychiatric evaluations. These evaluations, done by counselors rather than physicians, invariably suggested hospitalization rather than outpatient treatment when patients had good insurance.

Quantitative studies suggested that this pattern was pervasive throughout the entire state. Vandenburgh (1999) found that the number of admissions was highly correlated with the amount of stipends paid psychiatrists by hospitals, and that these tended to rise based on the amount of competition the hospitals faced in their markets, bearing out Vaughan's thesis #1 regarding causal factors. Other Sunbelt states had similar patterns, especially those that had "sunsetted" (gotten rid of) legislation regulating new construction or controlling medical prices. Permissive attitudes toward new construction of psychiatric hospitals had quickly doubled or even tripled the number of profitable hospitals in many southern and western cities, causing competitors to fear for their ability to earn profits, or even to stay in business.

After 1992, most scandals disappeared because (1) new regulations in most states prohibited exploitative practices, and (2) "seed" money to drive heavy expenditures needed to furnish high stipends and buy expensive advertising was no longer available because of diminished revenues caused by tighter managed-care supervision.

TRUE WHITE-COLLAR CRIME

Many of the practices we saw above were actually legal when they occurred. But quite a number of business practices are illegal. These constitute **white-collar crime**, defined as crime committed as part of one's job or vocation. They often involve betrayal of trust by white-collar criminals (Sutherland 1983, Friedrichs 1996). Interestingly, white-collar crime does not need to be perpetrated by a middle-class or rich person. Many "white-collar crimes" are carried out by blue-collar employees. Although the list of white-collar crimes could go on and on, some key classifications are listed here:

Corporate Crime

Crime by big business, or **corporate crime**, is not at all unknown. It may come as a surprise, particularly after reading Vaughan's theory, but large, secure corporations sometimes commit crimes. Some of these crimes involve violence directed against consumers, the public, or the corporation's work force. Violence against consumers occurs when shoddy products incorporating safety hazards are sold. A case in point is the Bridgestone/ Firestone tire scandal. Here, a tire company furnished tires for sport utility vehicles (SUVs) that tended to blow out in hot weather. The SUVs' high centers of gravity made it likely that vehicles with blown tires would then roll over. For reasons that are not clear, these incidents happened more frequently when the SUVs were Fords. In spite of a pattern of accidents dating back to the early 1990s, Bridgestone/Firestone and Ford kept silent. It was not until publicity led to a series of lawsuits that people became aware that there was a problem. Following legal advice, the companies involved denied responsibility, instead pointing their fingers at each other. In some jurisdictions, courts are considering preferring criminal charges against Bridgestone/Firestone and Ford.

Another type of corporate violence is less direct. Here, the public falls victim to what economists call an "externality." This is usually pollution. It's called an economic externality because the polluting company saves the costs of cleaning up the mess associated with making products and passes these costs on to the public in the form of diminished quality of life, or even sickness and death. If this seems extreme, consider the case of Love Canal. In the 1940s, Hooker Chemicals purchased a location in Buffalo, New York, and began using it as a toxic chemical dump. Later a residential neighborhood was established there. A variety of unusual diseases and deaths began to occur, and it slowly became clear that pollution was the cause. Hooker ultimately had to pay damages to the residents, although many critics believe that the corporation got off too lightly.

Corporate violence can also result from failure to safeguard employees. Karen Silkwood worked in a nuclear plant in Oklahoma. She and several other employees were contaminated with atomic material, which is radioactive and can be harmful, during the course of their duties. Silkwood became involved in the union effort to resolve this and other employer-employee issues. During the course of her union-building efforts, Silkwood was killed in an automobile accident. Some critics have gone so far as to suggest that this "accident" was an attempt to cover up the pattern of corporate abuse first demonstrated by the poor nuclear safety standards.

Still other corporate crime can take the form of anticompetitive strategies corporations use to gain unfair advantage. The famous electrical scandals of the early 1950s saw some of the country's largest electrical corporations engaging in "phase of the moon" bidding: Each company in turn was allowed to furnish the low bid in secret collusion with the others. In the late 1990s and early 2000s, Microsoft Corporation was indicted for attempting, among other maneuvers, to become the major provider of Internet browsers by unfairly bundling them in its Windows operating system, which is used on most DOS-based computers. More alarming was Microsoft's attempt to require bulk purchasers of Windows to refuse to put competitors' software on the initial desktop that users saw when turning their machines on.

Corporate fraud is another key area of interest. In early 2002, the Enron Corporation suddenly went bankrupt. A year earlier, Enron had seemed to be one of the most successful companies in the United States. But in 2002, its executives were charged with using illegitimate accounting practices to make the company appear to be more successful than it actually was. Enron, like Bridgestone/Firestone in many ways, turned around and accused its auditing firm, Arthur Andersen, of having committed malfeasance.

Enterprise Crime

Enterprise crime is setting up a fraudulent business. Many telemarketing businesses are, in essence, fraudulent, although occasionally telemarketing workers may not be aware of the extent to which they are shams. All manner of worthless or nearly worthless products and services are sold, often to those most vulnerable to come-ons—the elderly. A telemarketer may offer such items as a discounted vacation plan having very little real value but requiring a hefty sign-up fee. The series of vacations offered could almost always be purchased for the same price through a travel agent. In one case, salespeople sold "dance lessons" to elderly widows in Florida through telemarketing and advertising. When the widows took advantage of the offers of free lessons, they were swept off their feet by handsome young dance instructors, who invited them to sign up, not only for a series of lessons, but for special dinner-dancing dates and tours with their dance teacher. On instructions from the company, the dance instructors also plied these lonely women with gifts and personal notes sent to their residences. Occasionally they intimidated women who tried to back out of the arrangement. Victims often ran through $100,000 in nine months.

Some telemarketers sell "gold shares" that, when the victim tries to redeem them, turn out to be worthless. Others sell "employment services" in which the only service the customer ultimately receives is a generic handout describing standard methods for getting a job. Still others sell worthless stock shares (see the film *Boiler Room* for a realistic portrayal of this). Some sell products that fall apart overnight. Telemarketers often rely on their victims' need for someone to talk to in order to establish the connection that lets them make the "close." They often have an initial goal of just keeping their customer on the phone. Because many older people expect others to behave honestly, seniors are particularly vulnerable to this type of fraud. Telemarketers are often coached by their companies to turn abusive, if need be, in order to cow victims into agreeing to a sale. Once a senior has formed an emotional bond with a telemarketer, who may call repeatedly, he or she is particularly susceptible to phone strong-arming.

Lists of telemarketing victims are frequently sold to other companies. Some of the cruelest maneuvering is the phone sale of "recovery services," in which, for an up-front fee, a telemarketer offers to try to recover a portion of the money a victim has lost in a previous scam. Such recovery, of course, is never forthcoming.

Telemarketing companies, almost always located in either New York City or one of the Sunbelt states, are nothing if not mobile. A company with too many complaints against it can simply change its name and locate to a new office three blocks east or west. If judgments are filed against these companies, they can simply disappear, often without even bothering to go through legal bankruptcy, only to reappear in another guise somewhere else, perhaps another Sunbelt state, where a high rate of office vacancy makes short-term leases easily available. Because the business community in these states is transitory, there are fewer chances that local business leaders or authorities will take much interest in the activities of the new telemarketing company. It should be no surprise that many telemarketing employees are chemically dependent, and that their drug of choice is cocaine, which gives them the gift of gab they need to ply their trade.

Similar to telemarketing is fraudulent television advertising. This can range from selling worthless products for "$19.95 with an extra set thrown in if you call now" (many of these cheap products do not work or break immediately) to selling worthless items for which payment is collected through a victim's telephone bill. Many of the items sold this way are massively overpriced, especially if the number the victim calls is in a foreign country—which may not have laws against this type of fraud. People have been charged several thousand dollars for valueless items or services. If the billing company is in a foreign country, the American phone company may feel obliged to try to collect on the bill as though it were legitimate. The upshot is that the victim may lose his or her phone service or be faced with a collection action should he or she not pay.

Another enterprise crime is the West African Letter Scam. Here, the perpetrator sends out a huge number of e-mails (often to people on politically liberal mailing lists) claiming to be a politically powerful or wealthy person in a West African country who is temporarily unable to recover his or her investments due to legal or financial woes. The investments are always "worth" several million dollars, and victims are promised a substantial percentage if recovery takes place. The scamsters ask for no money at first, just advice—and the victim's bank account number (for later "deposit"). Once a relationship is formed, they request money to tide them over, or to finish recovery. They may loot the victim's account through forged wire transfers. This scam can also have an extremely dark side. American investors journeying to Africa to meet perpetrators have been kidnapped and held for ransom, even killed.

State Crime

In **state crime** the emphasis is on criminal behavior by government itself. For Friedrichs (1996), some states, such as Nazi Germany or the former Serbian government in Bosnia, are fully criminal organizations. They maintain power repressively and often commit genocide (mass murder) in order to continue their regimes. The Nazis, not content with war on segments of their own population, pursued external wars as well. The fact that their transgressions were punished by war crimes trials following World War II, just as Bosnian Serbs are now being tried for war crimes, shows that these acts were truly criminal.

State crime, however, often takes the form of the "merely" predatory state. Here, regimes use their position at the top of the political hierarchy to essentially loot the country in question. These regimes are often found in formerly colonized countries where neither economic nor political institutions have had a chance to fully develop to modern standards. In these countries, control over the military becomes a key factor to maintain power. Becoming head of state is probably seen as something like a business venture. The idea is to capture as much wealth as possible for oneself and a few cronies before being deposed by the next military government. Perpetrators often ship much of their looted gains out of the country, so that, if they survive the coup that deposes them, they can pursue a wealthy lifestyle in, say, the south of France. Key to survival of the predatory state is the cult of personality. Leaders maintain their power partly by garnering the support of peasants or primitive people likely to respect the outrageous displays of wealth made by the leader and his cronies, and to fear the power of the military, which is controlled by the leader.

Finance Crime

Because it's largely hidden from public view much of the time, and represents much wealth, finance presents a ripe environment for various sorts of crime. One prime example of **finance crime** was the massive **savings and loan scandal** during the 1980s (Pontell and Calavita 1992). President Ronald Reagan had swept America with a message of economic regeneration, and had won the 1980 election by a landslide. The administration believed that markets should be as free as possible. One industry subsequently deregulated was the savings and loan (S&L) system. These "thrifts" had previously been the most conservative businesses in the country. They were restricted to making home loans. When sunsetting these regulations allowed them to behave more aggressively, they did so with a vengeance. In fairness, the high interest rates existing across all financial markets at the time were partly responsible for their behavioral change (since S&Ls now had to try to keep pace with other competitive opportunities in order to keep their investors), but much of their behavior was unethical and outrageous by any standard. This included making extremely risky loans. In Oklahoma (much of the S&L "action" took place in the Sunbelt states), it was not uncommon for oil riggers to obtain several S&L loans on the same portable oil rig. They would pull up in front of an S&L, get a $100,000 loan for 100 percent of the rig's value, then drive the rig to another S&L and repeat the operation. In this profit-hungry atmosphere, normal oversight and escrow procedures were put aside in favor of making as many loans as possible as quickly as possible. When oil exploration companies went out of business in the middle 1980s, due to a downturn, the loans came a cropper too, bringing down many S&Ls.

Sometimes, S&Ls were systematically looted by owners or officers. One said, "The best way to steal from a bank is to own it." Loan company owners made extravagant personal purchases as business expenses. They often required kickbacks from customers as a condition of making loans. Double sets of books were kept to disguise these maneuvers. Many, however, were content to steal from customers. The prime example was Lincoln Savings. Its president, Charles Keating, forced his workers, including tellers, to try to get customers to switch from federally protected accounts to much more risky unprotected instruments offered by Lincoln. Salespeople did not inform customers about the greater risk involved in the switch. Most of these instruments turned out to be worthless. The Keating family, however, realized $34 million in three and a half years (Friedrichs 1996).

Keating was one of the few perpetrators of the S&L scandals who ever saw the inside of a jail. Some previous perpetrators, however, were able to benefit when the federal government decided to bail out the S&Ls with a $250 billion payday. The government's judgment was that S&L failures should not be allowed to scuttle the entire thrift industry. In some cases, the individuals who looted or bankrupted an S&L were allowed to reacquire it at fire-sale prices, thus getting value out of it twice.

Other types of finance crime are not specifically linked to a unique period, as was the S&L crisis. One such is **insider trading**, the use of privileged information to gain an advantage in financial markets. "Insiders" can be owners of a company, its officers, employees, or even journalists who report the financial news, all of whom may gain access to information before the public does. The insider uses his or her prior knowledge of a company's current circumstances or likely impending behavior to make investments (or divest them) before the public gets the information. In the late 1980s, for example, officers of the restaurant chain Carl's Jr. divested much of their company stock the day before an unfavorable financial report was published. Thus they gained an unfair advantage compared with other stockholders who did not have access to the information. It should be noted, however, that insider trading is not illegal in every country. Other countries reason that, since a stock market is a place where information about investments becomes known (through fluctuations in stock prices), insider information is as good as any other kind, in spite of possible unfairness. Insider sales may cause the value of a stock to drop, registering its real value more rapidly. In these countries, the value of the market's receiving information as quickly as possible is placed ahead of investor fairness. Another problem with insider trading is defining it. It's sometimes not clear where "astute investor" stops and "insider" begins. An investor gathering too much direct information about a company, perhaps by visiting it repeatedly and asking questions—which might seem perfectly reasonable in commonsense terms—could probably be defined as an insider by an ambitious prosecutor.

Although they are not white-collar crimes most of the time, leveraged buyouts and corporate takeovers often occur in a gray area. They are frequently very hostile activities where the "players" involved try to obtain advantage by fair means or foul. Takeovers can occur because the people who run corporations usually control only a small amount of their stock. Ownership of stock determines who appoints the management group to run the company. The buyout begins with the acquiring firm making a very high offer for shares of the target corporation's stock. If the target decides to resist, it makes a counteroffer for its own stock. The ensuing bidding war can artificially inflate the price of the company's stock, which sometimes doubles or triples. Frequently, other companies interested in acquiring the target join in the bidding. Should the firm be acquired, or even if it remains in the hands of its original management group, it now has to make good on the newly high-priced stock it paid for. To do this, parts of the company are frequently sold off, and/or large numbers of employees are laid off. The acquiring company frequently issues "junk bonds" to make the purchase. Bonds are loan promises to pay the purchaser later with interest. Junk bonds are bonds that carry high risk. The implication of leveraged financing is that the company to be acquired is the security for the bonds. Hence, it's possible to acquire a company using very little of one's own money, a situation many think unethical.

Advocates of takeovers, on the other hand, argue that they create a healthy economy by breaking up old, inefficient conglomerates (collections of different types of companies under one "holding company") and that "debt tightens a company." While this *might* be true from the standpoint of efficiency or profitability, it becomes less attractive when we consider all of a firm's stakeholders—persons affected by what happens to the firm: stockholders, customers, employees, suppliers, and the public in communities where the corporation has plants. Many of these groups may be adversely affected by buyouts and breakups. Entire plants may close; communities may be devastated. From this standpoint, takeovers may seem less than attractive to society.

The most famous case of finance crime involved Michael Milken, who committed a series of spectacular maneuvers involving junk bonds, insider trading, securities fraud, and stock manipulation from his Drexel Burnham office in Beverly Hills. Like Keating and a few others, Milken was one of a very few finance crime perpetrators ever to see the inside of a jail. He served 22 months.

Embezzling

Donald Cressey's classic study, *Other People's Money* (1973), sheds much light on **embezzling**—the misappropriation of funds or property by a person who has been put in a position of trust in order to watch over these assets. Typically, Cressey found, the embezzler must (1) believe that he or she has a financial problem that cannot be shared with others, (2) believe that he or she is "merely borrowing" the funds, and (3) use rationalizations or excuses for his or her misappropriation. These can range from "everyone in this industry does it" to "I haven't been compensated well for this work." In spite of the fact that Cressey's approach to crime is to affix individual responsibility, he is clear that these rationalizations are social in nature. That is, they are available in culture before the misappropriation takes place.

Organized Crime

Although we don't usually think of **organized crime** in these terms, it can be classified as a type of white-collar crime because it provides an organizational vocation for its perpetrators. Technically it should be part of enterprise crime because illegal businesses commit the crimes. The difference, as everyone knows, is that organized crime frequently uses violence in its operations, while ordinary enterprise forms of criminality do not. In the United States, and also in some foreign countries, organized crime is recognized as a "normal," but not desirable, form of ethnic succession—a process whereby foreign immigrants arrive at the higher levels of the economic structure (Bell 2000). Typically, new immigrants are not well received in any but the most menial economic niches. In America, where the late 1800s and early 1900s were characterized by wave after wave of immigrants coming to New York City, the process took place as follows:

The first ethnic group to arrive in New York in great numbers was the Irish. As they were able to better themselves, they took jobs on the police force and in the fire department of the newly burgeoning city. They also took jobs in city government, or in the Irish city machine that competed with other political interests for control. Irish capture of city government used up positions available in public life. The next ethnic group to arrive was Jews from Eastern Europe. Many of them turned to organized crime, providing gambling, prostitution, and labor violence (working as "goons" for either management or labor during strikes). The essence of organized crime is the accumulation of capital by preying on others, usually one's own ethnic group. In many cases, the second or third generations of descendants enter perfectly legitimate businesses and become indistinguishable from other Americans. Because of a scholastic tradition involving achievement on an individual basis, most Jewish gangsterism disappeared by the late 1920s. Successful young men were more likely to take up business, medicine, or engineering. The Italian immigrants, however, were a different story. Arriving after the Jews, they emphasized young men working for the family as soon as they were able, de-emphasizing the educational aspirations that moved Jews up and out of working-class life. The Italians from Sicily brought the nuclei of organized crime families with them, as similar structures had existed in the old country. Another factor responsible for Italian organized crime persisting longer than Jewish crime is that Italians were not averse to making huge profits from alcohol sales during Prohibition. Liquor sales extended the reach of the Mafia from neighborhood operations to interstate businesses. Jews were lukewarm about profiting from alcohol. It just didn't fit into their cultural ideas about how alcohol should be consumed (Abadinsky 2002, Cohen 1998).

Today, organized crime persists as an American style of economic and cultural life. As Bell predicted, new ethnic groups have followed in the footsteps of Jewish and Italian gangsters in establishing themselves. African Americans, who entered the cities starting in the 1910s (before that, they were almost exclusively rural), and Cubans represent groups that came to organized crime late in our history. To a great extent, they found that they had been preceded by Italians, who still continued to occupy key positions in the "ecology" of this activity. Nevertheless, newly burgeoning drug networks provided opportunities for the expansion of new ethnic organized crime. Black drug dealers found that they could use the loose networks of "Blood" and "Crip" gang affiliations to extend drug distribution across the country, including to cities where it had previously not been a problem. In some ironic cases, young men taken by their mothers to "safe" towns in the country to get them away from gang activity became the new nuclei for distribution to those towns. It didn't help that local young people wanted to be instructed on the latest gang styles they'd seen in the media, and became recruits for the new gangs. Cuban organized crime, more like the original Italian variant, confined itself to Cuban enclaves like Miami.

Employee Crime and Professional Crime

Employee crime consists of using one's job illegitimately for gain. Authorities (Friedrichs 1996) suggest that 1 percent of our gross national product may be pilfered every year by employees who amplify their salaries in this way. This inflates prices by 10 to 15 percent, inflicting additional costs on consumers as a whole. Seventy-five percent of inventory

...age is from employee theft. The other 25 percent is from theft by outsiders, such as hijacking or shoplifting.

Professional crime is crime committed as part of one's professional practice. Physicians, for example, can direct patients to consume excessive amounts of medical care paid for by insurance. They can cross-refer to other physicians in a process known as "ping-ponging." They can also defraud Medicare or Medicaid, inflating the number of services they actually perform. Attorneys can defraud the public in similar ways. They can inflate the number of hours they work for a client, or embezzle (steal) funds from client trust accounts over which they serve as trustees.

Gerald Mars (1982), a British sociologist, classifies employee and professional thieves in a schema that uses fictitious animal types to illustrate various crime styles, as shown in Figure 10.2.

The dimensions Mars considers are (1) the degree of supervision one experiences and (2) the degree to which one works as part of a group. People who work without instruction and who also work independently are "hawks." These include fraudster doctors and lawyers, who use their professional standing to defraud the public in ways that hardly ever come to

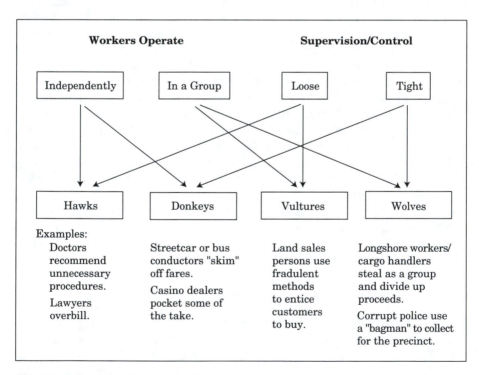

FIGURE 10.2 **Mar's Scheme for Workplace Theft**
Source: Mars 1982.

light. People who work with a great deal of instruction but work alone are classified as "donkeys." This category includes people like bus drivers, who pocket some of the fares they receive. The reason for fare machines on public transport is to prevent this type of pilferage. People who work without a great deal of instruction but work together are called "vultures." Certain salespeople fit this model. (The movie *Glengarry Glen Ross* shows land sales people committing crimes while selling.) Each shares (and is free to learn) deviant techniques from the others, but each is basically an independent operator when it comes to his or her ill-gotten rewards. The last group is "wolves." These are individuals who work under a high degree of instruction, and also work together. Work-groups of longshoremen who steal in gangs, under the direction of their legitimate foreman, are an example.

Cons and Conning

Cons consist of making money off victims in face-to-face situations. The term comes from "confidence game" or "confidence man," and is based on the fact that the victim must give the criminal his or her confidence in order to be taken. Often, the victims of con games are motivated by get-rich-quick or criminal impulses themselves, accounting for the fact that they rush into these games, only to lose their money. Technically, cons are a form of fraud, but here the con artist directly uses his or her acting skills to manipulate the victim into paying. Cons can be classified into two general categories; short cons and big cons.

Short cons consist of brief face-to-face situations. One such is the pigeon drop. Here, the con artist pretends to find a wallet containing money in the presence of the intended victim. The perpetrator is usually accompanied by an accomplice, who pretends to be another bystander. In one variation, the accomplice leaves; then the con artist proposes to divide the money among the three of them, but says he wants to find the other party. He proposes to put up some of his own money as "security" and entices the victim to do the same. Even if the money remains in view the whole time, it's switched and the victim's money is stolen.

Big cons require props such as an office and more players. One fraudulent Syracuse, New York, "medical imaging firm" had a series of offices with no real equipment in them. Impressed by the multiple locations the firm offered, investors gladly gave up their money. To be successful, these cons often require actors to play a series of roles. One such is the "roper"—the salesman or saleswoman who is responsible for getting the "mark" or victim interested. Other roles depend on the nature of the con. The most successful big cons "cool the mark out" following the "sting"—the point at which the mark loses his or her money. If the con is based on what the mark thinks is illegal activity, this could take the form of a staged "police raid," where the mark just barely gets away. The perpetrators count on the fact that the mark will never come looking for them or go to the police, since the mark believes that he or she has been party to illegal activity.

POLICY REACTIONS TO ORGANIZATIONAL DEVIANCE AND WHITE-COLLAR CRIME

For Cressey (1969) and others, white-collar deviance and crime are essentially individual activities. Common among theories concerning individual misbehavior are justice theory and deterrence theory. Both emphasize individual punishment as the appropriate technique to deal with illegality. There is no doubt that many white-collar crimes represent the activity of one person or flow from one person's design. But frequently they are also group activity. Some telemarketers are not even aware that they are engaged in a criminal enterprise. More common, no doubt, are employees who are aware that they are engaged in shady practices, who then put it out of their minds. Not infrequently, modern critics of business ethics state that industry in general seems to be marked by a lack of norm-defined moral behavior. Because of this, Fisse and Braithwaite (1993) want to specify sanctions for organizations over and above individual sanctions.

Some of the criticism of the deterrence or justice theories directed toward a culpable individual is that they frequently do not touch the organization that benefited. Deterrence theory advocates often think that this is permissible. One argument they cite is that to punish an entire organization, perhaps through a fine, is to hurt innocent stockholders if their stock plummets as a result. But the counterargument is that the stockholders should be responsible for discerning the ethical value and ethical risks of corporate activities, just as they are for its operational value and risks. Another argument is that deterrence measures directed solely against individuals usually involve scapegoating. Here a lower-level manager (or group of managers) becomes the fall guy for the whole organization, even when higher-level individuals are directly culpable.

A classic example is the My Lai massacre. Here Lieutenant Calley, a rifle platoon leader, directed his men to "waste" an entire village of men, women, and children. At trial, it became clear that Calley's company commander, Captain Medina, had probably ordered the massacre, possibly on orders of the battalion commander. None of Calley's higher-ups were ever tried. Public perceptions of the "unfairness" of trying only one of the people at fault probably led to the court's giving Calley only a year of house arrest. A presidential pardon soon followed.

For these reasons, Fisse and Braithwaite (1993) recommend that justice measures targeted against both individuals and organizations as a whole be used. Their approach goes beyond being punitive, being, in their own description, "nuanced." They acknowledge that organizations under great legal threat may "stonewall"—hire lawyers and hunker down to defend themselves legally. Fisse and Braithwaite believe that organizations can be worked with to bring them into compliance. They advocate on-site regulation by compliance officers who help the corporation obey the letter and spirit of the law. Rather than making laws or punishments more stringent, they advocate an increase in regulation and close scrutiny of corporations.

SUMMARY: ORGANIZATIONAL AND VOCATIONAL DEVIANCE AND CRIME

We have examined organizational deviance and criminality on two levels—first as merely deviant behavior breaking social norms, but not the law; second as behavior that is actually illegal. We defined organizational deviance as behavior that breaks social norms for businesses, and we saw that falling profits, lack of regulation, and decentralization could lead to this behavior. We examined different types of white-collar crime, investigating corporate, enterprise, state, finance, and organized crime. We inspected employee and professional crime, and we examined cons and conning. Lastly, we looked at different social policies dealing with white-collar crime and organizational deviance. We examined strategies designed to punish the specific offenders or the organization, and also reviewed nuanced, more nonpunitive regulatory strategies suggested by Fisse and Braithwaite.

11

Cults, Charisma, and Terrorism

Encounter with a Cult

Sue has just moved to the big city from her home in the rural Midwest. A new secretary in a large firm, she knows few people in town. She's always been a little shy anyway, and tends to stay to herself. One night, leaving the public library, she sees two young women on the sidewalk handing out small booklets. They work for the People of Light, and they engage Sue in an enthusiastic, friendly conversation about how she can better her life by coming with them. They are followers of "Father," they say, a spiritual leader with enormous healing power. She agrees to attend a meeting with them. When she meets Father, an energetic, bearded middle-aged man, she feels warm and nurtured by his smile and obvious concern for her. It doesn't take long before Sue quits her job, which she hated anyway, and moves into the group's house. When not walking the streets looking for potential recruits, she attends hours of "class" each day, where Father or one of his higher disciples explains the true meaning behind various religious teachings.

Father forbids outside friends or even contacts with family members, explaining that these are distractions from the "true path." He also forbids male and female partnering, or any other kind for that matter. People who seem to be best friends are assigned to different details and made to sit apart. Sue sinks into the routine, completely giving herself to recruiting, classes, and selling small crafts to support the house.

After six months, Mary, an acquaintance, whispers that Father has become displeased with Jean, a woman always seen with him, and is looking for a new "acolyte." Sue wants to know what the acolyte does, and Mary laughs sarcastically. "What do you think?" she snorts softly. Sue is amazed. Father has spoken over and over about purity in sexual matters, and of the need to transcend worldly things. Now this. She falls into a deep depression.

On a selling detail later that week, Sue tells her partners she has to use the bathroom, and sneaks away instead. Calling from the bus station, she asks her mother to wire her money so she can go home. Months later and a thousand miles away, Sue still has recurrent nightmares that the cult will find her and bring her back.

Cults have been a problem throughout history. **Cults** are small groups that carry out deviant activities under the direction of a charismatic leader. Under some circumstances, they can be dangerous environments for their members. They can also occasionally pose dangers to nonmembers: Extremist cults may use assaults or even murder against their "enemies." Cults commonly adhere to unusual practices, often based in religion, although some political organizations can probably also be included. They are usually "total institutions" (Goffman 1961), expecting their adherents to reside on cult property, be under the direction of senior members (a "cadre"), unquestioningly believe in a supreme leader, give all of their worldly belongings to the cult, either participate in sexuality at cult direction or abstain totally, and adopt unusual terms of speech. Families (couples or couples with children) are rarely permitted within cults, because family units tend to break down cult authority, which depends on a supreme leader having direct emotional access to all followers.

Cults almost always believe that the world outside is corrupt and ungodly, and frequently hold that it is their mission to change society, or, failing that, to leave to found a new, more pure social order. Most cults have turned out to be harmless to society, although they often have devastating effects on the mental status and fortunes, and sometimes even the physical survival, of their adherents.

CASE STUDY: THE HEAVEN'S GATE CULT

In the late 1970s, Marshall Applewhite, a former Texas music teacher, arrived in Southern California and began holding meetings of a "new age" group. This group, known as Heaven's Gate, settled in the San Diego area and recruited on college campuses. Although he appeared kindly and compassionate, Applewhite's approach was nothing if not controlling.

His lectures involved learning how to do everything in intricate detail. In addition, every cult member was given a "check partner," who made sure his twin performed according to Applewhite's lists. This cult was one of many forbidding sexuality utterly, and some members later theorized that this was so because their leader was embarrassed by his own homosexuality. Over the years, many male members were castrated, including the leader. He proposed that humans were here as imperfect beings from a more celestial plane to which they could return under the right conditions. In his teachings, he was aided by a female co-leader, Bonnie Nettles—"Ti," named after the musical note. (Applewhite's cult name was "Do.")

In 1992, after Ti's death from cancer, Applewhite decided that the cult needed to go to a higher level. He had long since cut cult members off from their families. After eating a lavish dinner at a restaurant one evening, cult members killed themselves using a combination of drugs and suffocation. A member who did not participate was instructed to visit the house and find the bodies after the mass suicide. In all, 39 people lost their lives (Moran 1999).

The suicides took America by surprise. Many of the members were from sound, middle-class families, with everything to look forward to. They often had parents and siblings who loved them, good educations, and productive skills. Why then, had they destroyed their lives?

THE HISTORY OF CULTS

The first cults were probably the first religions. Another way of saying this is that all religious movements probably start as cults. When cave people looked up at the stars and wondered where the next bison would come from, it helped to have a notion of how nature was organized, and how it could help or hurt them. As we saw earlier, a religious leader, a shaman, frequently could give meaning to the world, making it seem more secure for the tribespeople. As civilization came to the ancient world, cults persisted. The Roman Empire tolerated the religions of captured peoples. A huge number of groups practiced a wide variety of religious teachings. Some of the groups were extremely small and were characterized by extreme religious beliefs. As in modern-day Los Angeles, a citizen of Rome could pick and choose his or her religion, and many did. Some of the groups interested themselves in prophecy; others gave themselves over to pleasures of the flesh, including unrestricted sexuality and drinking (Cahill 2001). It's not unreasonable to suggest that most of major religions had their origins as cults. All were at odds with the mores of the societies in which they developed. All held themselves out as having a superior set of beliefs and practices that should be adopted generally.

During the Middle Ages, new cults continued to emerge. In the Islamic world, the Old Man of the Mountains cult used hashish to carry out assassinations, promising followers a return to paradise in return for their obedience. In Christian Europe, the Albigensian Heresy (Catharism) decreed that some souls were already perfect, and that they would reveal themselves through saintly behavior on earth (O'Shea 2001). The "lights," as these people were called, abstained from sexual relations and meat and cultivated a detached and saintly attitude. Most Albigensians, however, were mere believers, who had a chance to elect the full version of this religion on their deathbeds. As in many other European cults of the time, Albigensianism was probably a reaction to the pervasive corruption of the Roman Catholic Church. Pope Innocent III put an end to the movement by launching a crusade against its homeland in southern France and putting its adherents to the sword. Later, many Protestant groups would come into being as cults. The early Quakers, dismayed at the worldliness of post-Elizabethan Britain, often attended the services of rival churches completely naked in order to underscore their belief that God intended humans to live simply and in poverty.

Cult activity has been used to establish groups interested in racial separation as well. White separatist groups often have physical enclaves where followers live under conditions similar to those found in many cults. The Manson Family, one of many modern cults, was under the control of Charles Manson, an ex-convict with the gift of persuasion. He used drugs and sex orgies liberally to break down the personality structures of his followers, until all bonds of loyalty were connected to him and him alone. In order to begin a race war Manson thought inevitable, his followers murdered the inhabitants of two residences in Los Angeles, one of them the home of director Roman Polanski and his wife, actress Sharon Tate (Bugliosi and Gentry 2001).

Another famous killer cult is Aum Shinrikyo, an organization led by a charismatic leader, who, like Applewhite and Manson, believes it his mission to reform an evil world. In order to spark the transformative conflagration, the Aum cult dispersed Sarin, a highly deadly military nerve gas, on the Tokyo subway in 1995. Eleven people were killed. The cult had been experimenting with nerve gas and with other weapons of mass destruction for quite some time. The leader and several followers faced prosecution, but the cult still exists (Lifton 2000).

At times, cults take on a political character. A series of social service organizations that developed from a farmworkers' organization have a cultlike nature. These include organizations of service workers and several similar groups. Recruits are drawn from college campuses. They are usually upper-middle-class youth who lack direction. Over time, they are persuaded to abandon their studies and live at the offices of the organization. In keeping with the total institution nature of the organization, all of their movements in and out of the building are monitored. Once captured by the cult, followers have tremendous difficulty leaving. The organizations probably do some socially beneficial work for the poor, but their main purpose seems to be to gather recruits who obtain money that the leadership needs to continue the cult's activities. In addition, the organization attempts to strike up relationships with college professors and others from whom it might be possible to recruit students. In order to maintain these relationships, the organization keeps up a perpetual stream of correspondence, sends gift calendars in the mail, and so forth (Markon 1996).

CHARACTERISTICS OF CULT LEADERS

Cult leaders are frequently **charismatic**. That is, they seem to have attractive personal qualities that transcend those of ordinary people. The particular charisma at issue here is not the benign charisma of a Martin Luther King or a John F. Kennedy, however. Like hypnotists, these negative leaders attempt to control the details of their followers' lives. They often seem obsessive or driven, as was David Koresh of the Branch Davidian cult in Waco, Texas. Koresh had an uncommon memory for biblical scripture, and could quote it for hours without repeating himself. To a clinical psychologist, many cult leaders would seem to have narcissistic personalities. That is, they have fairly stable notions of their superiority and higher mission. At times, however, their self-delusions may be threatened, and, for this reason, they attempt to increase control over their followers. Because part of the charismatic leader's mind can see the falsity of his (the leader is usually male) position, however, this leads to increasing paranoia. The paranoia is what makes cult activities dangerous. The leader usually takes the position that the outside world is evil and dangerous. Usually, also, practices of the cult, especially unusual sexual practices, help create the leader's growing sense of fear. The leader senses that society would disapprove of the cult's style of life, and this fuels his or her uneasiness. Under the right conditions, this can spill over into violence (Cohen 1994).

The Reverend Jim Jones founded a religiously based social service organization that became quite successful in the San Francisco area. Of mixed parentage himself, Jones was skillful in bringing blacks and whites together. As Jones's People's Temple evolved, however, he began to see himself as more and more at odds with society. True to one type of classic cult form, Jones had engaged with quite a number of his followers sexually. In addition, the cult was attempting to gain political power in San Francisco. Suddenly, Jones's paranoia became too great, and he relocated his group to South America. Moving the cult geographically did not resolve the increasing sense of alienation and paranoia, however. With the

People's Temple now located in a rural setting, Jones's extreme behavior began to know no bounds. He worked cult members for long hours while placing them on a subsistence diet. He deputized a corps of men to act as enforcers/overseers. (This was particularly ironic because many of the members were African Americans whose ancestors had been freed from slavery in the United States.) He had large sex orgies in which he participated with both male and female partners.

As is common, relatives of members became concerned about the fate of their loved ones, and they contacted Congress. When a congressional delegation arrived to see what was going on, Jones decided to take action. Concerned that the United States government would move against him, Jones sent an armed team to the local airport as the delegation began its return to Washington. Many members of the delegation were killed. Now Jones went into action against his own people. Marshaling them all, he instructed them to drink poisoned Kool Aid. The enforcers made sure everyone complied. Drinking simulated poison was a ritual the community had practiced many times. At the end, Jones himself died as well (Layton 1999).

Jones had been well thought of as an effective, if somewhat unconventional, community activist in the early 1970s. By the late seventies, however, he had turned into a paranoid who was willing to kill his followers and die himself because of his growing perception that he was becoming more and more unlike those in normal society. This sense of alienation led to paranoia. The paranoia made him believe that the United States was about to invade his community and obliterate it. In order to retain control, Jones was willing to destroy his own community. Characteristics of both cult leaders and followers are discussed in Table 11.1.

TABLE 11.1 Characteristics of Cult Leaders and Followers

	Leaders	*Followers*
Personality	Narcissistic and/or antisocial	Dependent
Motivation	Change society Create pure society Conquer "evil"	Fit in Belong Become part of movement greater than self
Religious orientation	May have political or religious preoccupation	May have political or religious preoccupation
Self-presentation	Self-confident Cool Controlling	Nervous Dependent

CHARACTERISTICS OF CULT FOLLOWERS

Given the will to dominate shown by cult leaders, it should come as no surprise that cult followers are frequently drawn from people who have been unsuccessful. They have typically had problems fitting into society. Often they have experienced depression, broken families, lack of economic success, and the like. An unexpected characteristic is that cult members frequently come from affluence (Cohen 1994). Many members of the Sun Myung Moon cult, founded on the belief that this Korean minister is Christ reincarnated, are drawn from upper-middle-class young adults looking for meaning.

A total institution, the Moon cult takes up all of a recruit's time. New recruits are socialized through meetings that run from early morning until late at night. They live collectively, often packing an apartment with 25 people sleeping side by side in sleeping bags. Relationships and couples among these recruits are not permitted although long-time members may be permitted to form couples and marry. When not in the long indoctrination meetings, followers are "dropped off" at airports to sell flowers, often for 18 hours at a stretch. This explains why "Moonies" make money, much of which goes to fuel the lavish lifestyle of their leader. It costs next to nothing to support a house full of followers.

One might fairly ask, "Why do people join cults?" People give up much of their freedom to do so—sometimes, as we've seen, even their lives. The answer is that cults provide total definition of what one is to do from moment to moment, and, provided one follows the myriad cult rules and defers to the leader, total acceptance. Since followers have typically had problems with lack of meaning in their lives (as in the case of upper-middle-class youth), or being accepted (as in the case of followers from the margins of society), cults provide an environment where meaning and acceptance are guaranteed. Often the cult also provides a hierarchy for advancement, offering followers who might otherwise have had little prospect of advancing in society a chance to gain status. As total institutions, cults have strong sanctions against trying to leave. In Synanon, a cultlike drug treatment program in northern California, people who attempted to leave were referred to as "splittees," and were considered particularly contemptible. In most cases, splittees were pursued by Synanon members, and, if caught, were often persuaded to return, sometimes by threat of force.

Some cults have used means other than simple charisma (of the leader) and peer pressure (from the other followers) to impose discipline. One cult, for example, has its members disclose all of the embarrassing secrets about themselves they can recall as part of their progress to becoming "empty," a process costing thousands of dollars. Implicitly the secrets become items that could be used against the cult member should he or she defect. This partly explains why a number of movie stars have remained cult members for years. The cost to them should their personal information become public is too great. Another reason is that the stars are celebrities within the cult just as they are in society. Because of their fame, they are relieved from some of the onerous tasks assigned to other members, and are treated as royalty, because of the public relations benefits that the cult gains.

Other cults have a higher percentage of working-class and lower-class followers. These tend to focus on Christian or right-wing political preoccupations. Here the Bible is interpreted in a literalist way and used to advance the power of the leader. In David Koresh's Mount Calvary in Waco, many of the rank-and-file cult members came from modest backgrounds. Koresh so dominated the cult that he was able to force all of the men to sleep in a dormitory, apart from the women. As leader, he was the only male permitted to have access to females. He accomplished this by using Scripture to argue that he was the reincarnation of Jesus Christ. Some of Koresh's sex partners were as young as 12 years old. This pattern of ignoring age norms in sexual relationships is not unusual in extreme religious cults. Many try to evoke the social conditions that prevailed in early America, when girls married at puberty (Linedecker 1993).

POLYGAMY: THE FAMILY AS CULT

Polygamy, the practice of having plural wives, was eliminated from the doctrine of the Church of Jesus Christ of Latter-day Saints, also known as the Mormons, around 1870. However, some individuals in this tradition continue to practice plural marriage. Although many of these relationships seem to be stable and relatively benign, many are troubled.

Practitioners of what polygamists call celestial marriage often have arrangements where several women live in a household as wives to one man, or live in several households with one husband who visits them on a circuit. A family that has taken the cult of polygamy to an extreme is the Kingston family of Utah. Some of the men in this family have as many as 10 wives. Although men are free to acquire new wives outside of the family, women are required to marry men who are Kingstons.

Generally, the husband is selected for a young girl by her father. This practice has led to situations where underage girls have been forced to marry their uncles (Tracy 2001). Some anecdotal evidence suggests that men in these families may be likely to molest their offspring because the group is inward focused with few contacts outside the family, has an ideology of total deference to the father (so wives and children are likely to accept abuse), and has already relaxed sexual boundaries between family members because of the plural wives.

These practices are cultlike because the husband acts as a charismatic leader for family members, who are allowed to function only within narrow limits. Due to the tense relationships existing in these plural families because of jealousy, the emphasis, as in any cult, is on living daily life according to minute rules. If a wife or child attempts to leave the family, they are prevented from doing so and punished. Some estimates are that as many as 100,000 residents of Utah are polygamists today (Tracy 2001).

A major problem with polygamy is that typically, women who have been raised in the system or who have married into it are incapable of assuming productive roles in the larger society. Women are usually allowed only to stay at home and bear and raise children. In largely polygamous communities in Southern Utah, these women still wear dresses suggesting the late nineteenth or early twentieth centuries. As is usual in patriarchal groups, women are required to bear as many children as possible. Ex-polygamous wives have formed a support group, Tapestry of Polygamy, attempting to transition polygamous women back to productive lives in society. Tapestry retrains these women for adult life and provides psychological counseling.

Although illegal in every part of the United States, polygamy has proved difficult to prosecute because it is usually not set up as bigamy. A man wishing to take on additional wives may divorce the first spouse, while continuing a married relationship with her. He may then divorce the next in turn to marry an additional wife, and so on. Alternatively, he may marry only his first wife, or none of them. Eschewing actual plural marriage has another side benefit. If they are not formally married and if they are without jobs, these "wives" can claim welfare payments. Although nominally conservative and hence opposed to social programs in general, many polygamous husbands warmly support these payments, sometimes claiming that they are a gift from God especially intended for polygamists.

Because of the fact that legal bigamy is rarely committed, few prosecutions have occurred since 1953, when the last major attempt to exorcise polygamy in Utah occurred. Prosecutors jailed hundreds of polygamous spouses then, but the public relations fallout was a disaster. Television cameras captured hundreds of parents being taken to jail in front of their children. Isolated prosecutions now occur, but these are typically for the rare cases of child abuse that come to the attention of the authorities.

TERRORISM AS CULT ACTIVITY

Terrorism is advancing a political agenda through fear and using methods such as bombings, assassinations or threats. On September 11, 2001, 19 terrorists boarded four jetliners and attacked two different targets in the United States—the World Trade Center in New York and the Pentagon in Washington, D.C. Theirs was a suicide mission. The two planes destined for the World Trade Center under terrorist control flew into the sides of the buildings, killing everyone on board. One of the other planes hit the Pentagon, and the fourth crashed in Pennsylvania, after some of the passengers jumped the hijackers. The passengers had discovered by cell phone that the agenda of the captured flights was a series of suicide missions, and decided to risk overpowering their captors. It's clear that their heroic actions prevented another destructive crash.

What motivates young men, and sometimes women, to take the drastic steps the hijackers took on September 11, 2001? We should not jump too quickly to the conclusion that they were purely politically motivated. Many of the young men involved in the attacks were from the middle or upper classes in several Muslim countries, including ones allied with the United States. They were not, as one might have supposed in the first moments following the attacks, all from the poor sections of Palestine occupied by Israel—heavily supported by the United States—or from Iraq, where the United States exercised military control over the country's airspace, and where resentments against this country were particularly high. For these individuals, and for many other terrorists, participation in terrorist activity was tantamount to participation in a cult.

Many of those who join terrorist organizations, like many cult members, are taken to locations completely isolated from normal life activities. They typically have been motivated by outcries of injustice related to political or religious causes. As in a cult, the terrorists in training are completely cut off from others. As in a cult, there is usually a charismatic leader. Osama Bin Laden served as such a leader par excellence for hundreds of recruits training at his terrorist camps in Afghanistan. As is also usual in these types of total institutions, there is a cadre of trusted followers who have complete control over recruits. As in cults, recruits rid themselves of the speech patterns and culture they have previously used and adopt the parlance of terrorists. As in military training, which always has cult aspects, recruits are tumbled out of bed at odd hours, trained under privation conditions, taught to hate enemies they've never met, and so on. As in any cult, the outside world is represented as under the grip of evil and in need of deliverance. The same drama repeats itself frequently in other parts of the emerging world, as other terrorist organizations rise up and try to establish power in places where the old political empires of Europe and America are withering away (along with the social relations established by them) (Robinson 2002).

As we've seen, these political cultists are among the most dangerous people on the planet. Because they justify their actions by an overarching political ideology, it becomes possible for them to kill men, women, and children in great numbers in service to a higher cause. When the cult political ideology is tempered with religion, as it frequently is in the case of Islamic terrorists, cult members become even more dangerous. It is likely that the only way to end this behavior is through meaningful economic and political development in the parts of the world likely to generate terrorist cults. This development would incorporate a strong economy, a strong state, strong representative democracy, strong unions, a strong military, and a lack of corruption. Most likely, these states would tend to be secular (nonreligious) or moving in that direction, and would recognize the rights of various ethnic groups living in their borders. These are tall orders for countries moving out from under colonial domination, with leaders anxious to live in the manner of their European predecessors. In addition, neighboring countries or even Western countries sometimes surreptitiously prevent the development of modern states because it is to their economic advantage to do so. This practically ensures the development of more terrorists.

THE BASIS OF CHARISMA IN THEORY

Max Weber (1970), one of the founders of modern sociology, explained why charisma frequently emerges as a form of authority. There are three types of authority, which is the basis of all social groups. (Weber did not have a particularly democratic vision of social life.) The first type, **traditional authority**, is based on custom. A man might become the leader of a tribe because he is the chief's son, regardless of his fitness for leadership. The second type, **rational-legal authority**, goes with modern bureaucracies. Here authority is derived from a code of laws or procedures, which is usually written down. As with the first type of authority, leaders often lack ability, but this may be a secondary consideration because the main source of authority is the written procedures. Thus a poor shift-leader at a McDonald's may make little difference if all of the workers do their jobs according to the written policies and procedures for each station. Usually, however, persons in positions of leadership must at least demonstrate their fitness in terms of some form of credentials, or at least in terms of tenure (length of time) on the job. In spite of drawbacks, these two forms of authority are relatively stable. Importantly, they allow for transmission of leadership from generation to generation, preserving the basic structure of institutions and organizations.

For Weber, there is a third type of authority—the subject of this chapter: **charismatic authority**. Charisma, as we've seen, depends on the special qualities of a leader that are attributed to him or her by followers. Unlike the first two types of authority, it's based on irrational considerations and has a personal quality, even in a large organization. Because authority accrues to a specific person, rather than to laws or customs, succession—the replacement of one leader by another—is a major problem. The Oneida Colony, for example, was a colony based on free love, operating a very successful farm and producing fine silverware in upstate

New York. It was a very financially secure and stable organization, except in one regard. It was founded on the charismatic authority of John Noyes. As Noyes aged, succession to leadership of the community began to loom larger and larger as a problem. Noyes and some of his followers wanted to see the leadership pass to his son, who, unfortunately, had few of his father's captivating personal qualities. The colony subsequently broke up, demonstrating Weber's pronouncement that charismatic authority is unstable.

If charismatic authority is unstable, does it ever serve a purpose? Weber believed that charisma is a way to occasionally break through the moribund patterns through which societies typically reproduce themselves from day to day. In order for charisma to become stable, it has to become "routinized" as either traditional or rational-legal authority, however. Although many charismatic organizations are destructive, as we've seen, it is possible for cultlike organizations to occasionally facilitate social change for the better. Early Judaism, Christianity, and Islam, to name just three religions, initially emerged as charismatic organizations. It can be argued that these religions have had positive effects in world history, even if not every action taken in their name has been beneficial. So occasionally charisma makes a contribution for the better.

THE ISSUE OF DEPROGRAMMING

Not all family members of cult participants sit idly by when their loved one joins a cult. Many turn to **deprogrammers**—people who specialize in detaining and working with cult members to bring them back to normal ways of behaving. These deprogrammers, many of whom have backgrounds in the police or the military, often pick up a cult member (sometimes with a legal conservatorship furnished by the state to do so), take him or her to a motel, and work with the person psychologically, sometimes around the clock, to break down his or her defenses. This may last for a week or two. The deprogrammer hammers away at the cult member's belief system, reminding the person of his or her family, previous life, and so on. He frequently asks questions designed to get the cult member to see the flaws in his or her adopted belief system. Deprogrammers frequently report that the individual "snaps" back into reality when confronted with these flaws in cult ideology. Often, however, ex–cult members need assistance to begin a normal life once again. At first, they are in a state that Ted Patrick, a well-known deprogrammer, describes as "floating." As such, they are susceptible to recapture by the cult, but they may simply drift, traumatized by the cult experience. They may continue to meet with the deprogrammer or consult a more conventional psychotherapist for "exit counseling." Here, the cult member is gradually helped to rejoin society (Tobias and Lalich 1994).

Because deprogramming constitutes a forcible intrusion into a victim's life, it is controversial. Kidnapping is sometimes used, and deprogrammers have spent time in jail or been successfully sued by cult members or cults. Critics have charged that, no matter how bizarrely they are doing so, cult members are merely exercising their religious freedom. Deprogrammers respond that the total mind control exercised by the cult is not the practice of religion, and that strong methods are needed to counter the brainwashing the victim has undergone. It is not clear that deprogramming is always successful. Many victims return to cults in spite of being deprogrammed. Nevertheless, deprogramming has worked in quite a number of cases, and may be beneficial when it can be carried out legally.

SUMMARY: CULTS, CHARISMA, AND TERRORISM

Cults are and always have been a social problem. Although few people are directly affected by cults, they continue to pose a threat to public safety and personal liberty. Cults depend on charismatic leadership for their structure; this tends to be unstable. In addition, cult leaders tend toward paranoia, which tends to be dangerous to followers and to the public, should the leader decide to take on society directly and violently, or to order group suicide in the face of what he or she perceives to be irreconcilable differences between the cult and society. Followers tend to come either from upper-middle-class backgrounds offering little life experience or from the margins of society. While in cults, they are subjected to total mind control, with all details of their daily lives supervised by leaders and cult cadre. Many types of organizations can be cultlike. These can include religious organizations, polygamous families, and terrorist organizations, among many others. Deprogramming can be used to extract members from a cult, but it is controversial. Deprogrammers break the law if they kidnap cultists without a court conservatorship, and they may be sued successfully by the cult in any case.

12

Domestic, School, and Workplace Violence and Abuse

Abusive Relationship

Karen and Jim have been married for 12 months. At first, Jim seemed one of the most traditional men Karen had ever met. He opened the door for her and brought her flowers when they dated. Since marriage, however, he's been changing. Lately he's told her he doesn't want her to have friends or go out when he's not involved. These ideas are foreign to Karen's idea of how marriage should go, and she's shocked and frightened by them. When she goes to the store on a legitimate errand, Jim is waiting for her when she gets back demanding to know where she's been. He drops home from work unexpectedly, or calls to check up on her.

Last month it finally happened. She told Jim she wasn't willing to live like this, and he hit her across the face. She spent several days at her mother's, with Jim phoning frantically every day, promising to act better in the future. Karen relented. She moved back in. For a while Jim seemed to treat her as an adult, but lately, he's gone back to his old ways. In a screaming argument, he swears that he'll pursue her if she goes to her mother's again. "I'll hurt you and I'll hurt her too," he promises. Completely out of options, Karen gets a referral to the city's battered women's shelter and goes to its secret location when Jim is at work.

The issue of violence and abuse directed toward spouses, children, fellow students, and even coworkers has become increasingly public. To choose one example, 16 percent of couples experience at least one violent act in a given year (Straus, Gelles, and Steinmetz 1978). Around 50 percent of parents physically discipline a child (Gelles 1980). Abuse and occasionally violence are endemic to much school experience (even leading to a few well-publicized school murders, and many that are not publicized). Workplace abuse and assaults are fairly common. These phenomena are not new. They are becoming increasing concerns due to advocacy and research. Much of this violence has been present throughout our history.

BIOLOGICAL THEORIES OF AGGRESSION

Although violence and abuse are facts of life, they should be seen as phenomena people can control. It's not clear how much tendency toward violence is natural to humans. One school of thought, exemplified by Konrad Lorenz (1974) and some of the sociobiologists, holds that humans, particularly human males, are relatively aggressive. (In modern life, there is no requirement that aggression automatically turn to violence.) They argue that our closest relatives are chimpanzees, known for forming male gangs that often rape and murder other chimps. Others, such as Erich Fromm (1991), stress that humans have evolved completely new brains, capable of actions different from animal behavior. For Fromm, tendencies toward violence result from a competitive social order, not from anything dictated by genes, although "genes" may be used as an excuse by people who don't wish to improve society. There is evidence from biology that we are not the direct descendants of chimps. We are the same genetic distance from bonobos (pygmy chimpanzees) as we are from true chimps (Diamond 1992). Unlike patriarchal chimps, matriarchal bonobos use little violence, although females do jockey for power in various ways based on alliances. It's thus not clear how much aggression is "nature" and how much is "nurture," in spite of the current spate of science television programs promoting the idea that everything derives from genes.

Sociobiologists claim that aggression results from male competition over females. Recall that sociobiology says that men want to procreate widely while women want to select the right mate (although they may occasionally select one mate for his genetic attributes and another for his wealth—as long as the two are not aware of each other). So when men are together with women, there is competition to see which men can secure women. Men are not free to appear interested in more than one woman (although they usually are) because women will then lose interest in them. Men need to form alliances with other men for purposes of defense and aggressive behavior toward others. They are also interested in policing their female mates' attractions, and sociobiologists believe that spousal abuse may derive from men proactively punishing their wives for imagined infidelity. In school or work situations, abuse results from men competing over women they encounter there, trying to make other men look bad to improve their reproductive chances. Women, despite protestations, may be more interested in dominant men than in "wimpy" ones. In all-male settings, abuse results from forging male alliances, and may use the victimization of subdominant males as the basis for group solidarity of more dominant ones. Again, it's not clear how much of this behavior is truly genetic and how much is a product of societies that are unequal and competitive. Diamond (1999) identifies societies where there is little competition or aggressiveness, so there may be less real genetic basis for aggression than there sometimes appears to be.

PSYCHOLOGICAL THEORIES

Psychological theories paint a picture of the ways violence may occur. They stress the roots of aggression that exist within the individual. There are three general types of ideas: (1) psychiatric, (2) behavioral, and (3) cognitive (Mignon, Larson, and Holmes 2002).

Psychiatric Roots of Violence

Violent behavior can stem from at least two types of psychiatric problems. Usually, the behavior is caused by a disordered personality, which in turn may be prompted by issues of misdevelopment. The prime example of this is perpetrators with **antisocial personality disorder (APD)**. These individuals, perhaps due to abuse or neglect in childhood, are exploitative, lacking the ability to feel guilt or remorse. Men are more commonly affected by APD, and there is evidence that family patterns of alcohol abuse are correlated with it. Especially dangerous are antisocial individuals who fail to become aroused by normal stimuli that would cause fear in most individuals (the "flight-or-fight reaction"). These people are capable of doing considerable damage because they have few feelings of conscience and may seek excitement by committing sadistic acts. The portrayal of Hannibal Lecter in Thomas Harris's novels is accurate when it mentions that this serial killer maintains a normal pulse rate while attacking a nurse in prison. Some psychologists speculate that fetal alcoholism syndrome plays a role in developing these individuals. Others believe that the chaotic home atmosphere APDs may experience as children inures them to feelings of empathy. Because of their early experience with violence, they are incapable of feeling afraid in situations most people would dread.

Another, less common psychiatric source of violence is true **psychosis**—schizophrenia or bipolar disorder. Only about 1 percent of the population suffers from each of these conditions. **Paranoid schizophrenics**, especially, are quite capable of acting violently. In 1999, Andrew Goldstein, a mental patient living in the community, pushed Kendra Webdale in front of a subway train in New York City. He had never seen his victim before the moment he murdered her. He had been hospitalized many times. Because of the revolving-door situation in community mental health, he was living in the community when he committed this crime. He had stopped taking the medications that might have prevented this senseless act. Paranoid schizophrenics like Goldstein commonly hear hallucinatory voices conveying uncomfortable or threatening messages. They sometimes hear "command hallucinations" ordering them to hurt or kill someone.

People with bipolar disorder, characterized by periods of manic excitement, can be also be dangerous because they lack compassion for others and insight into the effects of their behavior. In the past, scholars believed that people with mental problems were less dangerous than average people, but recent studies have changed this finding. People with frank psychoses are actually somewhat more dangerous than the average person (Cockerham 2000). By and large, however, most mental patients do not act violently. And mental illness is not the major cause of most violence in society. According to Gelles (1973), probably no more than 10 percent of domestic violence, to choose one example, results from frank mental illness.

Behavioral Theories

In **behavioral** theories, the idea of reinforcement—that is, shaping perpetrator behavior through rewards or punishments—is key. If a perpetrator abuses an intimate and obtains increased compliance or deference, it's likely that he or she will repeat this behavior. The victim's behavior acts as a reward. On the other hand, if the victim fails to respond, or takes action other than the one the abuser wishes (for example, by punishing the perpetrator in return, or by escaping from him or her), the perpetrator may decrease the abusive behavior. The behavior may go on what psychologists call "**extinction**," meaning that it subsequently occurs less and less. The extent to which reinforcement is central in shaping perpetrator behavior is not clear, but it's sure to play a role.

Cognitive Theories

In **cognitive** theories, models and images of violence that perpetrators and victims experience are central. If perpetrators or victims grow up in households where violence is common, they are likely to become willing participants in violence as adults. In addition, the media bombard children with programs in which violence is used to solve virtually any problem. Children have generally seen many acts of violence by the time they reach puberty. This may not always cause a person to act violently; but, in the absence of strong, nurturing family, neighborhood, and school relationships, there is no doubt that atavistic media images loom larger in the consciousness of young people (Comstock and Strasburger 1990). If positive relationships are not there to counterbalance media, young people are likely to turn into young perpetrators.

SOCIAL ROOTS OF VIOLENCE

Social models of violence can be both global and social-psychological. Global models posit all of society as causal. Social-psychological models assume that smaller social formations, such as the family or workplace, contribute to violence.

Global Theory: Wilhelm Reich's and Erich Fromm's Theories

Wilhelm Reich (1980) believed that violence, especially domestic violence, occurred in modern society because of the abuse that men encountered in the workplace. They often worked under alienating conditions on production lines. Frequently they were required to get passes even to go to the bathroom. In the 1920s when Reich wrote, some workplaces even used physical punishment. Key to abuse, Reich believed, was the Freudian defense mechanism of **displacement**. When workers (at this point mainly men) suffered abuse in the workplace, they took it out on their spouses and children at home. Getting rid of alienating forms of industrial production was key to ending violence, particularly domestic violence. Although this theory intuitively makes some sense, it still doesn't explain why men who work outside of industrial production commit domestic violence.

Erich Fromm (1994) emphasized how authoritarian child-rearing methods used by the working and lower classes set a person up to fear violence and authority, but also to believe in these methods. He stated that, in particular, these patterns of child rearing prepared common people to tolerate, even venerate, authoritarian political figures, even when it was not in their interests to do so.

Global Theory: Stress Theory

Stress theory extends Reich's idea of displacement. In this theory, the total amount of stress emanating from all of a person's social circumstances inclines him or her to engage in violence. This theory goes beyond Reich or Fromm because it emphasizes how global stress can account for all types of violence. Thus it helps describe how men or women from affluent circumstances can perpetrate violence, an issue not covered by Reich or Fromm. Still, there is evidence of more direct personal violence in the working and lower classes, in spite of frequent claims by moral entrepreneurs that such violence knows no class. Since lower-class life may indeed be more stressful, this in no way invalidates stress theory. Another underexplored aspect of stress and violence is the idea that much aggressive upper-middle and upper-class behavior is expressed in ideas, speech, writing, or business practices. John Braithwaite (1992) has written about the crimes of the upper classes (many of them not identified as crimes) as motivated by greed as opposed to psychological or physical need. If greed is prompted by a need to "keep up with the Joneses" or by a need to obtain payback for the alienation inherent in management jobs (similar to that in working-class jobs), then "violent" behavior in the form of immoral or exploitative management practices expresses the same reactions that overt abuse does in lower-class people.

Global Theory: Feminist Theory

For the last 5,000 years or so, men have tended to occupy superior positions in developed societies. This does not mean that women were always powerless, but it does mean that culture and political structure in society have favored men. The values offered by strong patriarchal societies may emphasize men as parental, women as childlike; men as rational, women as emotional; men as moral, women as disorganized and immoral; men as able to work outside the home, women as able to work only within it; and women and children as the chattels (possessions) of men (sometimes sexual chattels).

Feminist theory, which facilitates analysis of psychological and physical abuse of women and children, fits with Wilhelm Reich's theory. For Reich, the lid is kept on in modern society, which might otherwise be quite vulnerable to uprisings by disgruntled workers, by a system in which every man is a king at home—able to do anything a king could do during the age of divine right of kings. This could include violence or sexual abuse of the children as well as the spouse. Patriarchal values prompted by this structure carry over into all realms of life. Men often have social lives apart from women in which they participate in activities emphasizing and exaggerating their masculinity. This leads to aggression and violence against other men as well as women, and to a culture where "wimpiness" is not tolerated. Inability to tolerate emotional softness or sensitivity in other men (the psychological mechanism of projection is at play here, by which a given man may hate and fear his own vulnerability) means that there is little chance for true emotional bonding with others to promote pro-social values, even if these might benefit society.

Naturally, the attractions of patriarchy sometimes trickle down to women and children as well. In highly patriarchal lower-class communities, women may act as aggressively as men, particularly toward children, although patriarchalized men may find this unacceptable when it's directed toward them and may attack these women for doing so. An afternoon spent watching *The Jerry Springer Show* is instructive. Sub–working-class couples with messy life problems are placed on display. These problems usually have to do with breaking sexual norms, usually in grotesque ways. The partners rage and storm at each other, often with a third party brought onstage to escalate the conflict. The audience hoots at any particularly obscene or strange material the couple discloses. In general, the audience is only slightly better off than the participants in terms of social class, and one can theorize that some audience members indulge in some of the same behavior themselves behind closed doors. Typically the women on stage are as aggressive as their men.

When raised in a patriarchal family, children, too, become more likely to use aggression. Randall (1997) shows how corporally disciplined children are more likely to become bullies and abusers. When the family is wealthy, physical aggression may be less an issue, but the family may be even more patriarchal than a poor family in terms of sex roles. In wealthy families, the father may exercise detailed control over all aspects of family life. When women in these families do not work, they are sometimes subject to male authority to a greater extent than even in very poor families. This implicitly infantilizes women, even if they have a wealth of club activities to consume their time. Detailed control is extended to children, who are expected to conform closely to father's life plan for them. A vivid example of this is offered in the film *Dead Poets' Society*, in which a wealthy, controlling father drives a student to suicide. Although direct violence is seldom an issue, the amount of patriarchal control exercises a similar effect as in poor families because it heavily constrains choices women and children make about their lives.

DOMESTIC VIOLENCE

It may come as a surprise that much violence in society happens within families. When one considers that the majority of murders are perpetrated by persons well known to the victims, the frequency of domestic violence makes more sense. The family is an area of life likely to be rife with emotion. As we've seen, frustrations acquired in the world outside the family are likely to be expressed within it. The family is also an area not subject to outside scrutiny. Indeed, custom and law over centuries have frequently held that it should not be. Aggressive behavior that wouldn't be tolerated if it occurred between persons in public is frequently tolerated within the family. For these reasons, violence is relatively common. It's estimated that about a quarter of families experience interspousal violence at least once in the course of a marriage. At least 16 percent experience at least

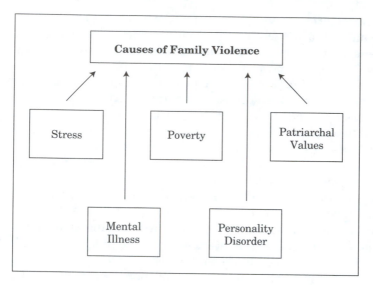

FIGURE 12.1   Causes of Family Violence

one violent episode in a given year (Straus, Gelles, and Steinmetz 1980). Some of the causes of family violence are shown in Figure 12.1.

Spousal Abuse

Spousal abuse is most often perpetrated by men, although there is also growing evidence of abuse perpetrated by women. Some of the key elements contributing to acts by men include belief in male authority, the feeling that men should be masculine at all times, the relative economic helplessness of a female partner, a female partner being burdened with child care, the belief that the woman should fill the "wife-role" only, negative female self-image, the belief that the woman is like a child in the relationship, and the idea that the justice system is male oriented (Strauss 1976). We've already seen that belief in male authority and compulsive masculinity can set men up "not to take any lip" from women. Since women are often more verbally skilled than men, and men are more likely to act out physically if they feel at a loss for words, this creates potentially dangerous situations because it prompts men to act out physically if they feel bested verbally. In the lower classes, the fact that women often talk aggressively makes for frequent explosive situations in families. That current-day families are more isolated means that the control and support once offered by friends and relatives may not be as present as it once was. This means that neighbors or relations may not be available for either marriage partner to turn to in order to air their grievances.

There is no doubt that women are more vulnerable than men economically. Thus they may see their possibilities for independence from abusive mates limited by the fact that well-paid employment is more difficult for women to obtain. Children, if any, almost always accompany their mother if she leaves an abusive husband. This puts women at a double disadvantage. Their income is reduced if they leave, but they must also assume the economic burden of providing for their children. They may feel that the loss in status accompanying separation or divorce is too much to be borne, or that they do not want to become a stereotyped "single mother." They may identify with the role of "wife," particularly if they have had no other job training, and be reluctant to give this up, even after abuse. For Strauss, too, the negative self-image likely to form as a result of patriarchal values may persuade the abused wife that she does not deserve to be treated with respect. Infantilization of women suggests the same idea: the wife is another of the children, in essence. She "is, and ought to be, subservient," waiting for direction from her husband. If she internalizes this value, she is likely to experience trouble asserting herself or leaving the relationship.

Like drug or alcohol addiction, patterns of marital violence often follow a cyclical pattern. As partners wear on each other's nerves (or as one partner becomes irritated by a passive partner), tension escalates. There may be verbal exchanges involving one or both parties. Finally, an episode occurs in which one or both partners act out violently. Injuries occur; perhaps the police are called; occasionally an arrest results; feelings are hurt. After this, the perpetrator, usually male, feels remorse. He makes a concerted effort through good behavior to get back on the good side of his partner. If the couple has separated as a result of the incident, he resolves to "win her back." If the couple stays together, they often enjoy a "honeymoon period." It's as though the relationship is new and exciting again. Sexuality between the partners may improve. Over time, however, tensions in the relationship, which have not really been dealt with, reemerge. One thing leads to another, and violence recurs, often perpetuating yet another cycle of events.

Abusive husbands often become especially dangerous to wives after separation or divorce (Meadows 1998). Ex-husbands have spied on former wives, stalking them from place to place, even when they moved secretly, and beaten or even killed them. Ex-husbands can become particularly dangerous if separation was the wife's idea. The stalking and murder of Nicole Simpson was most likely such a case. Her ex-husband stalked her for extended periods of time, at times entering her house unannounced, even after the divorce was final. He beat her on many occasions, although the bulk of these beatings happened before the divorce. As a civil trial finally determined, O.J. Simpson probably killed his former wife and a young male restaurant employee who was returning a pair of glasses. Even before separation, their relationship followed a typical cyclical pattern of escalation, abuse, breaking up, getting back together, and brief honeymoon periods, followed by re-escalation.

Strauss's last point, the male orientation of the justice system, has probably changed somewhat since he wrote the classic article on this subject. There is no doubt, however, that the justice system has problems being equitable toward women. In spite of a spate of sensitivity training courses, the fact remains that the orientation of police departments is patriarchal. After all, the police themselves are drawn largely from the lower middle class and the working class, where these values are likely to be particularly strong. This means that the police, when called to a scene of spousal conflict, may favor the man, or that prosecutors or the courts may not be energetic in pursuing abusive husbands.

Fortunately, options for intervention in spousal abuse have developed in the last 25 years. In general, the legal system has grown more sensitive, and the police and other justice personnel have typically been given classes in spousal abuse and better intervention techniques. Sometimes, specialized officers dedicated to dealing with spousal abuse are found in larger departments. Because complainants may retract their charges once police arrive at the home, some departments have a mandatory arrest rule, directing that an arrest must be made if there is evidence that abuse occurred.

The courts have generally improved the ways they deal with spousal abuse and battery, as well. Procedures to obtain a restraining order against an ex-spouse have been streamlined. Laws against stalking have been implemented in quite a number of states. Most cities have battered women's centers where women can seek shelter while transitioning out of an abusive relationship. In these centers, women are housed anonymously, so that they cannot be tracked down by abusive partners. Counseling and housing for dependent children is also provided. Another exciting new trend involves providing mandatory counseling for wife batterers. Because more effective enforcement activities may cause increased reporting, it's not actually clear whether increased measures against spousal abuse are working, but it's likely that they are. Community members are now more aware of the problem of spousal abuse.

Child Abuse

Child abuse is another key area where family violence occurs. Occasionally children are badly injured or are killed by parents. Children who live with stepfathers are more likely to be grievously injured by abusive discipline than are those who live with their natural fathers. Sometimes, it's hard to know where to locate physical discipline on a scale of abuse, and this topic is controversial. In a given year, around 60 percent of parents discipline a child physically. This is not to argue that all physical discipline is abuse, but we can place physical discipline on a continuum with abusive practices. Around 13 percent have used an object such as a belt or switch to punish a child. Around 3 percent have hit or kicked a child (Gelles 1973). Some authorities such as Finkelhor (1990) are totally opposed to any kind of physical discipline, claiming that it's all, in essence, abusive, and that we have difficulty perceiving this because we're a relatively violent culture. Others draw the line between discipline and abuse at other points, some arguing that spanking is appropriate for children between toddlerhood and puberty, some that the use of a lightweight switch or belt is permissible.

Like spousal abuse, child abuse can be related to stress. Parents sometimes express reactions to difficulties outside of the family by their behavior within it. Also, children themselves can be a source of stress. Young parents, in particular, may be unaware of the demands that raising a child, even a very well-behaved child, will place on them. Children intrude on adults frequently. They have more energy than adults do. They are not very reasonable. Because our culture romanticizes children and childhood, parents may not be prepared for the fact that children are frequently not soft, cuddly, sweet, or docile. Certain types of parents are at greater risk than others for acting out physically toward children. These include single parents who must work, parents who live in isolation, parents with several children, parents of children with disabilities, parents who "expect too much" of their children, parents who discipline inconsistently, parents who were themselves abused, and parents who have low incomes (Ziegler 1980).

Not commonly known is the fact that more child abuse is perpetrated by women than by men (Barnett, Miller-Perrin, and Perrin 1997). Given the fact that men are more aggressive, this may seem unexpected, but it's easy to explain. Women spend much more time in the company of children than men do. Not only do they experience more stress from dealing with children and their demands, but since they spend more time with children, they have greater opportunities to abuse them.

Child sexual abuse is another very serious social problem. It usually consists of activities such as fondling of genitals and oral sex. Intercourse takes place in only about 5 percent of cases (McCaghy and Capron 1997). Like child abuse in general, it's massively underreported. Studies indicate that many girls are likely to have been abused before achieving adulthood. Boys, too, are abused more often than one might suspect. A small but significant percentage have typically been abused before becoming adults. Like assaults against children, incestuous abuse is more likely from stepfathers than from natural fathers. Non-incestuous abuse also occurs between other adults (typically known to the child) and child victims.

One might ask: When sexual abuse does no physical injury, why is it as grievous an issue as researchers say? The answer is that sexual contact with adults is invariably psychologically unhealthy for children, in spite of arguments to the contrary by sexual liberationists or pedophiles. Sex is a matter of risk and trust under the best of conditions between adults. Even if an adult is very gentle when sexually abusing a child, the child almost invariably concludes that he or she has been taken advantage of, even if at the time the child may have enjoyed the experience or felt neutral about it. There are several reasons for this:

1. Children rightfully expect that adults will care for them and look out for their interests. This is the foundation of children trusting adults. When an adult takes advantage of a child sexually, the child knows that the adult has violated this trust, and is less likely to trust adults in the future.

2. Children expect that there will be "good boundaries" between adults and children. Adults have positions of authority, but they are expected to use this authority to protect children. When boundaries disappear, the child loses his or her sense of security.

3. Children become aware that they have participated in a forbidden activity, which they are likely to conceal (often because of prompting or threats by abusers). Because of the natural narcissism (self-centeredness) of young children, they are likely to blame themselves. This causes feelings of shame and guilt, likely to reverberate for years.

4. Children participating in sexuality with an adult are at great risk for injury or even murder, if the abuser is sadistic and/or decides to cover up his (or sometimes her) crime.

5. When sexually abused children compare their experiences with those of the majority of children not abused, they feel a great sense of loss in discovering that they have been singled out for this experience and other children haven't. This leads to feelings of depression and self-doubt.

Usually perpetrators act alone, although there are a few instances of two or more men abusing children as a team. Reports of nursery school abuse by mixed groups of men and women have generally turned out to be manufactured, as we saw earlier. Although "reports" of satanic ritual abuse against children (children "penetrated by objects" while lying on altars, children "killed and eaten" during ceremonies) were common during the early 1990s, there is scant evidence that much of this ever occurred. These reports were probably concocted by ambitious therapists, then spread by consultants and trainers—usually ex–police officers—who received lucrative fees for conducting satanism seminars. The few instances of satanism actually verified usually involve teenage boys interested in "heavy metal" music and culture, who may or may not abuse animals or vandalize cemeteries. Sometimes, however, a solitary male perpetrator enlists a female accomplice, usually his wife or girlfriend, to help abuse, even murder, young women or girls. The accomplice is invariably an abuse victim herself, and has typically been subjected to sadistic and controlling physical and sexual abuse over a long period to prepare her for her role as assistant. These women may not become murder victims themselves because perpetrators are aware that the police look at partners first as likely suspects.

Authorities split on whether sexual abusers can be treated successfully. In cases of incest, some argue that the family should be preserved, with the perpetrator receiving treatment. Others (Herman 2000) say that once incest has occurred, trust within the family is impossible, and that the perpetrator should be removed. As with many other such issues, the final answer is not clear. When children have been abused, either physically, sexually, or both, they generally must receive treatment. Some children are more resistant than others, but most require intervention in which they are aided in making sense out of the experience and working through the emotions that result from it. Failing this, they are likely to suffer negative effects for years, and may be subject to re-abuse as adults. Absent treatment, victims are likely to unconsciously seek out the same sorts of people as their previous abusers. Abusers may seem fine when first encountered, but the victims identify the subtle signs that mark them as abusers. These seem familiar, and victims experience familiarity as attraction, although this is really the first step in a return to abuse. With therapy, victims can move away from these patterns.

SCHOOL ABUSE

Many of us remember school as a place fraught with occasional danger. On one hand, there are always a few frank bullies who physically intimidate or assault other children. On the other hand, the process of joining other children and forming groups, although not as extreme as physical intimidation, can sometimes feel like bullying as groups and individuals jockey for status in an environment made insecure by the immaturity, lack of experience, and lack of power of children. In addition, schools have harbored more and more reactive types of violence as children have brought weapons to school, and sometimes used them. Most children have experienced fear at one time or another in school. It's not uncommon for children who feel great fear to bring weapons to school to defend themselves.

Bullying

A small percentage of children are out-and-out bullies (Randall 1997). Typically from abusive families where violence is glorified, these children, usually boys, pick fights for no reason. They often invent offenses others have supposedly committed against them as a pretext for physical attack. They also take offense and attack if someone bumps into them accidentally or jostles them in a lunch line. They often have the ability to single out children who are shy or retiring, who make especially convenient victims. In many cases, school officials are insensitive to the problem of bullying and tend to believe that the victim is the one with the problem. Because American society is individualistic and because it promotes self-reliance, it emphasizes the idea that each individual should defend himself (sometimes herself). Bullies, however, are often stronger and more aggressive than victims. Although bullies have average popularity in the elementary grades, they tend to have fewer friends as they age because other children perceive the drawbacks involved in associating with them. By high school, they may be limited to two or three other bullies as friends. Societies where bullying is prevented, like Norway, are characterized by teachers and groups of children intervening assertively when one child is being picked on by another. In these societies, bullying is reduced, leading to more civil behavior in general (Eckstein 1975). In spite of universal tendencies for some children to act in a bullying manner, some societies do a better job than others at preventing this problem.

Groups and Gangs

Children are often desperate for order. Everything is changing, including their bodies, their knowledge and opinions, and their place in society. Because of this, social groups are important; they provide a sense of belongingness and often also physical security, because they provide protection from other children who act aggressively. But joining a group as a new member is not always easy. There are always informal processes through which one must go before he or she is finally included. These may involve being assessed and judged by members of the prospective group. The new person is often evaluated as to his or her clothing, attitude, and demeanor, to see if these fit with the group's style. He or she may also be assessed to see how well he or she respects the authority of the group's leaders. These processes also involve a period of teasing or hazing, during which the prospective member must prove himself or herself by enduring some kind of test.

Teasing and hazing can also be hallmarks of a group's behavior toward members of other groups or toward independent students who do not seem to be group members. Here, the behavior has the dubious function of making the aggressive group feel good about itself. Picking targets outside the group obviates the need to select scapegoats from within the group's members in order to define the desired behavior of in-group members more precisely. But, as has recently become clear, teasing and hazing (even in some cases physically assaulting) out-group members can have devastating consequences. The mass murder at Columbine High School in Littleton, Colorado, was sparked in part by the harassment of members of the "Trench Coat Mafia," a group of "losers" (in this case boys with bohemian or gothic tendencies) by "jocks"—athletes. This in no way excuses mass murder, but it does illustrate the types of forces that can make it more likely.

Gangs are the lower-class version of groups found in more affluent schools and neighborhoods. As Chambliss's (1973) well-known study, "The Roughnecks and the Saints," states, there are often more similarities than differences between these two types of groups, although adult authorities tend to treat members very differently based on social class. Neighborhood adolescent gangs are formed for three basic purposes: (1) to provide neighborhood protection; (2) to operate illegitimate businesses (such as drug dealing); and (3) to consume drugs ("stoner" gangs) (Spergel 1995). Gangs also translate themselves into the school environment, since adolescents from local neighborhoods are likely to attend the same schools. Weapons are often brought to school by members of protection-oriented gangs, but they may be brought in by individual students as well. Many students say they have at some time brought a weapon to school. Invariably, the motive given is personal protection, although a few of the students who want to "protect" themselves end up using the weapons aggressively and tragically. Many of these incidents result from real or imagined insults directed toward students who are armed.

One factor leading to school violence is the size of contemporary high schools and junior high schools. If a school has from 1,000 to 5,000 students, as some do, it's difficult for teachers to be aware of and intervene in student conflicts. In addition, contemporary teachers often avoid conflicts involving students because of a history of lawsuits against teachers. If a teacher intervenes in a student fight, for example, and ends up defending himself or herself physically, he or she could be sued by a student or parents, as unfair as this might seem. The upshot of having a combination of large schools and loose supervision can be a social system in schools similar to that in large prisons, where the inmate social system is more important than the institution's formal organization. Teasing, hazing, intimidation, and assaults can occur because the institution has implicitly declared a "hands off" policy toward student conduct, in spite of policies stating otherwise.

Some contemporary schools have begun to change this system, however, in the light of the murders and assaults occurring on school premises. They use strategies ranging from dividing the school into more intimate clusters to sensitivity groups where students discuss violence and devise means to intervene—this is grass-roots intervention, not a policy forced on students from above. Some schools have trained students as mediators whose job it is to resolve conflicts among peers by using verbal techniques to defuse conflict situations as they occur.

WORKPLACE ABUSE

Many people think of the workplace as a rational environment. The world of working adults is supposedly very different from that of children, who lack the maturity to deal with their differences in an adult way. The problem with this shallow analysis, however, is that people do not check their emotions at the door when they arrive at work. And as we'll see, in some cases conflicts occurring outside the workplace can make themselves felt within it. Also, because the workplace represents a location where employees are rewarded differentially, it can become fraught with emotion if employees believe that they have been treated unfairly. Moreover, as in school, bullies and bullying behavior can sometimes occur in the context of one's employment.

Sexual Harassment

As feminism grew in popularity, women began to come forward with tales of supervisors pressuring them for sexual favors. Often, promotion or continued employment depended on a female employee's sleeping with a supervisor. Hollywood legend abounds with stories about the "casting couch," referring to male studio supervisors (or even agents) requiring actresses to render sexual favors before being considered for parts. Many of these accounts were, in fact, true. As the critique of sexual harassment continued, other types of situations emerged. One was the "hostile environment" workplace, where the atmosphere was charged with references to sexuality, with unwelcome flirtation, with attempts to grope female employees, with pin-up pictures, with the telling of "dirty" jokes, and so forth. Feminists correctly believed that many of these hostile environments were not sexually charged for the purpose of promoting sex with (usually new) female employees, but to make them uncomfortable—to drive them away from jobs that had previously gone to men. Later analyses extended "sexual harassment" to cover situations where supervisors unfairly favor employees who are willing sexual partners. In these cases, other employees can legitimately make claims that they were sexually harassed.

However, as with other areas developed by moral entrepreneurs, it's clear that "sexual harassment" claims can sometimes be taken to absurd lengths. The hostile environment category is vulnerable to a variety of interpretations because courts have, perhaps unfortunately, found that this type of sexual harassment depends on victim interpretation, rather than perpetrator behavior that can be objectively measured. Occasionally, employers fire "perpetrators" on the say-so of putative victims without determining the facts. A tenured technical writing instructor at Brown University was suddenly discharged when several women (women were new to his courses) complained about his use of colorful language—a practice he had employed over the years to get the attention of students in his formerly all-male classes. He was able to obtain a lawyer and be reinstated with back pay. Courts have fortunately found that in most cases the putative victim has a duty to warn the putative perpetrator that the victim finds his or her language offensive, and they have also found that sexual harassment can be female-male, male-male, or female-female, as well as its classic form of male-female.

Workplace Bullying and Assaults

It may come as a surprise to those who believe that bullying goes away in junior high or high school, but there are cases of documented bullying and assaults in the workplace (Randall 1997). Sometimes workplace bullies have been celebrated by management, since they are occasionally perceived as people who "make it happen" (sometimes the bully is a supervisor), in spite of management research that shows that teamwork is generally a better strategy for productivity. In other cases, workplace bullies operate outside of management's knowledge. As with harassment in schools, bullying can consist of physical intimidation, but it can also involve theft of another's property, interference with his or her performance of duties, ruining his or her work, or starting baseless rumors.

In extreme cases, bullies can perpetrate assaults against coworkers. In a given year, many workers are either victims of or witnesses to workplace assaults. Many companies, responding to these trends, have established firm policies calling for preventative training and disciplinary action against perpetrators.

Workplace Stalking and Murder

In 1989, Richard Farley, angry that a woman he wished to date had spurned him, came armed with a shotgun to her place of business and, pursuing her, killed seven other people who had the misfortune to be her coworkers. Because she would not go out with him, and would not even speak with him, he went to her workplace and opened fire. She escaped. The facts are that 35 percent of women who are murdered become victims in the workplace, and it's the largest cause of death of working women (Meadows 1998). For every woman who becomes a victim of murder on the job, many more are stalked at work by ex-husbands and ex-sweethearts, or by fellow workers. Another major problem in the workplace is assault, murder, or mass murder by disgruntled employees. Certain (almost always male) employees who have been disciplined or fired may return to the jobsite with a weapon and assault or murder other employees, most often supervisors but often others as well. Episodes of this sort have happened often enough in post offices that the phenomenon has become known as "going postal." Employers have responded by increasing security, and by increasing training of supervisors and coworkers. Some of the characteristics of perpetrators include:

1. Having a history of violence and fascination with weapons
2. Being angry, but with few outlets for it; having requested help in the past
3. Being socially withdrawn, with a history of interpersonal conflict, family problems, and marital strife
4. Making verbal complaints about and to management, stopping at some point to "stuff" the complaints after that
5. Exhibiting paranoia about others; engaging in alcohol and drug abuse (Meadows 1998)

SUMMARY: DOMESTIC, SCHOOL, AND WORKPLACE VIOLENCE AND ABUSE

We've examined biological, psychological, and social causes of violence, taking into account that each may contribute to cycles of abuse. In spite of the fact that violence is more common than most of us would like, it's frequently preventable if proper systems are in place and intervention occurs. We've seen how the home can frequently be a theatre for violence, and that stresses from other spheres of life may be expressed there. Spousal abuse can occur, and the physical or sexual abuse of children is also unfortunately not uncommon. Far from always being a setting for an idyllic childhood, school, too, can be an arena for violence. Not only are there occasionally bullies, but the process of joining groups of children is fraught with some degree of bullying as well. Gang participation may be mandatory for children from certain neighborhoods if they do not want to become victims, but it may also open them up to being victimized by other gangs. Unexpectedly, the workplace also turns out to be an important location for violence, with its own bullies in some cases. Also important is a growing incidence of workplace violence and murder. Women are sometimes stalked or assaulted at work, and disgruntled employees have murdered their supervisors or coworkers. Tightening security and putting prevention programs in place decreases these types of incidents.

13

Cyberdeviance

Internet Pornography Addiction

Bob has always been a loner. He's currently employed as a night watchman, working by himself. Ever since he bought a computer with a fast Internet cable connection, he's developed a new hobby: Internet porn. At first, Bob only hit a few Web pages, just messing around. Now, he can't wait to get home to get on the Net, which he does for as many as 12 or 13 hours a day when he works, or 20 hours a day when he does not. He belongs to five separate porn membership services, and spends much time surfing these as well as visiting the new sites added daily. Bob barely looks at many of the images, but speeds on to view others in a driven way. The pay sites cost from $30 to $75 a month, which Bob can't really afford because his pay isn't great to start with. Because of his hobby, he has virtually cut all ties to the outside world. He no longer accepts calls from his mother or his sister, leaving the answering machine to pick these up. Sometimes he calls in sick, which he can't really afford to do, just to hit more Web pages. He loses sleep, and seems only interested in getting back on the Web to view pornography. He rarely bathes, and his small apartment has been a shambles since this behavior developed.

CYBERDEVIANCE AND THE INTERNET

The **Internet** was invented in the late 1960s as a means for government research facilities to communicate with each other. By the early 1990s, it linked virtually all parts of government, virtually all large educational facilities, and most large companies. Communication took place through e-mail and bulletin boards, although the World Wide Web (a graphic way to display information as Web pages) became available with the invention of Web browsers. By the early 2000s, virtually every household owning a computer made extensive use of the Internet, usually through a combination of the Web and e-mail. The number of Web pages available for viewing ranged into the billions, with many servers (sites for Web pages) situated in foreign countries, not subject to United States laws.

Even home computers can link to other computers through phone or other direct connections. This makes for interesting types of deviance. Individuals of any age can access mammoth amounts of pornography in their own homes, much of it free. They can enter into chat rooms tailored to obsessions they may have, be they sexual, obsessive, or destructive. In some cases they can entice others, or be enticed, to physical meetings of a deviant nature. They can perpetrate fraud, have fraud perpetrated against them, or have their identities stolen by fraudsters anxious to make purchases using someone else's credit. They can enter computer systems belonging to major companies or government, sometimes merely as unauthorized visitors, sometimes as persons bent on destruction.

Because the Internet originally developed as a government project and cost nothing to users, many people believe that it should be an institution characterized by free communication and relaxed property relations. Some Internet deviance is facilitated by this belief. The Internet is free; therefore, it is thought, social control should be at a minimum. Anything should be allowed to be communicated over the Net. All information should be free and in open access, according to many users. And this reasoning is often extended to computers attached to the Internet. In the minds of hackers, who want to go wherever the "Information Superhighway" leads them, it's not legitimate to restrict access to cybernetic information anywhere.

However, in spite of its obvious appeal, this is only one side of the story. Harm can result from communication over the Net, particularly if victims are minors being stalked by sexual predators. Local communities may find that cosmopolitan, even perverse, views of sexuality or gender relations featured on the Net exceed their standards. Also, the Internet costs money. It is therefore only right that individuals and businesses should pay their fair share of the costs. And because information is crucial in business and personal life, it's not legitimate to argue that all data should be in the public domain if it's on the Internet. Much of this information has been expensively acquired and may demand client confidentiality or the preservation of trade secrets. Hackers and other, more destructive visitors to computers can cause huge personal and monetary losses. For these reasons, it's reasonable to regulate the Internet and to ask users to pay for access.

SEXUAL DEVIANCE ON THE WEB

The Web catapults sexual deviance into virtually a new dimension. One can access a variety of materials directly from his or her home in privacy. People can join bulletin board Web services where they can have virtual discussions on a variety of sexual subjects with like-minded others. At times individuals use the Web to meet others for sex, and sometimes victimization occurs, especially when one person is a minor. The Web has introduced a new level of "exchange" between consumers of pornographic materials and between people interested in joint sexual activities, whether on the Web or in person. At times, the Web has also meant increased access to vulnerable persons by predators.

Internet Pornography

Compared to pornography generally, erotica on the Web is plentiful and often free. It's estimated that fully 50 percent of Websites accessed in any given period of time are erotic ones (McBain 2002). In addition, the specific interests of any given segment of pornography consumers can be addressed exactly. A comprehensive search engine like Google can search by text as well as titles, so virtually any Web page containing a phrase like "sex with animals" or "sex in public" can be accessed in seconds. All one need then do is click on the URL that appears with the entry, and, *voila*, one is in a Web page specifically tailored to that interest. Although many erotic sites are pay sites (a monthly fee is typically paid by credit card), virtually all sites have a free area to entice potential customers. So customers not interested in paying can skip from site to site without furnishing credit card numbers. Because many sites are located in foreign countries, and because local enforcement varies, it's possible to view photographic or rendered (drawn) images of child-adult sex or sex with animals, even when these images are prohibited locally. Pornographers believe they are protected by disclaimers stating that users should not view this material if they live in areas where it's banned.

Many pornographic sites are characterized by endless **"pop-ups"**—full-page advertisement portals to additional sites. When one is closed, another pops up. Often pop-ups come so fast and furiously that the user is forced to turn off his or her computer to get them to stop. More pernicious is a tendency for some pornographic sites to quickly install programs on home computers, virtually without the user's authorization. (On some sites the user must quickly cancel the proposed installation, which takes place if this is not done.) Once installed, some sites automatically dial phone numbers to access more pornography, and the user is automatically charged on his or her phone bill. These programs may also install icons on the user's computer, or send pornography out to other sites from the machine. If a user is an unwitting recipient of child pornography (Jenkins 2001), this places him or her at substantial legal risk, since the Justice Department has made it a priority to prosecute persons dealing in or possessing this material. The user may or may not be aware that even looking at (not soliciting) Web-based child pornography stores images in the memory register of Web pages visited (the computer does this to speed up access time to revisit Web pages). Possessing these images (if photographic) is illegal in the United States, and law-enforcement officers may not believe the excuses that users give—that they visited these sites inadvertently, or that they did not mean to store such pictures. Those who store and exchange child pornography often conceal it with a technique known as *steganography*, in case their computers are searched by law-enforcement officials. Here, code describing a pornographic image is concealed inside another innocent-appearing picture file. Excess bytes of information are used to store the real picture, and a decrypting program is used to access this information. Police can decrypt these images, but only when they suspect that they are present.

Some Internet pornography sites are very elaborate. One fictitious but typical site, operated by "Jane," features a "tour" area and a "members" area. Jane, an attractive but rather ordinary-looking woman of around 30, slightly overweight, explains that she is a swinger and has parties at her house. Site members can tune in on her having sex or masturbating twice a week on a "live cam." They also have access to a number of frequently updated galleries and MPEG movies of Jane and her friends having sex orgies. They also can chat with her by e-mail. One of Jane's specialties is interracial sex; in her bio, however, she explains that she is not open to anal intercourse. She is also bisexual, and some shots feature her with partners of both sexes. Compared to many more kinky sites, Jane's site is actually rather tame. These kinky sites may feature all-interracial contacts, "family love" (simulated incest), bestiality, and a host of other attractions. Fees can range between $30 and $100 a month.

Chat rooms, most of which operate by posting asynchronous (not real-time) Web pages, often are organized around sexual topics. Incest-Taboo.com, for example, gets 30 to 60 postings in a 24-hour period. Many of these have pictures (typically of simulated incest between adult or teen "family members," older women as simulated "moms," or younger women as simulated "daughters" or "sisters"). Often URLs to other, usually commercial, incest sites are offered as well. When the postings don't contain pictures or URLs, they may offer stories, billed as either "true" or fictitious, about incestuous encounters. Much of the discussion is about topics like "family love," but many participants are adamant that their orientation toward the material is "fantasy only." For this reason, virtually all participants are adamantly opposed to child pornography (even though the emphasis on father-daughter sex or mother-son sex would seem to suggest the contrary). In fact, virtually every day's discussion includes threats by the more athletically inclined members detailing how they would physically punish child pornographers. Thus, participants (who may have tendencies to view child pornography, but may be reacting against them) are anxious to mark the difference between themselves and pedophiles, at least publicly. The site also offers "incest personals," where members list their personal attributes and invite e-mail, telephone calls, or physical meetings. Some invite other participants to form fictitious families for the purpose of acting out fantasies. Around 15 to 20 percent of the site's participants are women. Like the men, they post pornographic pictures and occasionally reveal fantasies about making love with fathers or brothers. The site also offers links to an anime bulletin board, where cartoon images of sexuality, often involving rape or very young girls, are a staple. In addition, there is a link to a bestiality bulletin board, featuring photographic images of women having sex with animals.

The Web As a Conduit for Molestation or Rape

Because computers are a popular pastime for children and adolescents, these machines sometimes open up new dangers when children access the Web (Aftab 1999). The availability of live chat rooms means that adolescents and children, many of whom have normal interests in sex and are interested in having sexual conversations with peers, can talk with a sexual predator without realizing it. In the chat room, the predator often impersonates a child of the same age, slowly getting the confidence of his intended prey (women virtually never engage in this behavior). Predators are often charming, and know just what to say to forge relationships with minors, especially if their intended victims come from troubled families or from families where good values have not been taught. A predator invests time in developing a relationship with a victim, frequently over months, and suggests a meeting. If the meeting occurs, the child is typically sexually molested, although there have been incidents of kidnapping, forcible rape, and even murder.

Fortunately, law enforcement has become sophisticated at locating and arresting sexual predators on the Web. Stings are often used to entice and catch perpetrators. Officers play the role of children interested in what predators have to offer. When a meeting is finally arranged, rather than the "child" being present, officers are waiting to arrest the perpetrator.

FRAUD ON THE WEB

One of the most serious problems with the Web is that it is a major conduit for **Internet fraud**. Just as the telephone opened up new forms of
fraud by direct solicitation, the Web opens up still more opportunities for
criminals to exploit victims by deception. Victims cannot actually inspect
the products or services they agree to purchase. For this reason, they may
order items that turn out to be worthless. Because Web merchants do not
necessarily operate out of a fixed or known address, it may be impossible
for angry customers to locate purveyors if they are dissatisfied with what
they receive. In the wake of September 11, 2001, and the subsequent anthrax attacks on a number of businesses and individuals, companies
began selling worthless "anthrax detection kits" over the Web. Because of
the level of fear concerning anthrax, these kits, not surprisingly, sold like
hotcakes. It took action by state attorneys general and law-enforcement
agencies to make these companies stop their activities.

Auctions

A common site of Internet fraud is **auctions**. In auctions, sellers post
items they wish to sell, and potential purchasers make bids on them. While
many Internet auctions are legitimate, worthless products are often sold
this way (Thomes 2000). Frequently the fraud is on the part of the person
offering the product, not the service that provides the bulletin board for the
auction; and auction services usually disavow responsibility for the quality,
or even the delivery, of items. On some occasions, individuals have "sold"
items that do not exist. Curiously, Internet fraud works in two directions in
regard to auctions. On many occasions, minors have made bids on items
they did not have the funds to purchase, or even the legal right to purchase,
because they were underage and not permitted to enter into contracts.

Come-ons

Often the Internet is used for fraudulent **come-ons** that are more
tragic. On such is the adoption agency scam. In this scheme, an "adoption
coordinator" posts a Web site on the Internet. The site has pictures of
many very young children, and often features valentine hearts and other
sentimental decorations. The Webmaster, usually a woman, often self-
described as a "social worker," offers to put prospective adoptive parents
in touch with young mothers who are not able to keep their children. The
"social worker" charges a fee, often between $5,000 and $15,000, which
must be paid immediately and is nonrefundable. Significantly, this fee is
not contingent on an actual adoption, but merely engages the services of
the perpetrator as a consultant. The scamster stays in constant contact
with the prospective parents by e-mail and phone, usually with tales of a
particular young woman who "just became pregnant" who seems willing

to give her child up for adoption. To safeguard the young mother's "confidentiality," her name and address are not to be revealed until the last moment. The perpetrator maintains her relationship with victims through constant communication, updating the adoptive parents with constant tales of the young mother's pregnancy, medical reports about the baby, and so on. As the "pregnancy" progresses, the scamster solicits additional payments to pay for the mother's care, unforseen problems, and so forth. At the end of this cruel scam, the prospective parents are usually shaken down for a particularly large payment for "the young mother," and are then "blown off" by communications saying the natural mother changed her mind at the last minute and no baby will be forthcoming. Often this end stage is prolonged by repeated demands for additional payments to get the "natural mother" to change her mind. Of course, the mother and baby usually don't even exist. When they do, another type of scam often takes place in which several sets of parents have the same baby promised to them exclusively. At the end of the scam, most or all of the prospective parents are blown off in the same manner as in the nonexistent baby version. These scams occur because the process of adopting a child through legitimate means is laborious and detailed. It can take years. The use of an adoption broker like these scamsters holds out hope of short-circuiting the process. Victims usually say that they found it almost impossible to believe that the warm, caring "social worker" they talked with on the phone would cheat them and break their hearts. Police have been able to intervene in these adoption scams, but it frequently takes years, and requires the willingness of victims to come forward, to catch the culprits. Many of the perpetrators go unpunished.

Similar come-ons occur when American men shop for Russian women or women of other nationalities on the Internet through ads for prospective brides. Many of the agencies posting these ads are reputable, but some of the parties signing up to meet these men may be less than honest. In several cases, Russian women used the process in order to come to the States and defraud would-be suitors. In another case, a Russian woman, who had no intention of marrying any American, enticed her prospective husband to come to Russia, and to bring money with him. Once there he was murdered by the woman's boyfriend.

Identity Theft

The Web can be used as a means to accomplish identity theft (Hunter 2002). To steal a victim's identity, a perpetrator uses the Web to search out personal and financial details. Although many of these are technically confidential, fraudsters can use various Web services to obtain them, often for a small fee, from commercial services not concerned about the uses to which such information might be put. Once a perpetrator has obtained a victim's Social Security number, it's relatively easy to steal his or her identity. This usually means that the fraudster secures false credit cards in the victim's name, charges the maximum amount allowed on each card, and subsequently abandons them once the bills begin to roll in.

For example, Martha's first clue that her identity has been stolen is a call from a creditor she's never heard of. When the woman on the other end of the line wants to know, can they expect payment for the entertainment center Martha received. Martha is flabbergasted. Frugal and conservative, she's never ordered anything of the kind. The angry collector at the other end of the line states that they've even had a problem finding Martha, and that Martha's number is not the one she's given them, which turned out to be a dead end. The collector refuses to believe Martha's answer that she's never ordered an entertainment center, and threatens legal action if payment is not immediately forthcoming. The angry collector refuses Martha's request to know the phone number and address listed on the bill. On advice from her lawyer, Martha obtains her credit report, and she sees that she has supposedly made quite a number of credit purchases recently, some already in arrears.

When Martha reports the problem to the local police, they seem uninterested. "This is really a problem for the stores, not you," they tell her. The unauthorized purchases continue. When Martha cancels the accounts, others are opened in her name, using her correct Social Security number. Finally Martha blocks access to any credit in her name, essentially denying herself her own credit, should she wish to use it. It takes her a year and $10,000 in legal fees to recover from this case of identity theft.

Other, more elaborate forms of credit can be secured as well. Fraudsters have purchased houses or cars with false credit. In one case, life insurance was obtained on an identity theft victim, leading one to wonder what the plans for her might have been had the crime not been discovered.

Interventions

Efforts have been made to make the Internet a more secure place for commercial transactions, but difficulties remain. Any time a secure technology is invented, another can be invented to defeat it. It is possible for encrypted (changed into code) credit card or other personal information to be intercepted by identity thieves. Law enforcement has become more proficient in tracking down perpetrators, but the huge amount of Internet traffic makes it difficult to make much of a dent in this activity. Similarly, other Internet criminals can be apprehended, but only when they come to the attention of law enforcement. Again, it is likely that the creative skills of Internet criminals will always allow them to evolve methods to get around new developments in security and detection. Part of the immense freedom conferred by the Internet is its capacity to facilitate literally millions of transactions outside the direct oversight of society. Criminality on the Internet can be defeated only if complaints are brought to the attention of authorities.

PHONE FREAKS AND FRAUDS

Although the phone system is not properly part of the Internet, it is still a significant part of cyberdeviance (Williams 1997). By the 1960s, the first well-known phone freak had been nicknamed Cap'n Crunch because he used a cereal box whistle to transmit audible signals to phone switching devices from phone receivers. He could make a normal phone call, and then use his whistle or even just his puckered lips to signal with a musical tone that the call had not been picked up, thus avoiding charges. Neglecting the dial or keypad, he could use musical tones to select complicated routing schemes (for instance, in phoning New Jersey from New York, he could first send the call to the West Coast by landline, then to Europe by satellite, then back to the United States by satellite, then to New Jersey by landline). This was necessary because, once law-enforcement or phone company operatives became aware of phone freak activities, they used call tracing to attempt to discover where the calls originated. It is very difficult to trace a call that has been directed through multiple switching devices.

Most phone freaks did not have Cap'n Crunch's virtuosity with lips or whistle. For them, computer buffs built "blue boxes," which could cost as much as a thousand dollars, even in the late 1960s. These were tone generators precisely matched to the phone company's switching devices. Among the more eager customers for blue boxes were organized criminals. Because of wiretaps, they did much of their business from pay phones, and they did not like paying the high coin-telephone tabs.

Blue boxes and whistles are now a thing of the past because the phone company has switched to digital equipment. It's probable, however, that phone freaks are searching for new means to hack phone switching systems as this is written.

New opportunities for fraud using phone equipment arose with the development of the cellular phone system, making telephones increasingly portable. Although these phones had been around for decades, older versions required mobile operators to complete calls. The newer cellular system used ubiquitous towers to receive short-range impulses from much smaller instruments, which were for the first time truly portable. (Older versions were actually two-way radio sets that needed to be able to reach a central radio station. As such, they were bulky. Usually the handset connected with a large box that needed an electrical connection or a large battery pack.) The new instruments are small, often no bigger than a large calculator. Because of this, they are easy to steal. They can be used for a short time, then discarded. More to the point from a criminal perspective, however, is the theft of either a cellphone's unique crystal or its crystal's identifying code. Either facilitates placement of the new crystal in a new phone, where it can be used to the thief's or his customer's heart's content, or at least until the cell company turns that particular crystal's access off. Stealing the code, usually by intercepting cell transmissions, has an advantage because it does not disable the victim's legitimate phone service. There are simply now two users of the code, one legitimate, one criminal. Phones with counterfeit crystals are sold in mass quantities to groups of poor immigrants, who use the phones to call distant locations in Asia and Africa, at least until service is turned off—as it will be when the legitimate user gets his or her bill.

UNAUTHORIZED USE OF COMPUTERS

Many of the well-known problems that come with computers involve unauthorized use of a computer belonging to someone else. As we saw, many computer hobbyists think it should be perfectly allowable to access a corporate computer by modem or network connection, obtain information, and leave. A few, motivated more by ideology, believe it's legitimate to access another's computer for destructive purposes. Destructive behavior with computers, as we'll see, frequently causes losses ranging into the billions of dollars.

Hacking

Hacking is simply the unauthorized use of another person's computer without his or her knowledge or permission. Hackers enter machines through modems (phone connections) or network lines (faster connections than phone lines). The Internet, itself, can now also be used as a conduit for hacking. A hacker uses various tactics to get on a remote machine. One method consists of obtaining passwords from internal registries. Here, he or she actually gets a list, often through hacking this or another machine, and puts one or more of the passwords to use. He or she can also use such probabilistic methods as repeated attempts to access the machine with likely passwords until he or she is logged on, although many machines will deny access after a certain number of failed tries. Hackers are aware that many mainframes (large business computers) have "backdoors" (ways for computer programmers or repair people to access the machine quickly without going through the normal protocols), and often take advantage of these to obtain access. Hacker Websites and hacker groups (often operated through a bulletin board or listserv) frequently provide kits with which members can speed up access. These consist of programs that contain code likely to permit access to mainframe systems, typically written in the Unix computer language, although other languages are also used. These may be available for purchase or exchange, or may be offered as "freeware"—that is, code in the public domain, which can be modified by end users. Once inside a system, hackers classically do no harm. They do, however, take it as a personal affront when they encounter encrypted or password-protected material, and they make every effort to access it. These protections are like thrown gauntlets to the dedicated hacker. He or she feels compelled to see what is behind them, even if the material turns out to be completely uninteresting. Even very well-protected, sophisticated systems such as ones belonging to the Department of Defense have been hacked—much to the dismay of system architects, who typically believe that they have constructed hack-proof systems.

Although their linkage may only be through computers, hackers constitute a definite subculture in which knowledge and hacking ability lead to prestige within the group. Participants make claims, sometimes false, about their accomplishments in order to attain status. As in many other subcultures, special language is used to mark the fact that hackers are distinct. It's likely that many people observing a discussion among hackers on a bulletin board would have no idea what the participants were talking about, so esoteric and strange is their language. Because the average hacker is a young male, either a late teenager or a young adult, there are frequently conflicts and competitions for status among members, just as there would be in any group of young men. These are marked by boasting about accomplishments and by personal insults (called "flames" when delivered by e-mail), just as they might be if the participants were young sportsmen or young management trainees. Of special concern is the problem of "wannabes"—members who fake their accomplishments. When these individuals are discovered, they are subject to intense criticism. In spite of the occasional competition that takes place, true hackers tend to adhere to an ethic that implies what in their minds is good behavior. According to the Hacker's Ethic, featured on a University of California Website (University of California 2002):

1. Access to computers should be unlimited and total.
2. All information should be free.
3. Thou shalt not destroy.

Thus we see that their interests are in complete freedom of access but not destruction.

In spite of the fact that hackers cost businesses and the public money because of the increased threat to security posed by the invasion of mainframe systems, they are acting ethically in their own minds. But it's clear that, however well-intentioned the invaders, organizations cannot allow unrestricted access to their secure files. For this reason, hacking must be seen as destructive regardless of its stated intentions.

Crackers—Destructive Hackers

A stage beyond hacking is the deliberate invasion of another's computer system for destruction. This has been called "**cracking**" (McCaghy,

Capron, and Jamieson 1999). Here, the same skills as used in hacking are used to create mayhem. Crackers can invade a system and delete or alter files destructively. Often, a time delay is used to put distance between the invasion and the destruction. There have been cases where information services employees of business firms have installed "logic bombs"—programs that destroy the employers' computer operating systems, if they are not periodically instructed to continue in a dormant state. If the employee is fired or laid off, the logic bomb is waiting to do its work after a suitable delay. Backdoors and other portals into computer systems are used in a similar manner by employees who are angry with their employers.

Probably the main problem is not so much cracking activity directed at a single employer, however, but virus and "worm" writers who design mini-programs that attack many end user systems. Frequently these programs don't completely disable the user's operating system; they merely interfere with it, using the host computer to send out replicas of themselves to other personal computers. Effects can range from annoying messages that pop up on the victims' screens to slow destruction of the victims' hard drives. These programs frequently use victims' address books to locate new targets. They are often transmitted as attachments to e-mail, so recipients are well advised not to open attachments when they are not familiar with the sender or aware of the attachment's contents. In spite of good antivirus software, writers create new viruses constantly. The very latest are usually not recognizable even by last week's software. Thus antivirus programs must constantly be updated in order to ensure protection.

There are other ways to attack computer systems. Crackers can precipitate "denial of service" attacks against e-businesses that have angered them. These attacks consist of secretly programming a variety of systems to make a great number of legitimate business requests or transactions impacting the target business simultaneously. Usually, operators of intermediate systems have no idea that they are being used as way stations in these attacks. Universities are prime intermediaries because they own complicated systems that are easy to access. The target business system is overwhelmed by the "legitimate" transactions and stops operating, often costing it tens of thousands of dollars in lost revenues. Similarly, Websites can be hacked directly by criminals who know how to do so. Even though Websites may seem to be impermeable to destructive hacking, an experienced cracker can sometimes jam his or her way onto them and reprogram them destructively.

INTERVENTIONS

Because computer systems are complex and technical, it is difficult for society to monitor, much less intervene, in every instance of destructive use. The Internet opens, as its proponents say, new realms of freedom for individuals and businesses. Along with that freedom comes the possibility for fraud or victimization. Internet users should be wary of situations in which they may be taken advantage of or victimized. In instances where users become aware of actual criminal behavior or are directly victimized by it, they should involve law enforcement. The National White Collar Crime Center, easily located by search engine, provides an excellent information and referral service for instances of computer crime. In addition, there are excellent programs that can block out minors' access to pornography, and possibly also access to chat rooms where sexual topics are being discussed. These services can be quickly located on the Web, and are usually a feature of large Internet service providers.

SUMMARY: CYBERDEVIANCE

The Internet, because it gives access to a world of information and communication from a variety of platforms, including personal computers, opens the door to various forms of deviance, including dangerous and destructive ones. Sexual deviance occurs on the Web just as it does in other areas, both in the form of pornography and in terms of developing connections for deviant sexuality. Some of these last can represent sexual victimization, and the Internet should be considered a possible conduit for dangerous sexual connections. In addition, varieties of fraud can take place on the Web. These can include the fraudulent sale of products or services, and also such cruel scans as adoption fraud, used to extract funds from vulnerable victims. The Internet can also facilitate identity theft because a large amount of confidential information is flowing through it on a regular basis.

Although it is not, strictly speaking, part of the Internet, the phone system offers similar opportunities. Rip-off artists have imitated switching signals to make free calls and to select call routings that make their activities hard to trace. Criminals have done a brisk business in digital boxes that imitate phone company signals. Also, cell phones are often stolen or their identifying crystals imitated. These devices can be sold by criminals to individuals who wish to obtain phone service at reduced rates.

In addition, hackers illegally explore computer systems for the sense of accomplishment they get from accessing systems to which entry is theoretically denied. More destructively, crackers invade systems to cause disruption or to shut the system down. Although the Internet is relatively free and is hard to regulate or police, users can take commonsense measures to avoid becoming victims, and can refer criminal behavior to law enforcement. A good point of contact is the information and referral service provided by the National White Collar Crime Center, which can be found by searching the Web.

14

Crimes Against Persons and Property

Robbery

Rob has always been a big man. As a child, he was something of a bully in the neighborhood and at school. He could often get other students to give him their possessions and lunch money, just by appearing threatening. Nowadays, he's become chronically unemployed. He used to do some construction work, but now foremen and other workers say that they just can't take his attitude on the job, and no one will hire him. A chronic user of drugs and alcohol in recent years, Rob has started hanging out near certain underlit ATM machines. When he needs money, he sneaks up on customers and takes the money they have withdrawn from the ATM. If the customer is male, Rob generally punches him to the ground so he'll know who's boss. Sometimes Rob has strong-armed his victims into taking out more money, if he doesn't like the amount they've withdrawn. Rob knows it's probably just a short time until he's caught, but it hasn't happened yet. He had a hot week last week and made $500 by hitting three customers.

Crime is deviance that breaks laws. Obviously, there's a continuum where some deviance is not criminal, some is mildly criminal, and some is very criminal. Fellatio, for example, is illegal in several states, but few regard it as a real crime. Murder, on the other hand, is regarded as a crime of great significance. In this chapter, we'll examine very criminal forms of deviance. Some earlier chapters have touched on crime, but this one is devoted to highly criminal activities, widely regarded as real crimes. I have placed it near the end of this book because I want to emphasize, again, that studying deviance is far more than studying crime. With that understood, personal and property crimes are major deviant activities and merit careful examination. In this chapter, we'll examine murder as an example of personal crime, and robbery, burglary, arson, and shoplifting as examples of property crime (see Table 14.1).

MURDER

Murder is taking a human life unlawfully. Although it's the worst, or one of the worst, crimes, in many ways it's also one of the most amateur because it often (around a third of the time) results from mundane arguments. Jail inmates say that they see little difference between most murderers and persons walking the streets. There is usually little of the professional criminal in the personalities of murderers, although murderers often come from poor circumstances and have a significant history of drug and alcohol abuse. Trivial disagreements often escalate to murder, especially if substances are involved, or if there is a history of bad blood between participants. Because it's committed in mundane and emotional circumstances, murder is perpetrated by family members or persons known to victims 47 percent of the time (FBI 1993).

Significantly, handguns account for around 68 percent of killings. Knives account for 15 percent, and other weapons, or hands or feet, account for about 17 percent (FBI 1993). Availability of handguns in the United States probably helps explain the fact that this country has a murder rate at least twice as high as that of any other in the Western developed

TABLE 14.1 Crime Categories

Crimes against Persons
  Murder
  Assault
  Rape

Crimes against Property
  Robbery
  Burglary
  Arson
  Larceny

world. Murders in the United States stood at about 10 per 100,000 in the early 1990s. The next highest rate was posted by Scotland, a country with similar cultural characteristics, at about 4 per 100,000 (Bennet and Lynch 1990). Some of the factors thought to account for the high U.S. murder rate include:

1. *Liberal policy on gun ownership and control.* Most other developed countries do not permit gun ownership or possession, especially handgun possession. (Rifles account for only about 3 percent of gun deaths) (FBI 1993). In some countries, you may own a gun, particularly a rifle, but it must be kept at a hunting club under lock and key when not in use. In Germany, hunting takes place under the supervision of a licensed hunter or *jaeger.* In Switzerland, much of the male population is in the army reserve, with guns at home, but these tend to be rifles, not pistols. But in America, we have a frontier tradition of gun ownership, which is still constitutionally protected. This happened, no doubt, because we believed that we needed to be able to defend ourselves. Obviously, there was much truth to this point of view historically, but it is not clear how applicable this point of view is to modern life. There is also contradictory information on carrying guns and crime prevention. Some research has shown that being able to display a gun, perhaps even to use it, has helped prevent crimes in some cases (Schulman 1994).

2. *The frontier tradition and individualism (even Protestantism with its deemphasis on hierarchy) helped to foster individual self-reliance.* This led to the idea that individuals, particularly men, should be able to defend their personal and property rights and those of their families. Individual defense is often seen in terms of violence. This perception is fueled by television, movies, and books that almost invariably show violence resolving conflicts.

3. *Some believe that cultural factors spur the high murder rate.* Scots-Irish culture (the Scots-Irish were a significant immigrant stream into the South and Midwest during the 1700s and 1800s) especially values masculine self-reliance. The Scots-Irish, who emigrated from Scotland to Northern Ireland, then to America, were originally cattle drovers. Where you find cattle in traditional societies, you find drovers stealing from one another. See the films *Rob Roy* or *Lonesome Dove* for graphic examples. Military skills become emphasized both as means to steal cattle and as means to prevent theft. In poor neighborhoods within the African American community, money, jobs, and respect are scarce. Male fighting skill becomes a way to protect oneself from predation by other poor men, to maintain respect, and occasionally to facilitate predation on others. In these cultures, men become protective of their reputations as fighters, and any serious insult is likely to lead to a fight, even to murder.

4. *As a competitive economic system and culture, America "teases" everyone with visions of success and power.* This is positive when it brings out the best in us in terms of competitive innovation and hard work. When it leads to self-definition as a "loser" and to criminality, however, it helps

provide an insecure environment where criminal violence is more likely—at least for the poorer classes, among whom violence is more accepted and failure to succeed is common.

Although it may seem incorrect in the light of television, movies, and novels, the bulk of murders are not committed for instrumental reasons (to achieve a nefarious goal). Murders thus are rarely committed to get an inheritance, kill a business partner in order to take over the business, or the like. Instead, about 30 percent (the largest category by far) are the result of arguments. Around 20 percent occur during criminal activity of another sort (robbery, burglary, and so forth). About 50 percent are distributed through a number of small categories (McCaghy, Capron, and Jamieson 1999). When a murder occurs as a result of an argument, the conflict is likely to go through a sequence of stages, according to Luckenbill (1977):

1. *Personal offense.* The victim insults the perpetrator, causing him or her to "lose face" (suffer injury to his or her self-image). Alternatively, the victim may refuse to comply with the perpetrator's orders, under circumstances where the perpetrator believes that he or she has the right to issue orders to the victim.
2. *Assessment.* The perpetrator assesses the victim's response as personally offensive. A key element is the perpetrator's deciding to believe that the victim's offense against him or her is deliberate.
3. *Retaliation.* Although the perpetrator can decide to leave the scene or otherwise to defuse the situation (say, by turning it into a humorous encounter), he or she decides to retaliate to regain "face" and to demonstrate "strong character." These are valued characteristics because they may prevent others from victimizing the perpetrator later.
4. *Working agreement.* At this point the victim may repeat the offense or otherwise repeat the provocation. This signifies an implicit agreement that violence is the way to proceed.
5. *Battle.* An attack ensues. If it turns into murder, more often than not the perpetrator has secured a weapon, since few murders occur bare-handed. The victim falls, dead or dying. (Alternatively, the attacker may be killed, under circumstances that may or may not legally be self-defense.)
6. *Termination.* The perpetrator is left to deal with the aftermath. What he or she decides to do is shaped by whether or not he or she knows the victim and whether or not bystanders are present. If the perpetrator knows the victim, he or she may remain, often even reporting the crime to the police himself or herself. If not, he or she may flee. The presence of bystanders may preclude flight.

Luckenbill's stages help explain why murder remains a crime likely to be committed by lower-class men, by men who are members of ethnic minorities, or by young men. These groups are more marginal than older or better-off people in terms of access to economic and political power. Because of this, issues of status or face become painfully important. Clearly, this analysis works less well for women, who are even more marginal than men when they are young or poor but are less inclined to use violence; so it's likely that biological and cultural factors also play a role in contributing to a high murder rate by young men.

SERIAL KILLERS: A SPECIAL CATEGORY OF MURDERER

Although very few in number, **serial killers** represent a frightening phenomenon in recent American life. In no sense is it a new phenomenon. A few such persons have always existed. Although the risk of being attacked by a serial killer is quite low, they command much media attention because of the horrifying nature of their crimes, and because they attack victims for reasons completely unconnected to any previous relationship—hence much more outside the victim's control. They are often prompted by sexual impulses, although this form of sexual expression is quite alien to most people's experience. The killer typically wants to own or possess the victim for all time, and so murders him or her, sometimes sadistically enjoying the victim's pain. He (rarely she) may keep the victim's body, or body parts, concealed either locally (as did Jeffrey Daumer in his apartment), or at a remote dumping ground where the remains can be visited repeatedly (as did Ted Bundy by depositing the bodies of many of the young girls he killed in remote mountain areas). Serial killers are hard to catch because of the lack of relationship between killer and victim and the unpredictability about where they will attack next. They tend to be either (1) organized—well-planned in their behavior, taking every precaution (like Ted Bundy), or (2) disorganized—unplanned and more emotional, less precautionary (like Richard Ramirez, who impulsively broke into victims' houses to kill men and rape women). Naturally, the disorganized type is easier to apprehend (Douglas and Olshaker 1999).

MASS MURDERERS

Another rare category is the **mass murderer**. These are individuals with deep psychological problems who frequently have also taken drugs, particularly amphetamines. When they snap, generally after an extended period of paranoia, they kill a number of victims, usually people unknown to them, in public places. Charles Whitman, a marine veteran, used amphetamines chronically while living in Austin, Texas, in the mid-1960s. One day he exploded, killed his mother and his wife, and then went on a mass killing spree, bringing a number of rifles and other types of equipment to the observation deck on the main bell tower at University of

Texas, shooting passersby from there. All told, he killed 14 people and wounded many others. Other mass murders have occurred in workplaces or schools; the perpetrator in these cases is more likely to know at least a few of the victims. In the chapter on violence, we saw that preventive measures can be used by employers and others to forestall some of the mass murders that occur in these environments.

ROBBERY

Robbery is using force or the threat of force to take money away from victims in face-to-face situations. Like murder, it's a crime most often committed by poor young men from ethnic minority groups. In the chapter "The Stickup Man" from his book *Seductions of Crime,* Jack Katz (1990) details how robbers construct their craft, asserting that, like many other jobs, robbery has its own intrinsic pleasures. Although the lifestyle is unstable, usually leading to personal undoing sooner or later, stickup men enjoy the feelings of power they get from plying their trade. We might almost compare robbers to addicts, which some of them in fact are. Taking a risk leads to a big payoff, providing enough reinforcement to induce the robber to repeat the behavior.

Unlike murder, robbery is almost always committed by people who are strangers to the victims, around 80 percent of the time (McCaghy, Capron, and Jamieson 1999). The majority do not involve injury to the victim. Paradoxically, the less well-armed the perpetrator is, the more likely the victim is to sustain injuries; in around 70 percent of incidents where the victim is assaulted, the perpetrator is unarmed. Aside from opportunist robberies, occurring when a nonhabitual robber comes across a drunk or an older person, robbery is typically planned. There are usually several stages (Best and Luckenbill 1994):

1. *Planning.* The perpetrator selects a victim based on the target's resources and vulnerability. The perpetrator should be unknown to the victim so that he or she can't be identified.
2. *Establishing co-presence.* After appearing to be an innocent participant in the scene, the perpetrator may rush the target using speed or stealth. Or he or she may maintain the illusion of innocence until the last second, as in passing a bank teller a note to hand over money.
3. *Developing co-orientation.* The perpetrator controls the victim through force or threat. This consists of displaying a weapon or assaulting the victim when no weapon is used.
4. *Transferring the goods.* The perpetrator either seizes the goods himself or herself or has the victim transfer them. This divides the robber's attention, so it can be a period of vulnerability.
5. *Leaving.* The robber makes his or her getaway.

As we see, robbery is frequently structured. Subject to more rational planning than many other crimes, it is an offense that can be deterred by increases in the levels of law enforcement or punishment. Katz would probably caution, however, that the sense of intrinsic reward and magical thinking that accompany robbery (perhaps robbery more than many other crimes because it offers a sense of power in dominating others) may obviate a too-rational interpretation. These crimes will probably occur as long as there are poor people willing to take a chance to get a quick score at someone else's expense.

BURGLARY

Burglary is taking someone else's goods or property by stealth, hopefully without being discovered. Where murder and robbery are often committed by young nonwhite males, burglary is typically committed by young white males. Like robbery, it can be seen as having several distinct stages (Best and Luckenbill 1994):

1. *Planning.* Offenders seek targets according to two criteria. First, there must be sufficient wealth to justify the risk. Second, the risk must be small. For Best and Luckenbill, the first criterion usually trumps the second, so if the potential take is good enough, risks will be taken. (This is another demonstration of the idea that rational deterrence may not always be the best way to analyze crime.) Informants or scouts may be used as a way to assess which locations are likely to prove fruitful.

2. *Entry.* The burglar enters the place to be burglarized. He or she must find either easy access, such as an open window, or a way to break in. Sometimes burglars' tools are used; sometimes forced entry consists of kicking in a door or window. Care must be taken to avoid observation, or if observation must occur, suspicion. Burglars may disguise themselves as delivery drivers or meter readers to throw potential observers off the track.

3. *Stealing.* The perpetrator usually locates ways to escape first. He or she must also find the actual location of valuables, often a formidable task. If these goods are large, stealing them may require equipment and time, making security more difficult than for a simple heist.

4. *Departure.* Once finished, the perpetrator cleans up the scene, attempting to pick up incriminating evidence. He or she tries to verify that departure will not be observed. A stolen getaway car may be used to ensure that the perpetrator will not be identified through vehicle registration. The goods may be exchanged immediately for cash (at a very reduced rate) through a fence (a receiver of stolen goods who resells them).

Burglary often works off tips—information from a variety of sources about where things worth stealing are located. Tipsters receive a small percentage of the burglar's proceeds. Because burglary is rational—perhaps much more so than robbery, which offers a larger emotional satisfaction at taking someone's goods away personally—it is more likely susceptible to deterrence. More so than robbery, burglary employs a large supporting cast of characters (Shrover 1974). These include tipsters, fences, lawyers, and sometimes the police or other authorities when corruption plays a role in precluding investigations or mitigating sentences.

Similarly, **larceny** is the theft of low price items typically from a place of business.

ARSON

Arson—the malicious or fraudulent burning of property — is an interesting crime that may be committed for a variety of reasons. On one hand, much arson takes place because of economics. On the other, some arsonists are motivated by the sorts of perversity that motivate rapes or certain murders. In Utica, New York, to give an example from the first of these categories, an enormous number of businesses have closed. This city has been called the "arson capital of the world," and its arson squad frequently trains investigators from a variety of locations. Once a thriving northeastern industrial city, Utica had successful factories, a symphony, a theatre, and thriving commercial and social communities with a great deal of prosperity and security. When more products began to be imported from overseas, the factories closed, dragging the entire community down economically. It wasn't long before businesses began literally going up in smoke. In some cases, owners were anxious to collect the fire insurance, the last "asset" the company possessed. Poor young men in the community began to imitate professional arsonists for the thrill of seeing a building go up and the fire department respond. In some cases, neighborhood people set buildings afire to run drug dealers out of condemned properties or because of grudges. Because much of Utica was older wooden building stock, a structure set afire tended to go up like a match, making arson all the more attractive.

A second type of arsonist derives a perverse, almost sexual, pleasure from seeing a building burn. These are true pyromaniacs, and only a small percentage of arsonists fit into this category. Around 15 percent of fires are set by these individuals (McCaghy and Capron 1997).

SHOPLIFTING

Shoplifting is a crime committed by many people who think of themselves as quite ordinary. According to Katz (1990), shoplifters derive the same sorts of pleasure from their occupation as do stickup men. The thrill of getting over on merchants is as at least as important as possessing a stolen item, if not more so. Shoplifters, like other criminals, can be categorized into several groups:

1. *Amateurs.* The great bulk of shoplifters come from all ages, walks of life, and social classes. These individuals probably steal for the thrill of it as much as for any desire for the items. Some are so caught up in the thrill of shoplifting that they fill their houses or apartments with items they never use. For these individuals, this crime has taken on addictive properties.
2. *Professionals.* These individuals, although rare, steal to maintain a livelihood. Few are accomplished enough to support themselves entirely through shoplifting, but some manage. These individuals use different sorts of equipment, ranging from special bags with false bottoms, to coats with "slashes" and internal hooks, to hatboxes with hidden compartments.
3. *Drug addicts.* These individuals (not to be confused with those "addicted" to shoplifting itself) steal to support drug habits. They sell the items at a radical discount to fences or others who agree to buy stolen merchandise (McCaghy and Capron 1997).

The losses from shoplifting are huge. When coupled with employee pilferage, they constitute a large portion of the total amount of theft that takes place yearly. Losses are passed on to consumers in the form of higher prices.

PUNISHMENT FOR CRIME

Mundane crimes (for example, shoplifting) are classified as **misdemeanors**, punishable by a year or less in county jail. Frequently, such offenses secure no jail time at all, particularly if the perpetrator has offended for the first time. He or she may be placed on probation instead. Other factors influencing punishment include court and jail overcrowding. If the defendant fights a conviction, it may take a long time before the case comes to trial. If he or she is sent to jail, the facility may be full, capable of absorbing few additional prisoners. In this atmosphere, prosecutors and public defenders are anxious to make deals. For this reason, many severe crimes are downgraded to misdemeanors in order to get the defendant to plead to a lesser charge.

More serious crimes are classified as **felonies**, defined as offenses that secure more than a year's incarceration. The offender is usually housed in a state penitentiary. Some inmates prefer such a facility over a county jail because penitentiaries are usually more comfortable, offering more programs and recreational activities. With a large influx of prisoners resulting from more stringent drug law enforcement beginning in the 1980s, however, some county jails have rented space to state authorities for long-term prisoners.

Overcrowding has also prompted the state to release prisoners more quickly. Perpetrators are placed on parole and supervised in the community by parole agents. However, this can set up a revolving-door phenomenon similar to that experienced with mental patients. Frequently, the prisoners are given little meaningful rehabilitation or job skills. Inevitably, many turn back to crime and are reincarcerated, perpetuating the cycle of prison-parole-crime-prison.

A disturbing factor is the current turn toward retributive punishment and its effect on prisons. A de-emphasis on rehabilitation has led to the idea that prison should be a miserable experience for inmates. This has often meant the removal of educational or athletic opportunities for them. In the minds of some, it has also meant that conditions permitting the victimization of one inmate by others should be tolerated. Abuse in the form of theft, beatings, and homosexual rape is fairly common. Some prisons have been referred to as "gladiator farms," where prisoners who do not wish to be victimized must fight, often against multiple attackers. Such events can be prevented by **"supermax"** facilities, where prisoners are confined alone. These are quite expensive to run, however, and are used only for prisoners who are extremely dangerous. This individualized form of confinement has become its own form of punishment, with some inmates experiencing psychiatric symptoms as a result of lack of contact with other people.

Some prisons, however, have been transformed into something more like college campuses or training schools—all prisoners are expected to attend classes, work, and support other inmates' rehabilitation. These types of prisons have been quite successful, and have lower recidivism rates than conventional prisons (Genders and Player 1994). They have sometimes succeeded with prisoners who did not seem likely to benefit from rehabilitation. Clearly they would not work for all prisoners, however. One way to conceptualize prison reform might be to imagine most prisons as being rehabilitative, with a few supermaxes, where some hard-core individuals are individually confined. Prisoners could graduate from supermax to rehabilitation prison if their behavior improved.

Another heartening trend is the improvement of technology for community supervision. Probation and parole officers now have more options than the occasional probationer visit to their offices. Clients can wear devices that alert law enforcement if they leave their houses. They also can be supervised by phone, with an officer calling to see if the prisoner is where he or she is supposed to be at a given time. These methods allow for a continuum of supervision in the community that allows much more flexibility in sentencing than previously.

CAUSES OF CRIME

As we've seen, such issues as poverty figure largely in the production of street or property crime. In the chapter dealing with white-collar crime, however, we saw that the losses from this form of crime actually are much greater than those from other property crimes. John Braithwaite (1992) expressed the difference simply when he said that the poor often steal out of need. The rich, however, may steal from greed. Even if they already have substantial goods, some want more. Thus the idea of poverty does not explain all crime, or even all motivations to participate in crime. Another variable that appears to drive much crime is youth. Crime is frequently committed by adolescent males between 16 and 20. Some have even called this variable the key factor in crime causation, against which all other potential variables pale (Bartol and Bartol 1997). A simple explanation for why crime rates have generally declined through the 1990s and early 2000s is that the cohort (group) of young males has declined in percentage of the population compared with other periods. However, while youth probably drives much street crime, it does not drive much white-collar crime, typically committed by older people.

FEAR OF CRIME

According to some authorities, fear of crime—the idea that crime is about to strike at any moment—is almost a bigger problem than crime itself. Fear of crime can keep people from going out at night, enjoying public places, or socializing. Paradoxically, this fear may actually lead to an increase in the very forms of crime it's a reaction to, as people socialize in public less and less, giving over public spaces to those likely to commit offenses. According to researchers, fears of crime are greatly overblown, although, curiously, people do not tend to fear the bad things that are more likely to actually happen to them, such as accidents or certain diseases (Warr 1987). Fear of crime, unfortunately, can often be tapped by politicians who want to be elected to office. It has often led to legislative climates in which sentences have been increased and judicial discretion—tailoring sentences to criminals—has been taken away in favor of mandatory minimum sentences. Currently there is a movement to reform harsh or unduly restrictive sentences, but this contends with a tendency for politicians to pander to fear of crime as a reliable way to gain popularity.

SUMMARY: CRIMES AGAINST PERSONS AND PROPERTY

Serious street crime can be classified as personal or property crime. Personal crime includes such offenses as murder. Property crime includes robbery, burglary, arson, and shoplifting, as well as other offenses. Crime may be punished by incarceration in a country jail or prison, depending on whether the offense was a misdemeanor or a felony. These prisons and jails can either be rehabilitative or punitive in nature, with the punitive facilities sometimes permitting exploitation of one prisoner by another. Supermax prisons have been constructed allowing for segregating individual prisoners who pose a threat to society, guards, or other inmates. Technologies also now exist that extend the ability of probation and parole officers to supervise their clients in the community. In general, the crime rate tends to increase directly with the number of young males in society. Fear of crime, often unfounded in its intensity, is frequently exploited by politicians desiring to be elected by citizens who believe that the crime rate is increasing.

15

The Future of Deviance Studies

AFTERTHOUGHTS

The purpose of this book has been an ecumenical one. We examined a number of types of deviance along with theories that explain, or try to explain, why it occurs. Because of this, I have muted the intricate critiques often applied to specific theories, reasoning that all are valid at least some of the time, and all have their uses. In addition, I pointed up the difference between deviance and serious crime—rather sharply, I hope. Many forms of deviance hurt no one; indeed, many forms exist as deviance only in the eye of the beholder. Some forms of criminality, however, injure victims substantially, and society should be concerned with and take action against them. Enlightened social policies, including amelioration of poverty, jobs for youth, and meaningful action against racism are likely to help. Still other helpful policies might include tighter surveillance of offenders, more treatment and rehabilitation during and after incarceration, more appropriate sentences (including shorter ones) for offenses—especially drug offenses—and more humane and motivating prison and probation regimens. Restorative justice—bringing together perpetrators, victims, and the community through steps that resocialize offenders and heal victims—offers much in this area. Some critics of contemporary criminology, the "left realists," charge that, although much crime seems to flow from social inequality, we should not romanticize working-class and poor people's crimes. Their victims, after all, are usually other working-class and poor people, and, even when the treatment of offenders is compassionate, the police need to be more diligent in solving these crimes and protecting these populations.

With mundane forms of deviance, we need to increase our sense of tolerance, while also increasing our attention to truly criminal activities. Many "deviant" activities hurt no one; they simply express individual preferences. Virtually no one's behavior could stand up to 24-hour-a-day scrutiny and not be seen as deviant by at least some of us.

We need to become less sensitive to fads and fashions in intervening in deviance. Many forms of deviance, when they really are in fact antisocial, need a measured and wise approach, not an approach based on ratcheting up punishment because the problem is the flavor of the month. Movements toward extreme forms of punishment, as opposed to wise and caring rehabilitation, need to be curtailed. Sexuality is an area fraught with fear and projection (Ch. 4). Intervention in this area, in particular, needs to be handled wisely. It is certain that the extremities of guilt and punishment associated with sex owe much to the fact that each person has sexual urges, but, at the same time, is often anxious to deny them publicly. It is virtually certain that the specter of guilt and punishment makes deviance associated with this area more likely, as the tension associated with such excesses adds to the addictive thrill associated with acting out.

Culture wars, whether the originators of these wars are liberals or conservatives, are particularly destructive. We should avoid labeling and casting into outer darkness persons whose behavior or alleged behavior is different. For this reason, the role of moral entrepreneurs in society should be examined carefully. There can be no doubt that they are enormously helpful in directing society's attention and resources toward worthwhile projects. It's clear, however, that, when moral entrepreneurs name new enemies for society to deal with, they can be destructive. The reason is clear. For the great Swiss psychiatrist Carl Jung, people have a tendency to project the dark sides of themselves—Jung called this the "shadow"—onto others. They are particularly apt to persecute individuals who represent aspects of themselves they have repressed. Marking some people as "enemies" or nonhuman is a distortion of the human truth that people are more similar than they are different, and that criminals, addicts, and "sexual deviants" are human, too. One of the great revelations here is just how mundane or ordinary deviance becomes when one observes it for a while.

Moral entrepreneurs need to be examined closely to ascertain the quality of their claims, to see how they make their money, and to assess their net benefit to society. Of particular concern is how resources and funds are used to benefit others or to accomplish worthy projects. In situations where moral entrepreneurs raise a hue and cry against others, sometimes without foundation, society should evaluate these claims wisely. The fashion for persecuting nursery school workers for alleged group child sexual abuse comes to mind. Many therapists, police, and prosecutors found such cases of "abuse" because discovering them was "in," and also because doing so enhanced their careers. When many of these cases were found to be spurious, they resisted restoring the liberty and property of the sentenced defendants because they had staked their reputations and careers on these cases. All of this speaks to a need to evaluate sensational cases of this sort—ones involving satanic ritual abuse, group child sexual abuse, multiple personality disorders, shaken-baby syndrome, and the like—scientifically, that is, by using teams of disinterested social and medical scientists who can evaluate such claims realistically before society takes action on a grand scale. The fact that one has basic clinical credentials in a field does not mean he or she is prepared to evaluate such claims, particularly in cases where he or she stands to benefit by finding cases. All too often, practitioners respond to distorted news reports or unsubstantiated claims from other practitioners in terms of what they believe to be important social problems.

None of this should detract from the important work moral entrepreneurs often do by bringing social problems to our attention and helping with their resolution. It simply means that we must be suspicious of moral entrepreneurs in the same ways we are of anyone else who has something to gain from getting the public to see things a certain way.

Restorative justice holds out a program for bringing criminal deviants back into the fold. With its principles of confrontation by victims, restitution, behavior change, and reintegration into the community, it is one of the best hopes for society in terms of creating individuals who, although once criminal, now are true community members. In order for restorative justice principles to actually work, alienation must be overcome in terms of the community actually being willing to work with ex-offenders in a close way, not hold themselves aloof. It is possible to envision a society where community bonds become strengthened again, not weakened through such methods as scapegoating putative criminals or deciding that some citizens are "good" and others are "bad" as permanent personality features.

WHERE THEORY AND RESEARCH ARE NEEDED

Theories still need to be generated for serious forms of deviance and crime, but they need, above all, to be practical. It is likely, after all, that there is no one "best" theory. Instead, all theories probably have something to offer, depending on what phenomena they describe. Attempts to minutely refine empirical theories in deviance, although interesting as exercises, should give way more and more to practical projects with troubled people that demonstrate workability through results and improvement of people's lives. Program evaluation should be the research model for a variety of different intervention models. At the same time, essentially victimless forms of deviance should not be targets for intervention. Although research on these topics, especially qualitative studies, is particularly interesting, society should think less and less along the lines of studying victimless deviance with a mind to inducing everyone to behave more conventionally. Deviance is a rich and interesting area of study. Hopefully, studying it makes us all more humane and tolerant.

References

ABADINSKY, HOWARD. 2002. *Organized Crime*. Belmont, CA: Wadsworth.

ABANES, RICHARD. 2002. *One Nation Under Gods: A History of the Mormon Church*. New York: Four Walls Eight Windows.

ADAMS, H. E., L. W. WRIGHT, and B. A. LOHR. 2001. "Is Homophobia Associated With Homosexual Arousal?" Pp. 213–20 in *Social Psychology and Human Sexuality: Essential Readings*. Editor R. Baumeister. Ann Arbor, MI: Sheridan Books.

AFTAB, PARRY. 1999. *The Parent's Guide to Protecting Your Children in Cyberspace*. New York: McGraw-Hill.

AGNEW, ROBERT. 1992. "Social Control Theory and Delinquency: A Longitudinal Test." *Criminology* 23: 47–61.

AKERS, RONALD L. 1990. "Rational Choice, Deterrence and Social Learning Theory in Criminology." *Journal of Criminal Law and Criminology* 81: 653–76.

ALCOHOLICS ANONYMOUS. 1997. *The Big Book of Alcoholics Anonymous*. New York: Alcoholics Anonymous.

AMERICAN PSYCHIATRIC ASSOCIATION. 2000. *DSM-IV-TR 2000*. Washington, DC: American Psychiatric Press.

ATACK, JON. 1990. *A Piece of Blue Sky: Scientology, Dianetics, and L. Ron Hubbard Exposed*. New York: Carol.

BARNETT, OLA W., CINDY L. MILLER-PERRIN, and ROBIN D. PERRIN. 1997. *Family Violence Across the Lifespan*. Thousand Oaks, CA: Sage.

BARTOL, CURT R., and ANNE BARTOL. 1997. *Delinquency and Justice: A Psychosocial Approach*. New York: Simon and Schuster.

BEATTIE, MELODY. 1987. *Codependent No More: How to Stop Controlling Others and Start Caring for Yourself*. St. Paul: Hazelden.

BECCARIA, CESARE. 1963. *On Crimes and Punishments*. Indianapolis: Bobbs-Merrill.

BECKER, HOWARD S. 1996. "Moral Entrepreneurs: The Creation and Enforcement of Deviant Categories." *Social Deviance: Readings in the Theory and Research*, 2nd ed. Editor Henry N. Pontell. Upper Saddle River, NJ: Prentice Hall.

———. 1963. *Outsiders: Studies in the Sociology of Deviance*. New York: Free Press.

BEHR, EDWARD. 1997. *Prohibition: Thirteen Years That Changed America*. New York: Arcade.

BELL, DANIEL. 2000. *The End of Ideology: On the Exhaustion of Political Ideas in the Fifties*. Cambridge: Harvard University Press.

BENDIX, RHEINHARD. 1990. *Max Weber: An Intellectual Portrait*. Berkeley: University of California Press.

BENNET, RICHARD R., and JAMES P. LYNCH. 1990. "Does Difference Make a Difference: Comparing Cross-National Crime Indicators." *Criminology* 28: 165–69.

BEST, JOEL, and DAVID F. LUCKENBILL. 1994. *Organizing Deviance*. Englewood Cliffs, NJ: Prentice Hall.

BLACK, DONALD. 1998. *The Social Structure of Right and Wrong*. San Diego: Academic Press.

BONGER, WILLEM. 1969. *Criminality and Economic Conditions*. Bloomington: Indiana University Press.

BRACKEN, MICHAEL B., and LYN WEINER. 1984. *Alcohol and the Fetus: A Clinical Perspective*. Oxford: Oxford University Press.

BRAITHWAITE, JOHN. 1990. *Crime, Shame, and Reintegration*. Cambridge: Cambridge University Press.

———. 1992. "Poverty, Power and White-Collar Crime: Sutherland and the Paradoxes of Criminological Theory." *White-Collar Crime Reconsidered*. Editors Kip Schlegel and David Weisburd. Boston: Northeastern University Press.

BRINKERHOFF, DAVID B., LYNN K. WHITE, and SUZANNE T. ORTEGA. 1995. *Essentials of Sociology*. St. Paul: West.

BRUMBAUGH, ALEX. 1994. *Transformation and Recovery: A Guide for the Design and Development of Acupuncture-Based Chemical Dependency Treatment Programs*. New York: Stillpoint.

BUGLIOSI, VINCENT T., and CURT GENTRY. 2001. *Helter Skelter: The True Story of the Manson Murders*. New York: Norton.

CAHILL, THOMAS. 2001. *Desire of the Everlasting Hills: The World Before and After Jesus*. New York: Knopf.

CARNES, PATRICK J. 2001. *Out of the Shadows: Understanding Sexual Addiction*. Minneapolis: Hazelden.

CENTER FOR MENTAL HEALTH SERVICES. 1992. *Mental Health, United States*. Washington, DC: United States Government Printing Office.

CHAMBLISS, WILLIAM. 1973. "The Roughnecks and the Saints." *Society* 11: 24–31.

CLOWARD, RICHARD A., and LLOYD E. OHLIN. 1960. *Delinquency and Opportunity: A Theory of Delinquent Gangs*. New York: Free Press.

COCKERHAM, WILLIAM C. 2000. *Medical Sociology*. Upper Saddle River, NJ: Prentice Hall.

COHEN, ALBERT K. 1955. *Delinquent Boys: The Culture of the Gang*. New York: Free Press.

COHEN, DANIEL. 1994. *Cults*. New York: Millbrook.

COHEN, RICH. 1998. *Tough Jews: Fathers, Sons, and Gangster Dreams in Jewish America*. New York: Simon and Schuster.

COLSON, CHARLES. 2001. *Justice That Restores*. New York: Tyndale.

COMSTOCK, G., and V. C. STRASBURGER. 1990. "Deceptive Appearances: Television Violence and Aggressive Behavior." *Journal of Adolescent Health Care* 11:31–44.

CORTES, JUAN B., and FLORENCE M. GATTI. 1972. *Delinquency and Crime: A Biopsychosocial Approach*. New York: Seminar.

CRESSEY, DONALD R. 1973. *Other People's Money*. New York: Patterson Smith.

———. 1969. *Theft of the Nation*. New York: Harper and Row.

DIAMOND, JARED. 1999. *Guns, Germs, and Steel: The Fates of Human Societies*. New York: Norton.

———. 1992. *The Third Chimpanzee: The Evolution and Future of the Human Animal*. New York: HarperCollins.

DIOP, ANTA. 1991. *The African Origin of Civilization*. Chicago: Chicago Review Press.

DOUGLAS, JOHN E., and MARK OLSHAKER. 1999. *The Anatomy of Motive*. New York: Simon and Schuster.

DUGDALE, ROBERT L. 1910. *The Jukes: A Study of Crime, Pauperism, Disease, and Heredity*. New York: Putnam.

DURKHEIM, EMILE. 1984. *The Division of Labor in Society*. New York: Free Press.

———. 2001. *The Elementary Forms of Religious Life*. Oxford: Oxford University Press.

———. 1976. *Suicide*. New York: Free Press.

ECKSTEIN, HARRY H. 1975. *Division and Cohesion in Democracy: A Study of Norway*. Princeton: Princeton University Press.

EHRENREICH, BARBARA, and DEIRDRE ENGLISH. 1983. *Witches, Midwives, and Nurses: A History of Women Healers*. New York: Feminist Press at the City University of New York.

EHRLICH, ISAAC. 1975. "The Deterrent Effect of Capital Punishment: A Question of Life and Death." *American Economic Review* LXV(3):414.

EKLAND-OLSON, SHELDON, WILLIAM KELLY, and MICHAEL EISENBERG. 1992. "Crime and Incarceration: Some Comparative Findings From the 1980s." *Crime and Delinquency* 38:392–416.

ERMANN, M. D., and RICHARD LUNDMAN. 1987. *Corporate and Governmental Deviance*. Oxford: Oxford University Press.

FARIS, ROBERT E., and H. W. DUNHAM. 1939. *Mental Disorders in Urban Areas*. Chicago: University of Chicago Press.

FEDERAL BUREAU OF INVESTIGATION. 1993. *Crime in the United States*. Washington, DC: United States Government Printing Office.

FERRI, ENRICO. 1917. *Criminal Sociology*. Boston: Little Brown.

FINKELHOR, DAVID. 1990. "Is Child Abuse Overreported?: The Data Rebut Arguments for Less Intervention." *Public Welfare* 48:23–29.

———. 1986. *A Sourcebook on Child Sexual Abuse*. Beverly Hills, CA: Sage.

FISSE, BRENT, and JOHN BRAITHWAITE. 1993. *Corporations, Crime, and Accountability*. Cambridge: Cambridge University Press.

FOUCAULT, MICHEL. 1995. *Discipline and Punish*. New York: Knopf.

———. 1988. *Madness and Civilization: A History of Insanity in the Age of Reason*. New York: Vintage.

FREEMAN, DEREK. 1999. *The Fateful Hoaxing of Margaret Mead: A Historical Analysis of Her Samoan Research*. Chicago: Westview.

FREUD, SIGMUND. 1989a. "Three Essays on the Theory of Sexuality." *The Freud Reader*. Editor Peter Gay. New York: Norton.

———. 1989b. "Totem and Taboo." *The Freud Reader*. Editor Peter Gay. New York: Norton.

FRIEDRICHS, DAVID O. 1996. *Trusted Criminals: White-Collar Crime in Contemporary Society*. Belmont, CA: Wadsworth.

FROMM, ERICH. 1991. *Anatomy of Human Destructiveness*. New York: Henry Holt.

———. 1994. *Escape from Freedom*. New York: Henry Holt.

GAY, PETER. 1989. "Introduction." pp. xiii–xlvii in *The Freud Reader*. Editor Peter Gay. New York: Norton.

GELLES, RICHARD J. 1973. "Child Abuse As Psychopathology: A Sociological Critique and Reformulation." *American Journal of Orthopsychiatry* 43:611–21.

———. 1980. "A Profile of Violence toward Children in the United States." Pp. 82–105 in *Child Abuse: An Agenda for Action*. Editors G. Gerbner, C. J. Ross, and E. Zegler. New York: Oxford University Press.

GENDERS, ELAINE, and ELAINE PLAYER. 1994. *Grendon: Study of a Therapeutic Prison*. Oxford: Oxford University Press.

GIMBUTAS, MARIJA. 1991. *Civilization of the Goddess: The World of Old Europe.* San Francisco: Harper.

GLASER, DANIEL. 1956. "Criminality Theories and Behavioral Images." *American Journal of Sociology* 61: 433–44.

GOFFMAN, ERVING. 1961. *Asylums: Essays on the Social Situation of Mental Patients and Other Inmates.* New York: Doubleday.

GOTTFREDSON, MICHAEL R., and TRAVIS HINSCHI. 1990. *A General Theory of Crime.* Stanford: Stanford University Press.

GOULD, TERRY. 2000. *The Lifestyle; A Look at the Erotic Rites of Swingers.* New York: Firefly.

GUSFIELD, JOSEPH R. 1990. *Symbolic Crusade: Status Politics and the American Temperance Movement.* Champaign: University of Illinois Press.

HANEY, C., W. C. BANKS, and P. ZIMBARDO. 1973. "Interpersonal Dynamics in a Simulated Prison." *International Journal of Criminology and Penology* 1:59–67.

HERMAN, JUDITH. 2000. *Father-Daughter Incest.* Cambridge: Harvard University Press.

HESTON, LEONARD L. 1977. "Schizophrenia: Genetic Factors." *Hospital Practice* 12:43–49.

HILL, GARY D., and MAXINE P. ATKINSON. 1988. "Gender, Familial Control, and Delinquency." *Criminology* 26: 127–49.

HIRSCHI, TRAVIS. 1969. *Causes of Delinquency.* Berkeley: University of California Press.

HOBBES, THOMAS. 1977. *The Leviathan.* New York: Penguin.

HOLLINGSHEAD, AUGUST B., and FREDRICH C. REDLICH. 1953. "Social Stratification and Psychiatric Disorders." *American Sociological Review* 18:163–69.

HOMANS, GEORGE C. 1992. *Human Groups.* New York: Transaction.

HUNTER, RICHARD. 2002. *World Without Secrets: Business, Crime, and Privacy in the Age of Ubiquitous Computing.* New York: John Wiley.

INABA, DARRYL S., and WILLIAM E. COHEN. 1989. *Uppers, Downers, All Arounders.* Ashland, OR: CNS.

JAYNES, JULIAN. 2000. *The Origin of Consciousness in the Breakdown of the Bicameral Mind.* New York: Houghton Mifflin.

JENKINS, PHILLIP. 2001. *Beyond Tolerance: Child Pornography Online.* New York: NYU Press.

JOHNSON, VERNON. 1990. *I'll Quit Tomorrow.* New York: HarperCollins.

KATZ, JACK. 1990. *Seductions of Crime: Moral and Sensual Attractions of Doing Evil.* New York: Perseus.

KEPHART, WILLIAM M. 1982. *Extraordinary Groups: The Sociology of Unconventional Lifestyles.* New York: St Martin's Press.

KINSEY, A. C., W. P. POMEROY, and C. E. MARTIN. 1948. *Sexual Behavior in the Human Male.* Philadelphia: Saunders.

KORNBLUM, WILLIAM, and JOSEPH JULIAN. 2000. *Social Problems.* Englewood Cliffs NJ: Prentice Hall.

KOSS, M. P. 1989. "Hidden Rape: Sexual Aggression and Victimization in a National Sample of Students in Higher Education." Pp. 145–68 in *Violence in Dating Relationships: Emerging Social Issues.* Editors M. A. Pirog-Good and J. E. Stets. New York: Praeger.

KROHN, M. D. 1986. "The Web of Conformity: A Network Approach to the Explanation of Delinquent Behavior." *Social Problems* 33:529–44.

LANGE, JOHANNES. 1931. *Crime As Destiny: A Study of Criminal Twins.* London: George Allen and Unwin.

LASCH, CHRISTOPHER. 1991. *Culture of Narcissism: American Life in an Age of Diminishing Expectations.* New York: Norton.

LAYTON, DEBORAH. 1999. *Seductive Poison: A Jonestown Survivor's Story of Life and Death in the People's Temple.* New York: Doubleday.

LEGOFF, JACQUES. 2000. *Medieval Civilization 400–1500.* New York: Barnes and Noble.

LEVINE, MELVIN D., and MARTHA REED. 1998. *Developmental Variation and Learning Disorders*. New York: Educators Publishing.

LIEBERSON, STANLEY. 1985. *Making It Count: The Improvement of Social Research and Theory*. Berkeley: University of California Press.

LIFTON, ROBERT J. 2000. *Destroying the World to Save It: Aum Shinrikyo, Apocalyptic Violence, and the New Global Terrorism*. New York: Henry Holt.

LINEDECKER, CLIFFORD L. 1993. *Massacre at Waco, Texas: The Shocking Story of Cult Leader David Koresh and the Branch Davidians*. New York: St. Martin's Press.

LOCKE, JOHN. 1988. *Two Treatises on Government*. Cambridge: Cambridge University Press.

LOMBROSO, CESARE. 1911. *Criminal Man According to the Classification of Cesare Lombroso*. New York: Putnam.

LORENZ, KONRAD. 1974. *On Aggression*. New York: Harcourt.

LUCKENBILL, DAVID F. 1977. "Criminal Homicide As a Situated Transaction." *Social Problems* 25:176–86.

LUSKE, BRUCE, and HENRY VANDENBURGH. 1995. "Heads on Beds: Toward a Critical Ethnography of the Selling of Psychiatric Hospitalization." *Perspectives on Social Problems* 7:203–22.

MACKINNON, CATHARINE A., and ANDREA DWORKIN. 1997. *In Harm's Way: The Pornography Civil Rights Hearings*. Cambridge: Harvard University Press.

MARCUSE, HERBERT. 1990. *Eros and Civilization: A Philosophical Inquiry into Freud*. Boston: Beacon Press.

MARKON, JERRY. 1996. "Party Just Like a Cult, Experts Say." *Newsday*. November 17.

MARS, GERALD. 1982. *Cheats at Work*. London: Unwin.

MARX, KARL, and FRIEDRICH ENGELS. 1965. "The Communist Manifesto." *Essential Works of Marxism*. Editor Arthur Mendel. New York: Bantam Press.

MASTERS, WILLIAM H., and VIRGINIA E. JOHNSON. 1966. *Human Sexual Response*. New York: Little Brown.

MAXMEN, JERROLD S., and NICHOLAS G. WARD. 1995. *Essential Psychopathology and Its Treatment*. New York: Norton.

McBAIN, MICHAEL A. 2002. *Internet Pornography*. New York: iUniverse.

McCAGHY, CHARLES H., and TIMOTHY A. CAPRON. 1997. *Deviant Behavior: Crime, Conflict, and Interest Groups*. Needham Heights, MA: Allyn and Bacon.

McCAGHY, CHARLES H., TIMOTHY A. CAPRON, and JAY JAMIESON. 1999. *Deviant Behavior: Crime, Conflict, and Interest Groups*. Boston: Allyn and Bacon.

McPHEE, STEPHEN J., VISHWANATH R. LINGAPPA, AND ANTHONY ROSEN. 1999. *Pathophysiology of Disease*. New York: Appleton and Lange.

MEAD, MARGARET. 2001. *Coming of Age in Samoa*. New York: HarperCollins.

MEADOWS, ROBERT J. 1998. *Understanding Violence and Victimization*. Upper Saddle River, NJ: Prentice Hall.

MERSKEY, H. 1992. "Manufacture of Multiple Personality Disorder." *British Journal of Psychiatry* 160:327–40.

MERTON, ROBERT K. 1957. *Social Theory and Social Structure*. Glencoe, IL: Free Press.

MESSNER, STEPHEN F., and RICHARD ROSENFELD. 2000. *Crime and the American Dream*. Belmont, CA: Wadsworth.

MIGNON, SYLVIA A., CALVIN J. LARSON, AND WILLIAM M. HOLMES. 2002. *Family Abuse: Consequences, Theories, and Responses*. Boston: Allyn and Bacon.

MILNER, CHRISTINA, and RICHARD MILNER. 1972. *Black Players: The Secret World of Black Pimps*. Boston: Little Brown.

MIZRUCHI, EPHRIAM H. 1983. *Regulating Society: Marginality and Social Control in Historical Perspective*. New York: Free Press.

MORAN, SARAH. 1999. *The Secret World of Cults: From Ancient Druids to Heaⁱ en's Gate*. New York: CLB Publish·

O'SHEA, STEPHEN. 2001. *The Perfect Heresy: The Revolutionary Life and Death of the Medieval Cathars*. New York: Walker.

PLUMMER, KENNETH. 1975. *Sexual Stigma: An Interactionist Account*. Boston: Routledge and Keegan Paul.

PONTELL, HENRY N., and KITTY CALAVITA. 1992. "Bilking Bankers and Bad Debts: White-Collar Crime and the Savings and Loan Crisis." Pp. 195–213 in *White-Collar Crime Reconsidered*. Editors Kip Schlegel and David Weisburd. Boston: Northeastern University Press.

QUINNEY, RICHARD. 1974. "The Social Reality of Crime." *Current Perspectives in Criminal Behavior*. Editor Abraham S. Blumberg. New York: Knopf.

RANDALL, PETER. 1997. *Adult Bullying*. London: Routledge.

RECKLESS, WALTER. 1961. "A New Theory of Delinquency and Crime." *Federal Probation* 25:42–46.

REICH, WILHELM. 1980. *The Mass Psychology of Fascism*. New York: Farrar, Straus, and Giroux.

REGOLI, ROBERT M., and JOHN D. HEWITT. 2000. *Delinquency in Society,* 4th ed. New York: McGraw-Hill.

ROBINSON, ADAM. 2002. *Bin Laden: Behind the Mask of the Terrorist*. New York: Arcade.

ROSENHAN, D. L. 1999. "On Being Sane in Insane Places." *Social Deviance: Readings in Theory and Research*, 3rd ed. Editor Henry N. Pontell. Upper Saddle River, NJ: Prentice Hall.

RUBOVITZ-SEITZ, PHILLIP. 1999. *Kohut's Freudian Vision*. New York: Analytic Press.

RUE, THOMAS S. 1983. "Invisible Victims: The Effects of Pornography on Women." Unpublished. Trenton State University, Trenton, NJ.

SAVITZ, LEONARD, STANLEY H. TURNER, and TOBY DICKMAN. 1977. "The Origin of ~tific Criminology: Franz Joseph ~ First Criminologist." Pp.
~ *in Criminology:*
s. Editor Robert
.lls, CA: Sage.

SCHEFF, THOMAS. 1975. *Labeling Madness*. Englewood Cliffs, NJ: Prentice Hall.

SCHULMAN, J. NEIL. 1994. *Stopping Power*. New York: Pulpless.com

SHAW, CLIFFORD R., and HENRY D. MCKAY. 1942. *Juvenile Delinquency and Urban Areas*. Chicago: University of Chicago Press.

SHELDON, WILLIAM H. 1949. *Varieties of Delinquent Youth: An Introduction to Constitutional Psychiatry*. New York: Harper.

SHROVER, NEAL. 1974. "The Social Organization of Burglary." *Social Problems* 20:499–515.

SPANOS, NICHOLAS P. 1996. *Multiple Identities and False Memories*. Washington, DC: American Psychological Association.

SPERGEL, IRVING A. 1995. *The Youth Gang Problem: A Community Approach*. New York: Oxford University Press.

SPITZER, STEVEN. 1999. "Toward a Marxian Theory of Deviance." Pp. 98–102 in *Social Deviance: Readings in Theory and Research*, 3rd ed. Editor Henry N. Pontell. Upper Saddle River, NJ: Prentice Hall.

SPRENGKLE, D. H. and C. S. RUSSELL. 1979. "Circumplex Model of Marital and Family Systems" in Family Process 18:3–28.

SROLE, LEO, T. S. LANGNER, S. T. MICHAEL, M. K. OPLER, and T. A. C. RENNIE. 1962. *Mental Health in the Metropolis: The Midtown Manhattan Study*. New York: McGraw-Hill.

STARK, RODNEY. 2002. "Deviant Places." Pp. 45–53 in *Deviance and Social Control*. Editor Ronald Weitzer. New York: McGraw-Hill.

STINE, GERALD J. 2002. *AIDS Update*. Englewood Cliffs, NJ: Prentice Hall.

STONE, MERLIN. 1990. *When God Was a Woman*. New York: Barnes and Noble.

STRAUS, M. A. 1976. "Sexual Inequality, Cultural Norms, and Wife Beating." *Victimology: An International Journal* 1:54–76.

STRAUS, MURRAY A., RICHARD J. GELLES, and SUZANNE K. STEINMETZ. 1980. *Behind Closed Doors: Violence in the American Family*. Garden City, NY: Anchor.

SUTHERLAND, EDWIN H. 1939. *Principles of Criminology*. Philadelphia: Lippincott.

———. 1983. *White-Collar Crime: The Uncut Version*. New Haven: Yale University Press.

SYKES, GRESHAM M., and DAVID MATZA. 1957. "Techniques of Neutralization: A Theory of Delinquency." *American Sociological Review* 22:664–70.

TANNAHILL, REAY. 1982. *Sex in History*. New York: Stein and Day.

TANNENBAUM, FRANK. 1938. *Crime and the Community*. New York: Columbia University Press.

THOITS, PEGGY A. 1995. "Stress, Coping, and Social Support Processes." *Journal of Health and Social Behavior* (Extra):53–79.

THOMES, JAMES T. 2000. *Dotcons: Con Games, Fraud, and Deceit on the Internet*. New York: iUniverse.

THOMSEN, ROBERT. 1999. *Bill W.: The Absorbing and Deeply Moving Life Story of Bill Wilson, Cofounder of Alcoholics Anonymous*. St. Paul: Hazelden.

THORNTON, RUSSELL. 1986. *We Shall Live Again: The 1870 and 1890 Ghost Dance Movements As Demographic Revitalization*. Cambridge: Cambridge University Press.

TOBIAS, MADELENE, and JANJA LALICH. 1994. *Captive Hearts, Captive Minds: Freedom and Recovery from Cults and Other Abusive Relationships*. New York: Hunter House.

TRACY, KATHLEEN. 2001. *The Secret Story of Polygamy*. New York: Sourcebooks.

UNITED STATES DEPT OF HEALTH AND HUMAN SERVICES. 2002. *Health, United States 2002*. Washington, DC: U.S. Government Printing Office.

UNIVERSITY OF CALIFORNIA. 2002. "The Hackers' Ethic" http://www. berkeley. edu.

VANDENBURGH, HENRY. 1999. *Feeding Frenzy: Organizational Deviance in the Texas Psychiatric Hospital Industry*. Lanham, MD: University Press.

VAUGHAN, DIANE. 1983. *Controlling Unlawful Organizational Behavior: Social Structure and Corporate Misconduct*. Chicago: University of Chicago Press.

VOLD, GEORGE B. 1958. *Theoretical Criminology*. New York: Oxford University Press.

WALDO, GORDON P. and SIMON DINITZ. 1967. "Personality Attributes of the Criminal." *Journal of Research on Crime and Delinquency* 4:202.

WARR, MARK. 1987. "Fear of Victimization and Sensitivity to Risk." *Journal of Quantitative Criminology* 3(1):29–46.

WEBER, MAX. 1970. "The Sociology of Charismatic Authority." *From Max Weber: Essays in Sociology*. Editors Gerth Hans and C. W. Mills. New York: Oxford University Press.

WILLIAMS, JOHN J. 1997. *Cellular and Cordless Phone Phreaking*. New York: Consumertronics.

WILSON, EDWARD O. 2000. *Sociobiology: The New Synthesis*. Cambridge: Harvard University Press.

WITKIN, HERMAN A. 1976. "Criminality in XYY and XXY Men." *Science* 193:547–55.

YOCHELSON, SAMUEL, and STANTON E. SAMENOW. 1976. *The Criminal Personality: A Profile for Change*. New York: Aronson.

ZIEGLER, EDWARD. 1980. "Controlling Child Abuse: Do We Have the Knowledge and/or the Will." *American Journal of Familty Therapy* 8(3):18–19.

ZITRIN A., A. S. HARDESTY, E. I. BURDOCK, and A. K. DROSSMAN. 1976. "Crime and Violence among Mental Patients." *American Journal of Psychiatry* 133:142–49.

Index